The Routine of War

How One Northern Israeli Community Coped During the Second Lebanon War

BETHE SCHOENFELD, Ph.D

ARTZY
BOOKS
JERUSALEM ◆ NEW YORK

The Routine of War
Published by ARTZY Books
Text Copyright © 2007 by Bethe Schoenfeld

Cover Design: Zippy Thumim
Typesetting & Book Design: Tiffen Studios
Editor: Shirley Zauer
Editorial & Production Manager: Daniella Barak

Cover photo of building taken by Lyn and Micha Baer

ISBN Hard Cover: 978-1-934440-10-0

E-mail: sales@ArtzyBooks.com
Web Site: www.devorapublishing.com

Printed in Israel

*I would like to thank my husband Asher
and my children, Lavie, Shanie, and Meshi
for their continuous support
in all of my projects
and the enthusiasm with which
they embraced this book.*

Thanks for the inspiration
to fulfill my dreams.

Table Of Contents

Prologue

The people who are interviewed in this book live on Kibbutz Gesher Haziv in the Western Galilee of Israel. It's a lovely area, and the kibbutz's location is especially beautiful. We are located on a hill overlooking the ancient village of Achziv (mentioned in the Book of Joshua) on the coast of the Mediterranean Sea, which is to our west. The beach at Achziv is one of the finest beaches in Israel and people spend many a lazy afternoon lounging on the sands.

To the north and east of the kibbutz is a flat valley surrounded by hills a few kilometers in the distance. Here you can find fields of wheat and other crops as well as groves of banana, avocado, lychee and persimmon trees. There are also a few other communities around us – kibbutzim, moshavim, closed communities and small towns. It is an extremely lush, green area, as well as being pastoral and quiet. On a normal day you would think you had found the Garden of Eden.

However, war has become routine here on the Northern Border. Gesher Haziv is located just a few kilometers south of the border with Lebanon. The Sulam Tsor mountain range, which fills my vision from the north, *is* the border. I have lived here permanently since 1981, when I immigrated from the U.S. The year before I made my life here permanent, in 1980, the Western Galilee and the kibbutz were tranquil. Since then we have had constant threats from Lebanon, first from the PLO and then from Hizbullah, usually in the form of Katyusha rockets. Katyushas are difficult to aim, but the fear and destruction they cause are remarkable. The noise is probably the worst. If it falls near you there is a loud crack and then deafening silence. If it flies over you, you hear the "whoosh" as it whizzes by. They are aimed from a mobile launch platform, often mounted on the back of a truck, which is quickly hidden after use (more often than not in residential areas, even in houses where people are still living). They are also usually shot in barrages, not individually, one at a time.

Since Lebanon and its governments are incapable or unwilling to take military control over its sovereign territory, especially in the south, militia factions rule the area, as they do in much of Lebanon. These militias feel it is their right to shoot rockets into Israel whenever they please. So, war has become routine for me and many others in the Western Galilee and other areas of Northern Israel, however banal that may sound. And no more so than in this last conflict with the Hizbullah in the summer of 2006.

During the war that lasted thirty-four days, each day blurred into the next; days became almost meaningless. We often had difficulty separating one day from the next and even the weekend was similar to the weekdays, except that more people left the community at the weekends. Thus, this narrative isn't exactly linear and I have divided it up into sections: Prologue, At the Beginning, The Middle, The End, and After the Cease-Fire. I included dates and a brief summary of Hizbullah's attacks on Israel to give the reader a better grasp of the war's development.

Before I begin, I think a little background about the community of Gesher Haziv itself is in order. Kibbutz Gesher Haziv was founded in January 1949. The kibbutz movement is based on socialist ideals espousing equality – "From each according to his ability, to each according to his needs." Under this system all monies were put into a communal account and divided up equally, regardless of the job one did. We had a communal kitchen and dining room, laundry, children's houses, administration, field crops and other agricultural products. It is a voluntary system for the general good of the entire community.

However, in the past few years Kibbutz Gesher Haziv (and other kibbutzim in Israel) has gone through a number of radical changes. The first was that in 1998 the kibbutz itself privatized. Now, we live from our own individual salaries. We no longer have a communal kitchen and dining room. The Laundry still exists, but it is run by an external company and use of its services costs money. However, we still have a number of communal responsibilities and pay taxes into the communal treasury in order to maintain them.

Then in 2000 the second change occurred. We began to build a new neighborhood in our fields as part of our renewal process. In recent years many younger people, children of members of the kibbutz, finished their military service, went to study, but didn't return to the kibbutz to live. This left a shortage in the population – we were getting older and there were few young people to continue the traditions. In addition, we owed a lot of money to the banks due to bad investments made over the years and exorbitant interest rates on loans we had taken out. We received government permission to sell plots of land and build a new neighborhood to be populated by people from outside the kibbutz itself, who chose to purchase a plot of land and build a house. There are four areas in the building process of the new neighborhood: *aleph* (the first stage), *bet* (the second stage), *gimel* (the third stage), and *daled* (the fourth stage). Sometimes I refer to the stages by their names in the narrative.

During the Second Lebanon War in summer 2006 we had approximately 130 new families living in the new neighborhood and these residents are a part of the community today known as Gesher Haziv. Thus, although in reality our expanded community is no longer a kibbutz, according to official records we are still known as Kibbutz Gesher Haziv. And while these new residents are not members of the kibbutz itself, which still exists as a subset, they are members of the greater overall community or municipality.

Since my husband, youngest daughter, Meshi, and myself were abroad when the war broke out, some people are probably wondering why we would choose to leave the relative comfort and safety of America to return to Israel during the conflict. Surprisingly, it never occurred to us to stay any longer than our original plan. Israel is our home, and while it's always wonderful visiting family and friends in the States, we still wanted to return to our own home, our garden, our animals (at least Meshi and myself) and our surroundings. Returning to Israel was natural; it didn't require any thought or deliberation.

My friend Beth Ann, whose house I always stay at when visiting Baltimore, kept saying: "Stay, stay. You know you can stay here for however long you want." And I knew she was truly saying this from the bottom of her heart. She has always opened her home to me and my family; I even lived with her and her husband for six months in 1981. Beth Ann has plenty of room and I knew that the three of us wouldn't be an imposition if we decided to stay longer with her.

An alternative plan could have been for Shanie, our older daughter, to fly to the States and meet us there. She's sixteen and has flown overseas without adult supervision twice in the past few years (once with her brother when she was twelve and then with a friend when she was fourteen), so I don't think that she would have been afraid of traveling alone. We could have arranged for a plane ticket and then picked her up at the airport near Baltimore or anywhere else that she flew into. However absurd it may sound, we never even entertained that possibility. It always seemed clear to the three of us that we were going home to Israel.

Life in America always seems so much safer than the way our lives in Israel are presented via the media. After all, what is usually shown are terrorists blowing up buses and killing scores of innocent Israeli civilians; or the big, bad Israeli army that indiscriminately kills Palestinians. However, that is not our day-to-day reality any more than it is safe to walk on the streets of most American cities. The Americans I know are afraid – of being mugged, of sexual harassment or being sued, having their homes broken into, losing their jobs, being randomly gunned down, or having terrorists attack the country again like the awful 9/11 atrocity. People are fearful and take precautions. Americans seem to be full of anxiety. Under the veneer of safety seethes danger and threat.

The international media offered a one-sided version of events during the recent Lebanon-Israel war in 2006, but this time it was even more skewed than usual. Having lived through the events, I can truthfully say that the sensationalism of the war was amazingly biased. The Israelis quickly turned from being the victims to being the aggressors. The war began with Hizbullah provocation when it violated Israeli territorial sovereignty, killed and kidnapped Israeli soldiers, and bombed the northern border of the country. Israel retaliated. Isn't that what any sovereign nation would have done? Doesn't Israel have the same right as all other nations to defend itself from attack?

The question was raised in the media about the proportion of Israel's response. Since when is a country judged on the intensity of its defenses? Not Russia exercising its right to quell insurgency in Chechnya, not the Chinese in Tibet or the Americans in Iraq. The Hizbullah continued bombarding Israeli cities, towns, and communities for over thirty-three days, but what was shown on the media were the poor Lebanese villagers of the south fleeing from their homes. What about the Israelis who had to flee their homes? Little or nothing was shown in the media reports about them or their plight.

And what about the Israelis, like my family, who chose to stay and suffer through the bombardments? There were a few documentary pieces shown about the citizens of Kiryat Shmona who were in the shelters, but nothing about the hundreds of thousands of other Israelis who were refugees for over a month, or about the fear and difficulties they faced during that time and after.

What wasn't presented in the media is the other side of Israeli society, the one that is warm, open and friendly, where we are the only liberal Western society and democracy in the Middle East. Israelis all over the country opened their homes to the refugees from the North; businesses and hotels offered discounts, and donations of all kinds (food, games, money, and live performances) flooded the North.

No one discusses the fact that in Israel all religions can worship freely and have free access to holy sites. Women are free to express their opinions, seek careers, get an education, and even drive a car. The educational system in Israel offers twelve years of education for both boys and girls of all religions; Jewish pupils are taught Bible along with Jewish history, world history and tolerance for other cultures and religions and the ministry runs an alternative Arab educational system that teaches in Arabic and offers other religious studies, such as Islam, Druze, and Christianity. And the judicial system is considered relatively fair and enlightened by many (including Harvard Law Prof. Alan Dershowitz) in its attempts to find the appropriate balance between security and liberty for *all* citizens, both Israeli and Palestinian.

In contrast, our Arab neighbors do not allow free religious worship or access to holy sites; deny women freedoms; have an unfair judicial system; and their educational and religious leaders spread hatred and lies about Israel and the Western world in general. There is no real democracy in these countries as there is in Israel, yet many countries of the world require Israel to abide by a double moral and political standard.

Due to media and political bias there is much information about Israel that is unknown to the world, which shows how affirmative Israeli society is in the world today. Israeli technology affects people's lives globally in a positive way since among the numerous inventions Israelis have created are: Pentium microprocessors and Centrino chips, disk-on-key (memory stick), and the video camera that travels through the intestine in a capsule. Economically, Israel has the highest average living standard in the Middle East. The per capita income in 2000 was over $17,500, exceeding that of the UK. Israel's $100-billion economy is larger than all of its immediate neighbors combined. Educationally, twenty-four percent of Israel's workforce holds university degrees – ranking third in the industrialized world after the United States and Holland – and twelve percent hold advanced degrees. Israel ranks second in the world per capita in the publication of new books. Moreover, Israel is the only country in the world that entered the twenty-first century with a net gain in its number of trees, made more remarkable because this was achieved in an area considered mainly desert. (However, from the damage done by the Katyushas to the forests in the North this summer it could take up to fifty years to regenerate.) Israel has more museums per capita than any other country. Israel has two official languages: Hebrew and Arabic. Israel is the only truly democratic state in the Middle East.

We are comfortable in Israeli society, although politically and socially there could be improvement. Knowing the "truth" about this country and recognizing its drawbacks, we couldn't have decided to stay in America during the war. And besides, our son Lavie is in the Israeli army. Although there was nothing we could do for him, none of us (Asher, Meshi, or I) could imagine leaving Lavie alone in Israel.

In retrospect it seems hard to explain our decision to return rationally, especially to someone who has never been in either Israel or in any country at war. I guess having lived through Katyusha bombardments before, we weren't really afraid. Or, maybe since we knew what to expect we thought we could carry on as usual. We wanted to be at home, our home. After traveling around the States for three weeks we wanted to unpack and relax, even if that meant being limited by the Katyushas. But as I said before, no one thought that the war would last as long as it did.

This narrative is non-fiction. As the subtitle states it describes the surreal reality of how the civilian residents of one Israeli community managed through this difficult time. It evolved from the first person impressions of the participants as we went through the routine of war. I interviewed people who chose to stay in Gesher Haziv, recording what they felt and what they did during this period of war, which lasted over a month. I tried to interview people of different ages, ranging from children to seniors so that a wider perspective could be seen of our situation and how people handled it. I also interviewed people from all areas of the community – the old kibbutz and the new neighborhood.

I have taken a little bit of literary license, sometimes

cleaning up sentences or deleting repetitive sentences, but I tried to keep each person's thoughts, syntax, and speaking pattern as intact as possible.

Most of the news items carried by the media during this period ignored what was happening with those Israeli citizens under constant fire. Hopefully, this narrative will offer a different perspective of how it felt to be in a constant state of war and how war became routine.

CHAPTER ONE
At The Beginning

Wednesday, July 12 & Thursday, July 13

Hizbullah sends dozens of Katyusha rockets into Israel. A number of Israeli citizens are wounded and two Israeli soldiers, Eldad Regev and Ehud Goldwasser, are kidnapped in the attack. Eight IDF soldiers are killed. On Thursday, direct Katyusha hits on Gesher Haziv including the Teacher's Room at Hofei Hagalil Elementary School. Hizbullah shoots dozens of Katyusha rockets into Israel all along the border, as well as at Carmiel, Rosh Pina, Mount Meron and Haifa. Numerous Katyushas hit Nahariya at least twelve times and twenty-three in the Western Galilee; fires started due to hits; at 12:01 there are 16 slightly wounded, ten suffering fear or panic attacks, one critical, one dead.

Shanie

My name is Shanie Coren. I am sixteen years old. I have lived all my life on Gesher Haziv. I have an older brother, Lavie, who is in the army, and a younger sister, Meshi. My mother is Bethe and my father's name is Asher (he was also born on the kibbutz). I am in the eleventh grade. I study classical ballet and theater, and am very active volunteering in the Noar Haoved Vehalomed Youth Movement (also known as the Noa"l).

This is the beginning of the war, for me, Shanie. I woke up that Wednesday morning. Everything was normal. I took the dog for a walk as I did every morning since my parents were abroad. While I was walking, I met a friend of mine who had just returned from our high school, called Sulam Tsor (which is located on the kibbutz). She was there in the middle of the summer to take a matriculation exam in mathematics. My exam was scheduled for an afternoon session. In the middle of her exam, the head of the mathematics department came into the classroom and said that Kibbutz Hanita and Kibbutz Matzuba (which are located very close to us) were under attack, but that the students shouldn't panic and the exam was continuing.

As my friend told me this, I realized I was home alone and that my brother was stationed at a military base on the Northern Border and might be in danger. I rushed home to call him. I saw that he had just called me on my cell phone, but that I had missed the call. I managed to contact him and he told me that he was okay and not to worry, and to let our parents know this information.

That afternoon I went to school to take the math exam, even though I was definitely not in the mood. I walked through a pretty woody area so I couldn't see much. When I got to school I could see where our army was stationed on the border and there was a lot of smoke coming out of that base. Besides that we were shooting towards Lebanon. There was a lot of booming and noise and a lot of rockets coming into Israel from Lebanon. During the entire exam I kept hearing the loud noises of rockets landing nearby. Let's put it this way, the math test did not go very well. (I found out recently that I got 100; I still don't know how since I couldn't concentrate very well that day.)

After that I went to the *ken* – the literal translation of the Hebrew word is nest, but it is used to identify a gathering place for youth in Noar Haoved Vehalomed a youth movement my siblings and myself are very active in. We were supposed to go out with our *hanichim* (our young charges) to a camp the next day and we had to prepare the activities. Then we were alerted to go into shelters and security rooms. I took Skippy for a walk because he had to walk, obviously. I walked in the direction of the Sulam Tsor Mountain (north) and I noticed that it was all burning up and full of smoke. All the smoke was very close to Kibbutz Hanita and, well, that basically told me that my brother was right and that there would be a war. Then I went to my friend, Smadar's house in the evening, since she is one of my best friends, and I was completely scared.

Later I went home. I spoke to my father on the phone and I must have been pretty hysterical at the time. He asked how the exam went and I said: "*Abba* (father in Hebrew), the whole mountain was burning and there were boomings. How do you think I did?!"

We were asked by one of the other teenagers in our group to make some phone calls to people in the community, to make certain that everyone heard the announcement on the loudspeaker telling everyone to go into the shelters. After that, our group decided to meet in one of the shelters. Unfortunately, it was still locked. While we were waiting for someone to come and open it, all my friends were making fun of the situation, and of course I was freaking out. However, believe it or not, we played board games throughout the night in the shelter to keep ourselves busy. Very amusing, very much fun, but I was still freaking out because I was alone.

Thursday was the day when everyone really starting getting scared because a Katyusha rocket fell 20 meters from the place where we were standing the day before, that same shelter. I was sleeping at home at the time. My room is a security room (more or less) and I woke up from the noise of the rocket landing. This was one of the scariest experiences of my life, especially since I was alone.

I started making phone calls to my friends when I realized that there was no way we were going out on the scheduled trip of our youth movement. Smadar called me at some point and told me to come to her house, so I wouldn't be alone. Rachel, our head counselor, called and told us that the buses weren't allowed to go north past a certain point, meaning that they couldn't get to the kibbutz. She also said that many of our younger members and their parents had fled the community.

Eventually it was just me and a few friends of mine who stayed on the kibbutz. From my age group only about three or four stayed; that was really sad. In the end we did go to the camp. But we had transportation problems – and we had to have some parents drive us to Moshav Regba (south of Nahariya) and then we took a taxi to Kfar Horesh where the camp was.

Terry

My name is Terry Hills and I am forty-nine years old. I immigrated to Israel from England with my wife Teresa and our two children. We came to live on the kibbutz in 1994, and have now lived here for twelve years. I work as a painter and carpenter.

On that first morning I drove to Shlomit (a town north-east of Gesher Haziv, about a ten-minute drive away) to pick up my son, Joseph (also called Yossi), who works in the carpentry business with me. Then Joseph drove to pick up one of our workers named Alla at his home in Ma'azra (a village just south of Nahariya), as usual. We had all arrived at the workshop around 8:30 as usual.

But afterwards we saw and heard two helicopters hovering above the workshop and firing into the Hizbullah towers located on the Lebanese side of the top of the hill to the north of us, the Sulam Tsor Mountain. They must have been Apache helicopters because they were hovering straight above us and standing still. That day we worked "normally," closing up shop around 17:00. I went home and Teresa (my wife) and I watched the news trying to figure out what was going on.

15

The next day, Thursday, I picked everyone up as usual. When we got back to the workshop it was only a matter of minutes before the first Katyushas started falling. We knew that there was a possibility that something might happen this day, so we weren't rushing to get to work. Once they started falling we tried to continue working "as usual," but we just couldn't concentrate; you can't when that kind of thing is going on. Forget the danger side of it, you just can't, and that's all there is to it. So I decided to give up on the idea of trying to work. Joseph and I took Alla home and then we drove back to Gesher Haziv. That's how stupid we were acting. Later that day, when Katyushas were falling everywhere and the electricity went out, all my wife Teresa was concerned about was the food defrosting. So instead of "forget the food or whatever," she wanted to drive where there are more Katyushas. "Let's go to Yossi's." Luckily, while we were driving there nothing fell.

We stayed there for a couple of hours (three or four) until we got bored – the conditions of Yossi's house were awful – we had to squeeze in between all the bottles on the floor to find a seat. But while we were there we heard what sounded like massive explosions. So we all ran outside, as you do, to see where the Katyushas had fallen. What it was, again, like the day before, were helicopters above Yossi's house firing missiles into Lebanon. But since we were in a valley there was an echo from the firing of the rockets. It scared the living daylights out of us for a while. We left there and came back to the kibbutz.

Teresa

My name is Teresa Hills and I am married to Terry. We have two children, Joseph and Gabrielle. I am a hairdresser by trade, but I also worked in the Baby House as a caregiver for many years after we came to the kibbutz.

I was at home that Thursday morning. When Terry and Joseph came home after dropping Alla off, I wasn't surprised. We were all panicking actually. We were all huddled in the security room while the Katyushas were dropping. Then suddenly the electricity went off. And I said: "Okay, so we're taking the food from the freezer and going to Joseph's house in Shlomit." Terry kept saying that we'd be safer in Shlomit because the Katyushas go over the houses. When we got there, though, all hell broke loose – Katyushas were falling all around us all the time we were there.

Judy

I'm sixty years old and my name is Judy Kasinetz. I grew up in New York, and first came to Israel on a Habonim workshop in 1963 for a year. I immigrated in 1969 with my husband, Mel, and our *garin* (*aliya* group). I have four children and have fulfilled a variety of functions on the kibbutz. My eldest daughter, Leah and her family live on the kibbutz.

The first day, when everything started happening, we had my sister-in-law here, Mel's sister. She was flying out that night and we had planned on leaving the kibbutz after breakfast. She had never been to the museums in the Tefen area, near Ma'alot (where I work), so we planned on going there. We were walking around the open museum and looking at the statues, and we visited all the different museums. And in the meantime we sort of heard some booming in the background, some activity. At Tefen we could hear a certain level of active fire and tried to keep my sister-in-law diverted, only talking quietly to the people working at the museum to find out what was happening. Then we left in the car and we heard on the Hebrew news that two soldiers had been captured. We did tell her this information and that apparently we were trying to get them back, or something.

We finished at Tefen around 13:00-13:30 and went down via Carmiel, had lunch, and then drove down to Netanya to my mother's house. After dinner there, the plan was to take my sister-in-law to the airport and then pick up my sister, Rita, and my mother in Netanya and come back north. Because we heard what was going on we convinced my mother not to come and brought my sister up because she was supposed to be having a reunion with her friends in Nahariya in the next couple of days.

Every time my sister Rita tried to get in the shower that Thursday morning Katyushas were falling in the area. So she started feeling kind of weird and paranoid. That day I wasn't supposed to be at work; it was supposed to be a vacation day. Meanwhile, things for my sister were very unnerving. All her friends who had planned to come up had to start changing their plans. She was extremely occupied with phone calls trying to reschedule the reunion. In the end they had to move the venue of the reunion south to Rehovot.

I am no stranger to Katyusha rockets being aimed at Gesher Haziv. I remember that in May 1970 the first Katyushas were fired on the Western Galilee and they landed in Gesher Haziv! Two months later, on July 12th, the night my son was born in Nahariya Hospital, there were more Katyushas in our area. I was concerned about people at Gesher Haziv, but in reality the Katyusha fell directly across the street from the hospital and I should have been worried about myself and my newborn. Since I didn't know the geography of the area well I was oblivious to the danger I was actually in. I have also been here through the Yom Kippur War, the Litani Operation (1978), Shlom Hagalil (the Peace of Galilee War, 1982), and so on until today, when we were also shelled. And I figured if I haven't left since then, and those events didn't drive me out of Gesher Haziv, then this is my home.

Ronny

Today I am thirty-three years old and am a relative newcomer to the kibbutz and the Western Galilee. My name is Ronny Livney. I was born in Herzliya, but have been living in Gesher Haziv for a year. I have an MA in social science and communications and a BA in psychology and communications.

That Wednesday afternoon, when the whole thing started, I was working as a supervisor for the math matriculation exams at the high school. As I was walking around, going from classroom to classroom, I heard the explosions from Zarit, which isn't far from here. Immediately everyone was asking everyone else: "What happened? What happened?" until we received word that there had been a kidnapping of soldiers and then our military responded with artillery into Lebanon. Then we had to decide what to do with the teens who were in the middle of the nationwide matriculation exam. Continue? Stop?

We tried to get whoever was walking around outside to go into the teacher's room, just so we knew where everyone was. Someone in charge stopped the exam and explained to the kids what had happened. We realized that this wasn't going to stop with a few far off boomings.

Carolyn

My name is Carolyn Danoff. I made aliya in 1980 and moved to Kibbutz Gesher Haziv in October 1982. I am a nurse at Nahariya Hospital in the Surgery B Ward, which is the Vascular Back and Chest Surgery Department. I'm fifty-four years old and married to Eugene. We have three children who are all in the army right now.

My ward is on the second floor of the hospital. First we moved all the patients to mamad rooms (security rooms with extra thick walls of reinforced metal and concrete). First they moved the top floors down to our floor, so we were with the eye unit on the second floor. There are fewer patients in a hospital in a war; initially, you release anyone you can and only do emergency surgeries.

As a nurse I am obligated to work during a state of high alert or a war. There was a memo in the hospital and the head nurses had meetings every day. They said it was like a *Tzav 8* (emergency call-up notice) – there are different levels of emergency situations. Nahariya was put on the most serious alert, although we never did twelve-hour shifts like I once had to do when I worked in Rambam Hospital. That might not have been a bad idea though, except for the people who had to work those long shifts, because there would have been fewer people on the roads. It really saves a lot of transportation and that was one of the big problems.

Eugene and I didn't even discuss going away. The question never really came up. First of all we had nowhere to go other than the offers that the kibbutz got. We are just not that terrified, and people respond differently. I didn't have three little kids this time around under the table like during *Invei Za'am* (The Grapes of Wrath Operation in 1996). Then the kids went away during the day but came back at night – which probably wasn't the best decision.

I worked a night shift between Wednesday and Thursday. That day, Thursday, my mother left for the States. She left Nahariya about an hour before a Katyusha fell right on the Ga'aton, which is the main street in Nahariya, near my parents' apartment. And then the minute I walked out of the hospital that morning, a Katyusha fell across the road in Moshav Ben Ami. There is this boom and it's frightening. But then it goes away and after 15 minutes you get in your car and drive home.

Eugene

I am seventy-eight years old and married to Carolyn. I made aliya in 1969. I have six children (three from a previous marriage) and my youngest son from my first marriage currently lives on the kibbutz as well.

I had no problem staying. I didn't want to go away. We spent one night in Tel Aviv and I'm not certain why we did that. I felt that this was my house and I didn't want to leave. We also don't have little children and that certainly would have been a factor in a decision like that. In previous years with me here and Katyushas falling, it has never been of this intensity. But this is home.

You have to use common sense with everything, especially in a war. When it was intense, and it was intense at times, I would go into the security room. So that became a routine as well.

Ishai

I am seventy-seven years old and I am married to Evelyn. My name is Ishai Harrari. I made aliya in 1948 with my garin and came to Gesher Haziv. I have been married to Evelyn since 1952. We have three children, two of whom are living on the kibbutz today.

We were lucky – our lives stayed more or less the same. I distribute the newspapers in the mornings, so no matter what the weather is or the situation, I have to distribute the papers. It reminds me a bit of how it was years ago when I was working with cows in the dairy. I had to milk the cows when it was time, regardless of the situation. It was the same thing now. We didn't have mail very often, but the newspapers came every day. That held me within a certain framework of routine all the time.

Noa

I am one of Evelyn and Ishai's daughters and I am forty years old. I was born and raised on Gesher Haziv and I have lived here for most of my life. I have one son, Kfir.

The war really began for me on Wednesday. I was at work in Nahariya, as usual. I received a phone call from Rhona, my sister, around 9:00, who said that a good friend of hers who works in Nahariya Hospital called and said that something had happened on the border and that the hospital was going on alert – to an emergency level of alert. She wanted me to do her a favor and go collect Lior, my nephew, from the summer camp because they were evacuating the children from the area. She wanted him to come home. The news of the kidnapping hadn't been aired on the news yet.

I called my boss and explained to him what my sister had said and that I had to leave. He said okay, but asked me to wait until my colleague returned. So I called my colleague and told him that I have to "fly" out of the office because my sister was under "atomic" pressure and any second they would be beginning the evacuation of the children and I had to get my nephew before they put him on the bus. He said he was on his way.

Around 9:30 my sister calls again hysterical, but I was finally able to leave the office. When I got to Kibbutz Sa'ar, where the camp was, they were indeed already putting the first groups of kids onto the buses. I turned on the radio in the car and there was still nothing on the news about the kidnapping. My boss called and I told him that I was at Sa'ar. He said that's it, the whole thing's over, you don't have anything to worry about. Lior arrived and then I heard the news report. Then I thought that if that's the situation then I'm not returning to work. The hospital was already on alert and now they've informed the public about the kidnapping. Then the residents of Shlomi (a small town in the Western Galilee near Gesher Haziv and the border) were told to go into the shelters and they closed the factories in the Shlomi area (not in Nahariya yet, though). I thought, there's no logic in me returning to work because by the time I get back they might send Nahariya residents to the shelters and the road North might be closed. So I just stayed at home.

I called my boss and told him I wasn't coming back. He then said that he thought that all would be over by the next day. Yeah, thirty-four days later.

Lyn

My name is Lyn Baer and I am originally from Australia. I am a nurse by profession and am forty-four years old. I am married to Micha and we have three children – Oren is thirteen, Ela is eleven, and Alon is eight and a half.

I was at work as the school nurse at Ein Hamifratz, a kibbutz south of Acco, and all of a sudden these news reports started coming through that something had happened on the border and that there had been some Katyushas into Shlomi. It was sort of discussed at the school, but these things have happened before. There were children at school in Galim, which is a special education school located on Ein Hamifratz in addition to the regular elementary school. I was also there for a staff meeting. Most of the children at the school are not from the Shlomi area, but they are from the Matte Asher Regional Council. But since they are from such a widespread area, there was no discussion about sending the kids home. We were aware of it, that it was happening, but at that point the children weren't made aware.

These were events that have happened before on the border. There had been numerous attempts to kidnap soldiers and soldiers have been shot at across the border, as well as Katyushas, which we've lived with for many years here. So people were made aware, but no more than that; it was at the back of my mind, though.

In the evening there were all the numerous news reports about the soldiers who had been taken and that eight soldiers had been killed, and everything else. We had the feeling then that something serious was going to be happening.

On Thursday, it all really started with the Katyushas coming over the border. Micha went off early to work at Kibbutz Evron as usual between 5:30 and 6:00, before anything fell. I got out of bed and started breakfast and did all the things in the house. Mid-morning and the Katyusha fell on the elementary school, Hofei Hagalil. That was the big bang for us. It was really quite scary. The kids were actually in the security room when it fell. They were in there watching TV, eating their breakfast in Oren's room because it is just something I let them do during the summer break.

I was in the lounge area when the Katyusha fell. And it shook our house, and it shook all the windows; everything rattled. I went into the security room and told the kids to lie on the floor because from past experiences, the Katyushas come in a set. I think it was the first time they really heard one go off *so* close – the bang of the Katyusha and that it actually shook the house like it did. We had bits and pieces of plaster come down, just little bits where the plaster meets the woodwork in our house. It was about 60 meters from here, and it was quite loud. It gave the kids quite a fright, also because I asked them to lie on the floor. That's the first time we've asked them ever to get down and be careful.

We waited in the security room and then heard reports that there had been Katyushas falling in Nahariya and that a woman had been killed on her veranda. Things started to look a lot more serious. We thought it was going to be a couple of days' activity or just returned fire; it just wasn't clear.

I called Micha and said: "Look we've got Katyushas falling around us here, I would like you to come home from work, just for you to be here," especially because they were landing in Nahariya as well. He came home. He actually got a *tramp* (ride) home with one of the guys who lives in Sa'ar who drove him into Gesher Haziv.

Then we went to the bomb shelter next to Aviva Amitai's house, but found we were ankle deep in water. There was a problem there with the pumping system. We spent most of the day cleaning the shelter. Micha worked on the pumping system until he had it working. It was Micha and I and our children and Aviva working on getting it habitable. They really enjoyed it.

The thing is that the Katyusha that fell on the school hit the electricity as well and we were blacked out – no TV, no radio, no computer – we were just all of a sudden cut off from everything. It took approximately four hours to fix the electricity because it hit a main line.

There was no air conditioning, no lights, no anything in all the shelters. So we went down there with camping equipment – battery lights that we brought back from Australia. So we hung a few of them up down there in the shelter and we cleaned up, which really kept the kids busy. It was sort of fun because it was in the dark with the lights and everything else. But there was that feeling of isolation because you didn't know how long it was going to go on for.

That first night we slept in the shelter. We decided to do that because we had never slept in a shelter before. And it was more like an adventure thing for the kids, so they could see what it was like. And we told them that if we need to do it again you will know where to come, where to be, the layout of the place – the toilets are here, the sinks are here, the taps, water, whatever. So we had it all set for them, so if there had been a heavy barrage then we would have returned to the shelter. But one night was enough for me – that was enough adventure for me. For the rest of the war I didn't feel the need to go down again.

Benny

My name is Benny Bodaga; I am thirty-seven years old and work for the Electric Company. I have lived in Nahariya all of my life; so has my wife, Orit, and I suffered through Katyusha barrages in the past, but this time the intensity of the barrages, the number of rockets shot at us and the length of time that we were under siege was unbelievable. I can't ever remember anything like this!

The first day of the war I was at work in Haifa when we heard on the radio about the kidnapping of the soldiers. At work we have two televisions, so after hearing the news on the radio we turned both of them on. All the employees began saying that we needed to respond, before we even knew what to expect. On the other hand we're the victims of this conflict.

Then all the telephone calls started. The children were in summer camps and Orit was at work. So I began making calls to the summer camp run by the Matte Asher Regional Council, which was in the eucalyptus tree grove here on Gesher Haziv, but they were evacuated. Then I called the kindergarten where my daughter, Shiri, goes and they didn't answer for close to forty-five minutes – they simply didn't answer the phone. They were at the pool. They were evacuated slowly and quietly in order not to make the children hysterical. They must have heard the boomings, but didn't understand what was going on and it took them some time until they returned to the kindergarten and into the security rooms. So then I calmed down a bit. Later, I arrived home as usual around 16:00. Orit and I were expecting our fourth child. During the first few days of the war, until the birth of course, we started to spend time in the mamad, but only the children slept there.

My mother lives in Nahariya. At the beginning of the war she suffered through a number of really bad Katyusha barrages. She lives on the sixth floor and saw them fall and cause a lot of damage, so she was pretty stressed. It didn't make sense for her to stay in Nahariya, so she came to stay with us. She did most of the cooking for all of us and was here the entire war. So we had seven people in our house during this period and we managed, even with all the pressure from the war and the boomings and the uncertainty.

Miri

My name is Miri Shulski Rashty. I am thirty-one years old and married to Ilan. I work in a bank and we have one daughter, Noa. On that first Wednesday, I heard on the radio that there had been a kidnapping. So I called the nursery school where our daughter goes and they said everything was okay. I came home early that day to collect Noa, and from then on no one from work saw me for a while.

On Thursday the nursery school on the kibbutz was already closed. I simply disappeared from my work at the bank, although I received a lot of support from the branch where I work.

I haven't experienced a lot of wars in my life, except maybe the Gulf War. I wasn't scared then, it was even a little bit funny. And then, suddenly, when it began here – I don't know – since I don't really know what a war is, or how to behave, and this wasn't a war like other wars.

I remember the electrical blackout that first Thursday morning when everyone fled the kibbutz. Ilan wanted me to come to the mamad because of the Katyushas that were falling close to us. Then a bit later we exited the mamad and we saw through the window that our neighbors were all packing up their cars, in panic. In that one moment we saw them running, really running. They put their things on top of their cars and left. Everyone just disappeared.

I said to Ilan: "I don't know," and Ilan says to me: "Let's take our things and drive to my parents' in Acco." And then, when we arrived there, he says: "Here the Hizbullah won't shoot. We'll stay here, nothing will happen to us here," which was a reasonable assumption. We were in Acco and then the Katyusha fell on Carmiel. So we said to each other: "Okay. If that's the situation, then it doesn't matter where we are, so we might as well be at home."

Hannah

My name is Hannah Troy. I am eighty-five years old (I was eighty-four when the war broke out) and I have lived here on Gesher Haziv since 1949, since the very beginning of the kibbutz. My two daughters, Naomi and Chava and their families, live on the kibbutz also.

The war caught me suddenly, like everyone – I was here – we were ordered to go to the security rooms (like a mamad, a room with reinforced concrete walls, floor, and ceiling) around noon or early afternoon. I still work a bit in the mornings in the Accounting Department, but by then I was at home.

I went into my security room when we were told to, but I don't trust it at all. It isn't worth anything. There is a story that someone once asked for a nail to be driven into one of the walls of the security room in order to hang a picture and just as the hammer hit the nail, it pushed the nail straight through to the other side! And in this situation it definitely wasn't secure. In the past, when it might have been able to protect me against shrapnel, then maybe I would have stayed there. Also, I would be alone. I know it is psychological; when there are more people around it's easier to handle this kind of situation, even though there is no rationale to this way of thinking. Still I felt safe in the shelter.

I think it was the next morning when we were told to go to the shelters, which I did. The shelter near my house isn't in good condition. It turns out in the end that it was full of water and we couldn't use it even if we wanted to. But it doesn't matter because I am registered for being in the shelter under the dining room. I was there in the past. Once upon a time when we were a more homogeneous society (just kibbutz members), then I might have used the shelter next to my house, but now when so many of the residents in my neighborhood are people I don't know, who are renting apartments, I didn't even bother to check it out. I also didn't want to be totally alone, which I might have been if I had used that shelter. I guess I could have gone there if it was only for a few hours. In the past Kopeet, another older kibbutz member, used to worry about bringing beverages to people in the shelters.

So I went to the dining room shelter directly because I knew that it was clean and organized. The Situation Room is also there. There is a telephone and TV so I wouldn't be totally disconnected from the world. Then a few more people came to the dining room shelter after me.

Shai

My name is Shai Grossman and I'm forty-three years old. I was born and raised on Gesher Haziv. My parents live here and so do my sister and her family. I am married to Tzofit and we have three children. For the past few years I have been fulfilling the job of executive director of the kibbutz (what used to be called the farm manager).

There should have been no formal connection to the day to day running of the municipality during the war, but since the municipality is in the hands of another person and wasn't functioning fully during that time, in my position I found myself as the person who was responsible for the functioning of the community during the war. This occurred without previous plan or forethought. It wasn't a formal appointment, but it more or less became that.

The first day of the war, on Wednesday morning, was the kidnapping and, via the security officer of the community, I understood that a high alert was being posted and there was an understanding that something was going to happen that might take longer than one day. In the afternoon we decided to convene the Security Committee of the community. By then it was clear that Katyushas were going to fall; there were alerts and warnings posted. So we decided to open the Hamal – the War Room, the Control Room (which will be called the Situation Room throughout this narrative) of the community during a war.

We sent out a letter to every resident of the community, and we went from house to house distributing it. The people who did this were members of the committee and we drafted teenagers to help distribute the sheet. What we informed people about was: 1) that there was a Situation Room open to any and every question that people may have – they could call there for an answer; 2) we informed people about the shelters; 3) we refreshed people's knowledge of the procedures – what to do if a Katyusha falls; 4) we also wrote that with any new development we would continue to inform people; 5) and that people must listen to the loudspeaker announcements in order to know what needed to be done. Then we arranged to meet at 7:00 the next morning.

A few minutes after the Security Committee met, at 7:15 on Thursday, the first Katyushas fell – one of which fell on the elementary school. At that point we realized that we were at a "different movie" from what we first thought, a much more serious situation. We started to get organized in a variety of ways. One, we tried to supply a response for people who were looking for a place to stay outside of the kibbutz; we networked among different kibbutzim or different places and paired the places with those families who wanted to be hosted somewhere else. We started to meet on a permanent basis every afternoon with a larger committee, the Emergency Committee (called Tzachi), which included someone in charge of the senior members, someone in charge of education and culture, maintenance, and all kinds of other people who had some type of duty. Every day we wrote up a summary of the meeting and distributed it among the members of the community. At the same time, on this Thursday, we decided that we were beginning to work on a system of phone messages that functions on SMS. We weren't organized for that.

Helen

My name is Helen Frenkley. I'm sixty-three years old and retired. I first came to Israel in 1960-61 on the tenth Habonim Workshop to Gesher Haziv. In 1965 I made aliya with my garin to Gesher Haziv. In 1973 I worked with Nogah Hareuveni creating Naot Kedumim (the Biblical Landscape Reserve in Israel located between Jerusalem and Tel Aviv with all plants mentioned in the Bible and Talmud – it's the only place of its kind in the world), where I was the director from 1993 until my retirement in 2004. Then I moved back to Gesher Haziv where I purchased a house in the new neighborhood.

I want to preface what I'm going to say throughout this book by stating that I was not stressed at all during the war. I can't say I had a routine because each day was different simply by the nature of the beast. I think that basically I am a fatalist, so I just don't stress out because of things like that. I'm just not afraid of dying. It doesn't bother me. It's not a fear factor for me – I just don't let it hurt a lot.

What I did think was important for me was to be as involved and as active as possible, because I am of the opinion that when you help others you are far less involved with yourself. Therefore, it was a completely selfish motivation to go do as much as I could.

The Situation Room got organized quickly. They set up a list of phone numbers and mobile phone numbers and made calls giving the community's residents all kinds of important information such as when the "SuperAlonit" store was open (a small market located at the entrance to the kibbutz next to the petrol station, generally referred to as "Alonit"), when to enter the shelters because of an imminent attack, when to exit the shelters. The Situation Room was operated twenty-four hours a day by two volunteers. That's where all information was gathered.

I had a guest staying with me those first two days of the war and she was supposed to stay another week. By that Wednesday evening, even I saw that she was getting antsy. So, Thursday morning I said: "Goodbye, you're going to your friends in Haifa." I shipped her out of here and I took her and someone else past Acco to a spot where someone was picking them up. I did this because I really didn't want the responsibility and I didn't want the pressure. She was an American and she was freaking out – and I thought that was kind of funny actually. I think this maybe because I lived in Ramat Gan during the Gulf War of 1991 when the Scuds were literally falling around us. I was the only one left in my whole apartment building, there was parking and I had a wonderful time. I thought it was terrific, so why should this time be any different?

This time the same thing happened. Most of my neighbors left and I was almost alone on my street. It's always quiet where I live, but now it was more so and it was wonderful.

But the real secret is I am the luckiest person, because I'm free. I have no obligation to a living soul except myself. I have no children, no parents nor siblings. It was my call – and that's a luxury in this situation. I mean, people had to make decisions about whether to stay or go; if they had only themselves to think about they could have decided differently than how they decided. I'm only responsible for my two cats and even I say that in the greater scheme of things, that's not the ultimate responsibility. I could do whatever I wanted. I wanted to stay home; I love my home. I was getting hysterical phone calls from friends in America and Jerusalem. I thought that was funny.

And then there were the cats I was feeding from around the neighborhood, one of which has since stayed on as an outside boarder.

Evelyn

I am seventy-three years old and I am married to Ishai. I made aliya in 1952 and I was one of the first volunteers on the kibbutz. I came to Israel because I was looking for an uncle whom both my mother and myself had never met, who was living in Haifa, and who had been born after my mother left Europe.

My routine was simple; I went with Ishai to deliver the newspapers in the mornings on a regular basis. And to my joy or not, the newspapers arrived every morning during the war, not like the mail. Ishai usually delivers the papers alone; now I went with him to help so that we could finish the job as quickly as possible. The newspapers arrived between 4:15-4:45 in the morning, just as always – no change in the schedule. Even though we knew that certain people weren't at home, it was still our responsibility to deliver the papers to them – so we did.

We did this each morning. It was an experience! We didn't know what would happen that morning. Our luck was that it was usually quiet (no Katyushas) during those hours at least until 9:00 (at the beginning). At 9:00 the "performance" began, so we tried to be done by that hour.

Sharon

My name is Sharon Cohen and I am thirty-five years old. I emigrated from Holland in the early 1980s. I lived in the center of the country for many years. I am a single mother with two sons and I am a chef by profession.

I got to Gesher Haziv because of my father who bought a house in the new neighborhood. Then I discovered the beauty of the place. Slowly, slowly my family has come after me, and so have friends. I haven't been living in Gesher Haziv for long, but I like the area immensely.

That Thursday I ran away because of the rockets that landed so close by. Two Katyushas fell close to my father's house on the east side of the community in the new neighborhood. By 8:30, my friend Ronny Livney and I were already on the south side of Haifa. I went to friends in the south. We finally understood what it meant to have a Katyusha fall on you.

M

I am a chiropractor; I am forty-four. Although I was born in the States, I grew up on the kibbutz from a relatively young age and have returned to live here as an adult. Also, my parents still live here today.

The first day of the war, Wednesday, I was at a seminar in Tel Aviv. Sometime during the seminar we were told that two soldiers had been kidnapped. I stayed that night at my girlfriend's in Tel Aviv, but that night her brother came from Kibbutz Evron (which is directly east of Nahariya on the main road and a few kilometers south of Gesher Haziv). He had already escaped from Evron, but I made the decision to go home.

And when I got on the train Thursday morning there was no train service past Acco, instead of up to Nahariya as usual. A friend picked me up from Kibbutz Beit Ha'emek in the Western Galilee, but we weren't certain if the road was open because that was after the first person was killed in Nahariya; Nahariya was basically closed. I was really in a hurry to get back to the kibbutz because I heard that there were big waves and that evening me and my friend, Chumpy, went surfing. The Katyushas that fell that day didn't bother us – we were going surfing! So we went surfing about 17:00 and we were sitting and waiting for waves and up near Rosh Hanikra (just beneath the border with Lebanon) there were two helicopters in the air firing all the time. When we got out of the water there were a few more Katyushas. You could always hear booming, but there was definitely a Katyusha hitting Nahariya when we got out of the water.

Aliza

My name is Aliza Elkon. I'm seventy-five years old and married to Zvi. I immigrated to Israel in January 1949 and am one of the founders of Gesher Haziv. We have four children.

We went to Tel Aviv the second day of the war, but that was a planned trip and we would have gone anyway. My narrative begins with a funny story that I love. Zvi writes here (in one of the e-mails dated July 14th, 2006 that they sent to their family and friends): "And so, we got onto the Acco train, but not before the lady guard at the station entrance, when hearing we were from Gesher Haziv, asked: Oh you're running away from the kibbutz?!? We retained our usual "cool" and instead of spitting on her and kicking her in the shins, smilingly answered that we would return Saturday nite. (sic)" That was just what we had to hear; it was so funny.

Danit

My name is Danit Cameo and I am a social worker by profession. I am married to Shlomi, who is in the permanent army, and we have two children, Gilad and Stav. We have lived on Gesher Haziv for many years and I am very active in the community.

We decided not to leave the kibbutz for two reasons: one, we knew that Shlomi, my husband, wouldn't be able to go with us and we are a very close family. As it was, Shlomi continued to drive to work as usual. We needed some kind of stable anchor so that the family unit would feel unified, and our home became that anchor. We felt safe in our home. And the second reason was that ten years ago we evacuated to Kibbutz Lohamei Hagetaot (some ten kilometers south of Gesher Haziv, but then out of the Katyusha shooting range) during the Grapes of Wrath Operation. We were living at Kibbutz Sa'ar then, which is next to Gesher Haziv. Since Gilad and Stav were born we've known Katyushas barrages extremely well. We decided that we didn't want that experience of being refugees again. It was very difficult for Gilad to be away from home that first time, and it was also very difficult for us to have the family divided. So this time we decided that we're staying home and staying together.

Micha

My name is Micha Baer. I'm forty-three years old and I was born and raised in Gesher Haziv. My parents live here also. I met Lyn twenty-one years ago, we got married sixteen years ago, and we have three children.

I was at work at the Bermad factory in Kibbutz Evron (which is south of Gesher Haziv and east of Nahariya) when the Katyusha fell here. We slept in the shelter that night. We weren't supposed to go to work that day, but I went anyway. I remember that the factory was closed for two days.

We, as a family, spent the first Thursday night in the shelter – we weren't so sure, but we decided that we wouldn't go back to the house. The next night, Friday, we slept at home. Basically, we spent one night in the bomb shelter and we were ready to go back to the shelter if we needed to. But then we stayed in the security room for the rest of the war.

Orit

My name is Orit Bodaga. I am married to Benny and I am thirty-seven years old. We have four children (aged nine, seven, four, and the newborn) and live in the new neighborhood. I work at Bank Mercantile Discount in Nahariya. I was right at the end of my pregnancy and that first day of the war I was at work, but then I had to go for a monitor check. The next day, Thursday, the bank was already closed.

On that first Thursday we brought my mother-in-law to live with us here. She lives in Nahariya. She was here the entire month. She didn't leave at all, except once for one day close to the end of the war. Even when we left for Eilat she decided to stay here. She felt safe here and was worried about driving on the roads.

My parents were here for the entire war, except for one day when they went to Tel Aviv. They live in the new neighborhood on Gesher Haziv as well, right next to us.

The mamad is usually the children's playroom. It is organized with a television, a table, all their toys, and a sofa that opens up. The children spend a lot of time there without any connection to the war. The thick metal door on the window is usually open, though, to let in fresh air. But during the war we kept the window closed so it was quite stuffy in there. They want to eat there normally – so they will take their plates there – so during the war it wasn't so different for them. However, during the war the three older children also slept in the mamad.

Ilan

My name is Ilan Rashty and I am forty-nine years old. I work at a bank, in the Carmiel branch. I am married to Miri and we have a daughter, Noa, who is one year and eight months old.

On Thursday, the morning after the kidnapping, we were both at home. We had just planted some trees in the garden around our house, so I went outside to water them. Miri kept saying to me: "Come in, there are Katyushas outside." I said: "It will be all right, leave it alone." And I continued to water outside. After the barrages intensified we decided to drive to my parents' apartment in Acco, where we thought it would be safer because the population is mixed (Arabs and Jews) and Katyushas would probably not reach that city. And we stayed there until the evening. Then the whole "business" escalated.

Friday, July 14; Saturday, July 15; & Sunday, July 16

Direct Katyusha hits in Gesher Haziv and numerous hits in the Western Galilee and neighborhoods of Nahariya. Hits in Shlomi, Dalton, Kiryat Shmona, Gush Halav, Safed, Hazor Haglilit, Yesod Hama'ale, Tiberias, Merom Golan, eastern Golan Heights, Amiad Junction, Toba, Emek Yizrael, Mount Meron, and in villages on the Northern Border, Carmiel, Ma'alot, Beit She'an, the Krayot and Haifa where a missile hit the train station in Haifa causing numerous casualties; 1,200 Katyusha rockets have fallen so far in Israeli territory.

Lyn

On the Friday we had Katyushas fall in the new neighborhood. That's when it fell in gimel – Friday mid-morning. And that's when practically all of the new neighborhood deserted the kibbutz. Some families were vacillating on the Thursday, when the Katyushas fell on the east side, but when it actually fell in the third stage, come Friday afternoon this place was like a ghost town. Really! It just emptied out. I was quite shocked actually.

We went for a walk on Friday afternoon – stay in the security rooms? We went for a walk! We went down to see where it fell in gimel and over to the school to have a look at the damage. It was probably after lunch, early afternoon; it wasn't 4 or 5 o'clock when most of the Katyushas were falling. We took the kids with us, but we talked to them on the way. Micha gave them the whole talk like: "If I tell you to get down, you get down," and "Try to get down behind a rock that's facing north." He gave the step by step of what to do. And we weren't too concerned when we were actually down in the

THE ROUTINE OF WAR

neighborhood because they have so many places that are being built which actually have built-in mamadim. So we knew that if they started falling we could just pop in to a mamad; that was okay.

In a way I think it was good for the kids to sort of have some perspective of the Katyushas, because the damage in gimel was fairly minimal and it was good for them to see, okay, it made a lot of noise, but it wasn't so terrible. When they saw the teacher's room they were actually more concerned about the teachers – "What are the teachers going to think?" "Wow, look at that!"

They had their own collections of shrapnel, shrapnel from the neighborhood and from the school – they bagged it and wrote down where they found it. Practically wherever they fell on the kibbutz they went and got their pieces of shrapnel and wrote down the date and whatever.

We did *Kabbalat Shabbat* (welcoming the Sabbath) at home and Chaya and Zvi (Micha's parents who live on the kibbutz) came over; that was fairly normal. We tried to keep our routine as normal as possible.

Terry

No one came and told me that I couldn't officially open the carpentry workshop. I took my cue from the information on the news. I didn't have either a security room or an internal room for safety, one of which was needed to keep a place of business open. I knew I couldn't open and then get any kind of compensation. It also wasn't very clear where the line was drawn which allowed a business to work or not. But I never believed that this situation would continue for so long, so at this point I wasn't very concerned.

Teresa and I had gone to Caesaria that weekend to see friends of ours who had come from Glasgow. But since we don't like to sleep away from home for more than one night, whatever the situation, we came home Saturday night. We wanted the comfort of our home and our own routine, however surreal it was becoming. As it turns out it became a routine for us to leave the kibbutz every weekend, at least on Saturdays.

Teresa

We saw on the TV that Nahariya was a complete ghost town. What was weird was that on the High Street (Ga'aton Street) all the coffee shops were still open the first day or two despite all the rockets falling. It should just be common sense that in that case businesses can't remain open. I was really scared at that point. We were alone on the kibbutz since our close friends were in the States. I couldn't wait for Bethe and Kathy to return.

32

We tried going into a shelter once, but that only lasted half an hour. It stunk and felt grimy. We felt better being at home in our security room, even if it was technically less safe.

Judy

I was supposed to have the hands-free speaker for my cell phone installed in my car at Regba. Without really thinking the situation through, that because of the shelling stores might be closed, I just drove to the store. When I got there, nothing was open but the supermarket. So I managed to get some food shopping in.

Somehow the day sort of passed with "normal" Katyusha-time activity with my daughter, Leah, her husband, Naphtali, and their two children. Every time there was an announcement from the loudspeaker about going into the shelters or security room we went – we were in and out all day. Leah and her "group" kept going back and forth from their house to mine throughout the day whenever it was all clear, but they slept in the security room in their house.

We tried to keep this normalish routine; just a normal Friday day – as normal as possible – cooking and cleaning. And in between I was walking Bethe's dog, Skippy, because Shanie was out on the camping trip and Bethe still hadn't come home from the States. I often take care of Bethe's animals when she isn't home – we're friends and neighbors. Things were getting hotter and hotter around here. Poor Skippy, he got very abbreviated walks. Normally, I would take him for a walk around the entire perimeter of the kibbutz. We walked closer to the buildings than usual, but I didn't plan the walk. I just waited for an all clear to make sure, or when things seemed to calm down I went out.

I didn't go to work that Sunday because my place of work was basically closed. I was home alone and still in the Katyusha-time routine I had gotten into over the weekend. I was also still in charge of Bethe's dog, Skippy, because Shanie was still on her camping trip.

Sometime mid-morning I took Skippy out walking from Bethe's house down to the main road and then around in a short circuit. Hopefully he would do what he had to in that short time. Meanwhile, there had already been one Katyusha that had fallen on the elementary school and one that had fallen in the third stage of the new neighborhood. I was walking up the road when I saw a senior kibbutz member, Margalit Bat-Adam, driving down the road on her *kalno'it* (electric motored vehicle like a small golf cart). So we stopped to talk for a few minutes. She said she was on her way to the third stage to check out the damage that had been done to the houses.

We parted, and I keep going with Skippy. All of a sudden I heard the whistling of a rocket coming in close. Skippy and I were right by

Haga (Haklaut Gesher Haziv – the agricultural business of the kibbutz). So I yanked Skippy over and we ducked behind the boulders that are on the old road. I didn't know if it was going to do any good or not. I crouched down very, very low, below the rock level. I figured that if I lay down I'd lose control of Skippy, and I didn't want that to happen. That was the whole thing – trying to be responsible and not let him go. We stayed until I didn't hear any more activity in the air. And I quickly walked home and put Skippy into Bethe's house. I'd decided that we'd had enough for today. The rocket apparently fell right at the Sa'ar-Gesher Haziv gate in the south of the kibbutz.

Meanwhile, there was no one at work in Tefen that day. We work on computers and we're fairly high-tech. I also have a connection, an on-line hook-up so that I can work from home. That Sunday I did some work on-line, what I had to do; some things were pressing, others weren't. I did anything that was pressing. On the other hand, my computer at home is in my security room. So I felt safer working in the security room than if the computer had been somewhere else. So it was very nice knowing that the computer was in a safe place.

Helen

I wanted to help, so when volunteers were asked to help clean shelters, I went. There were two flooded shelters, like Sisyphus, literally. I remember Naomi Benita, myself, Iris, and Zmira were trying to empty the water out. We were literally pouring the water outside, when we realized it was pouring in from someplace else. But besides those two shelters that were relatively unusable, there were enough shelters that were in good enough condition for everybody – had everyone wanted to be in shelters – and the rest of the shelters all had mattresses and all the other I accessories that are needed.

That Friday, Shai Grossman, the kibbutz manager, said we've got to know who's here. So I started walking the streets and knocking on doors – that was the only way to do it – going door to door. And then suddenly in the middle of this – walking around the streets – the loud-speaker would start making announcements which you really couldn't hear down here (in the new neighborhood). And we realized that this was nuts. So we decided to do a telephone thing. We started phoning people. But then you realized that by the time you finished calling the people on your list it's over or its fallen or whatever. It turns out that we were down to about twenty-five percent of the population.

And that's when Aaron Sharif fabulously started putting together the whole SMS connection. It took a number of days to get organized, but he got it through the Internet, so in one fell swoop you could send out a bunch of messages. And I don't know about you, but I never used SMS before in my life. I didn't know how to read the damn thing, but you really learn when you have to.

The animal part to this story is actually very interesting. On Friday, a Katyusha fell in gimel (the third stage of development in the new neighborhood) and I was in my bedroom. I was looking and I could see some smoke, so that is where the legend started, the myth that I'm the spotter, because I called the Situation Room immediately and I said it's about four houses down on the curve of gimel. The noise had been very loud when the Katyusha whizzed directly over my head. Both cats looked at me and since I didn't jump and I didn't do anything, so they remained calm.

Ishai

Pensioners do any work that other people don't want, like guard duty. But there was something else I could do to help. The caregivers in the old age home on Gesher Haziv wanted to get to work and were needed there. But the taxis weren't running, so I volunteered to transport them. I'd drive to Acco, Ma'azra and Shlomit, sometimes twice a day. That was also something that kept me busy. People said to me: "What? Are you an idiot? Why are you doing that?" My answer was simple – "If that woman is willing to risk herself in order to come to work at Gesher Haziv, then it isn't unreasonable that I should come and get her."

I didn't sleep much during the war, but then again normally I don't sleep much. In the security room it's almost impossible to sleep and is worse than anyplace else. I call it the torture room– there's no airflow, no air conditioner, and it's extremely uncomfortable. I learned that if there is an hour to spare and I'm tired, that I can fall asleep during that short period for at least half of the hour. I'm fine after that. And I'm like that even now.

Evelyn

After the first few days, maybe two, three, or four, no public transportation came to the kibbutz – no taxis or buses. Pnina, who is in charge of the old age home on the kibbutz, called me and other members of the board of the old age home and asked how we were going to solve the problem of how to bring the workers/caregivers to the kibbutz. I discussed this with my husband and we decided to take this responsibility upon ourselves. So we drove at least twice a day to Ma'azra or to Shlomit to bring the workers or take them home. We did this almost every day during the war. There were two shifts of 12 hours in the old age home. Sometimes the husband of one of the workers there would bring her, so then we had one less person to bring.

Eugene

I have a daily routine: I walk every morning and I said I'm going out there anyway. I walk around the residential area, not in the fields, but inside the kibbutz. It wouldn't have made any difference because we weren't getting bombed that early in the morning. I didn't realize it the first couple of times I went out – Israel didn't stop at 5:00 in the morning – Lebanon was getting pounded. However, I couldn't do anything else outside because around 10 o'clock things were happening and there was no guarantee – sometimes it was quiet sometimes it wasn't. The Hizbullah had a routine as well. The things I normally do outside I couldn't do because I felt that I was in more danger outside than in the house. Like I said before – use common sense.

Carolyn's parents live in Nahariya and they usually come to our house for Friday night dinner. Her mother had gone to the States and her father was home alone; he's ninety years old. As usual on Friday night he was planning to come visit. We said call a cab and come. He decided, all by himself, that he was going to walk from Sokolov Street, next to the beach, up to the taxi stand near the Egged Bus station (at the eastern entrance to the city), which he did, which we didn't know. And we get a phone call from him while he's there: "Listen, there's glass all around me, the whole place is a shambles." I said: "I don't believe it!" Then we said: "Go home! Go home, we didn't want you to walk there!" So he walked home since he couldn't get a cab. And we asked him to please call us when he got home.

Miri

Friday a Katyusha landed close, very close to our house; we felt it. We knew it was close. Stavi, who is a member of the kibbutz, a friend, and responsible for general maintenance of the community, called us and said: "Miri, a Katyusha fell close to your house." I said: "Stavi, I know, we're here in the house. Where are you?" Then we went outside and we were looking at all the people that arrived – the police, Stavi, Tzofit (the kibbutz nurse), and then all the curious on-lookers who came to see where it had landed. We were also curious; we wanted to know where it had fallen.

Danit

What happened at the beginning is that we were in a type of bubble. I couldn't work because the computer in our house was damaged and my clients were scattered all over the country and I couldn't make contact with them. We understood that we must just continue our lives. And correctly, even though Katyushas were falling around us.

Gilad was in the Situation Room, and there was a certain type of fun for him there. He had an important job to do there; he felt that he was contributing something of himself to the situation. From the point of view of passing time it was like being in an activity organized by the youth movement, but with a more active role. He likes that and he wasn't passive.

Our routine in the house was minimized. Now it revolved around one room – Stav's bedroom, which is a mamad. It became the room for the entire family. We slept there and spent many hours of the day there.

Stav

I am ten years old. Danit is my mother and Gilad is my brother. To my disappointment the entire family slept in *my* room, which is the security room or mamad. My mother was outside all the time when there was boom, boom, boom and I didn't leave the security room.

Gilad

I am sixteen years old. I helped out a lot in the Situation Room. It was really fun! I had something to do there. There was activity. We laughed a lot. It was like being in a summer camp. I wasn't at home very much during this time. Every once in a while I came home to eat or to sleep, and to play music.

Hannah

The way we lived in the shelter was established fairly close to the beginning of the war. Each of us usually went home around 5 or 6 in the mornings to shower and change clothes. And that's it; except for that short time, about thirty minutes every day when I went home to shower, I was in the shelter nearly all the time from the beginning to the very end of the war.

I received food in the shelter. In the Situation Room there were hot and cold beverages, white cheese, and things like that and for all the rest everyone fended for themselves. Noga had food that she kept in the refrigerator – containers and things like that. Evelyn would constantly ask if we needed anything or if they went shopping they would buy products that people needed. Noga was also there all the time.

I ate lunch with my daughter, Chava. She worked a little bit and the rest of the time she was at her house. I always ate lunch with her.

I left the shelter to go to her house; it's very close by. I would then take the food I wanted with me for dinner and the following morning's breakfast – usually a few slices of bread, cheese, eggs and vegetables.

So, except for the half hour in the morning when I went home and the half hour when I had lunch with Chava, I was in the shelter all the time.

Ronny

Sharon and I had left together on Thursday, and when we got to the center of the country we parted. But I came back on Saturday afternoon after I realized that I didn't want to stay in Tel Aviv for long. I was already on my way home. I stopped at my sister's house in Haifa and then took a *sherut* (large, shared) taxi, with seven other people to Nahariya. I got there about 18:00 or 19:00 in the evening and the place was deserted. I stood there on the main road looking for a way north to the kibbutz and there was nothing moving, absolutely nothing. This was just a few days into the war and Nahariya was already a cemetery. Also, throughout that first weekend of Friday and Saturday, Nahariya had really been pounded by rockets. It was really no wonder that it was so empty – just totally unexpected. So I called Sharon's father, Menno, and asked him if he could pick me up because I was stuck in Nahariya. So he came to get me.

Noa

My son, Kfir, wanted to leave the kibbutz on that first Saturday. He was supposed to go on Sunday to join my sister, Rhona, who was already South, but he wanted to leave early. My mother and I drove to Acco to take him to the train, since the train service had already stopped from Nahariya. I asked my mother to come with me to "hold my hand," so I wouldn't drive alone on the road. And it was a very unpleasant feeling because I think that Saturday we really started to feel the intensity of the Katyushas – that the rockets were hitting a much wider range of targets than in the past and this was before anything had fallen in the Krayot (the area between Haifa and Acco which has become a very densely populated area and which has conglomerated a few towns into a megalopolis), or in Haifa. Nahariya was hit really hard, even in the south part of the city; even Acco had been hit once or twice by a Katyusha or two, and that's what really made us feel the intensity. That it wasn't a situation where they shoot twelve or twenty rockets at us and it's over, but something that's going to continue.

The drive to Acco was very unpleasant. The hour that we drove was when Katyushas had been launched in the previous days – the late afternoon hours. Also the feeling that I had of putting my child on a train alone, in this kind of situation, and sending him away, was not such a nice feeling. I just hoped that the train would get moving already and go – and get out of this area. And then the following day was the direct hit on the train station in Haifa, and I said, what luck that we didn't wait until Sunday to send Kfir on the train.

After this major change in my life, I tried to make as few other changes as possible. But some things I just had to change. I began to sleep in the security room, which is my son's room, because I felt safer. I had decided that I wasn't going to a shelter no matter what happened. I didn't want the situation that if there were suddenly Katyushas falling close by, that I had jump out of bed and go the security room. So I decided to sleep there so that I could continue to sleep or continue doing whatever I was engaged in at the time. In Kfir's room I have a computer, TV, radio, music – everything that I needed was there.

The first week of the war I really didn't feel well and I was a bit sick, so that when someone first asked me if I would volunteer and since I didn't feel well, I told them that in another day or two I'd see what's happening. When I felt better I asked to be put on the work roster. The first few times I volunteered to work in the Situation Room I did the usual four-hour shift. It went by extremely quickly and I hardly felt the time pass.

Ilan

I remember seeing Margalit driving her electric motored vehicle. She was doing a circuit on the security road, as is her habit, and was just where the road meets the crossing to Sa'ar when the Katyusha fell. We saw the fall the rocket falling from the bathroom window and then we saw that there was another mushroom cloud from a hit. Margalit was really lucky that nothing happened to her, although she looked quite upset and unsteady. It caused a lot of damage, but only that. Later there was more intensive damage done in that area from other Katyushas.

It was on that first Sunday that my superiors decided to open our back-up bank branch in the Krayot, because of all the Katyushas in Carmiel. So, I was on the way South when I heard on the radio that Katyushas had fallen in Acco and in the Krayot. I flicked a switch in my head and I didn't continue south to the branch. I stopped at my parents' house in Acco to see that they were all right. There I felt tension. They had gone from the top floor where their apartment is down to the basement shelter, because they don't have a security room in their apartment. I stayed with them a bit. Then I called the bank and learned that because of the situation the back-up branch in Kiryat Motzkin wasn't going to open. So I stayed with my parents for thirty minutes or an hour and then returned home to Gesher Haziv. After that, it was decided to keep the branch in Carmiel open as much as possible – unfortunately more closed than open. In Carmiel we are located in a mall so we have a "safe area" but no security room or mamad.

Miri and I tried to continue living normally as much as possible and did our best to maintain a routine. We are usually connected to friends and family through the computer and e-mails, however during this period we weren't using e-mail any more than normal. We used the cell phones and regular phones more to be in contact, since we have a few family members abroad.

Sharon

I decided to return that Sunday and it was very difficult to get back – bus transportation was iffy from Haifa. It took me four to five hours to get back instead of the usual two and a half. That fact helped me make the final decision to stay on the kibbutz for however long. I didn't want to get stuck someplace that wasn't my home. And I love this place and I wanted to be here. I wasn't born here in Israel, although I've been here for twenty-five years. But when I first came to Gesher Haziv I realized that this was the first place in Israel that I could love. My parents are here and my son is here – the people, my parents, and the place. I have no other words for this community but a paradise on earth, really.

Orit

We chose to stay here during the war and specifically for me to give birth. Our normal routine was disrupted by a welcome and planned event– the birth of our fourth child. I went to Nahariya Hospital on the first Sunday of the war, on July 16th. I was three days after my due date and I went for a monitor check and I stayed in the hospital because the doctors decided that it was too dangerous to return home because the road was very dangerous then.

I usually only go to the hospital to give birth when my contractions are very strong; this time everything worked a little differently. That Sunday was the first time that rockets were launched at Haifa. I gave birth in the regular birthing rooms, not in a shelter. The Maternity Ward is on the first floor and there are three other floors above, so it was decided that it was safe enough to stay there at that point. All the other wards were moved down into the shelter. But it was problematic to move the Maternity Ward and the Children's Ward down into the basement shelter because they didn't want us to be with people who were sick. So we stayed there.

The Nahariya Hospital Maternity Ward is normally very busy. However, this time most women fled to the Haifa area hospitals or even went further south to give birth. I heard ambulances bringing the wounded to the hospital. And I heard the noise of the Katyusha rockets being fired at Nahariya and the Western Galilee area, including the ones that fell around the hospital. But I had to disconnect myself from all that and concentrate on giving birth and taking care of our new baby.

I can only talk about myself, but I was relatively disconnected because there wasn't any TV available and you know that when you watch television you're more "inside" and involved. I asked what was going on and people kept me informed, but I didn't get hysterical about the war.

After a birth friends and family usually come to the hospital to visit. But under these circumstances I couldn't expect people to do the normal thing. I knew it was dangerous and that I would be home in a few days. My parents took care of our other children when Benny went with me to the hospital to give birth.

Benny

The birth of our daughter was an exceptional event – both her birth and Orit giving birth during a war under rocket fire. Early in the day I was outside waiting for the results of all the tests and Orit was inside getting tested, and I heard the television in the Waiting Room report about the rockets that hit Haifa and that the war was escalating. It wasn't so pleasant, but there was the normal excitement of anticipation before a birth and the birth itself. They explained to us that the Birthing Rooms are extremely well protected, probably the safest, and the birth was relatively quick and everything was all right.

We had made a purchase for the baby for all kinds of things we'd need at Shilav (a baby supply store) in Nahariya. After the birth I called the manager of the branch and told him that the baby was born and that within two days the baby would be home and that we'd need the products. He said: "What do you want me to do, we're at war!" And I told him: "But my daughter is going to need things – I don't have anything at home for a baby like first clothes – I have to have these things." He told me that he couldn't get to Nahariya because it was being bombarded heavily and that he didn't know where my order was – whether they had packed the things in a carton in the store or if they were in the warehouse in north Nahariya. He wanted to check it out and asked me to call him back the following day.

Shai

In the first few days the Situation Room was staffed by Ma'ayan Shlossberg and Niria Ziv for the most part; everything was done voluntarily. When we decided to open the Situation Room, Rifi Shlossberg, who was in charge of Early Childhood Education in the community, suggested that we turn to Ma'ayan (her daughter) and that she would be happy to work there. Then she began calling around to get more people to help. During the first stages, when we started looking for volunteers, we found that many people were willing to help. At the beginning it was all very voluntary. Afterwards we decided that Tammy would be in charge of the Hamal volunteers so that their work would be professional and efficient, that there were standards. We decided also to change some of the volunteers so that the standards we set could be met; we didn't have a choice.

We attempted to improve the way we were working all the time. At the very beginning we sent out hard copy letters, later on we sent messages through the SMS network. Throughout the entire war, the Situation Room was manned twenty-four hours a day. It gave responses to people inside and outside the kibbutz.

Regardless of the war, my life stayed fairly the same. If Katyushas didn't wake me up first, I usually got up around 7 o'clock. The first thing I did was, without drinking coffee or tea, go to the Hamal to see what was going on there, to hear if there was anything new. Usually, in normal times, I manage to drink a cup of coffee first, take the kids to school on the way, and then go to my office. Now there wasn't any school and I didn't manage to drink a cup of coffee. It changed a bit as the war progressed; it wasn't always exactly the same in the mornings. Then I would go to my office and take care of all those things that were connected to the war, a lot of them concerning what was going on in the shelters, make sure what was happening with the activities – that things were happening with Rifi, if she needed help, with Effie, and not a little bit with those organizations that were offering to host families. I had very few meetings that were connected to my real job during this period, maybe five. In the afternoon, around 16:00 or 17:00 we'd have the Emergency Committee meeting. And then I'd get home somewhere between 20:00 and 21:00.

Hannah

Sometimes, now, I try to think about what I did all day in the shelter, and it's very difficult to describe, because the time did pass. We always wanted to hear the news, which is on every hour on the hour, even though most of the time nothing was new and the older information was repeated. I had a lot of luck because I managed to sleep well for the most part. Noga said she only slept for two hours every night, but I don't know if it's true, because I was asleep. We usually went to sleep around 22:30 or 23:00.

We didn't use an alarm clock or anything like that. We just woke up. At the beginning I woke up later than usual, around 7:00 or 8:00, and so went to my house a bit later in the mornings.

At the beginning Danit's son, Gilad, was around a lot and he really helped out. But there were other youth who were bored and who came to the central shelter for the "experience." So there were some things that really bothered me and the others. These youths came and went, in and out all the time. They left from the door closest to their homes in the new neighborhood, which was through the area where we lived. They said they were bored – what are we, the entertainment committee?

Carolyn

One night at the beginning of the war I went to work and the field by Kibbutz Sa'ar was on fire. It was just a scene out of a movie. Life imitating art, like 9/11; to me it was a scene out of a movie. It was 22:30 at night and I'm driving to work – there is nobody on the kibbutz, there is nobody on the road, anywhere – everything is shut down and in the distance you see a fire, and it was a big, big fire. There was a fire truck there trying to put it out, but there weren't any other people there or anything. And there was rubble all over the street. You feel like it's the end of the world. You're alone in your car and it's dark. And you feel like it's a scene in a movie. Is this the way the world ends or whatever? This really sucks, so to speak.

Helen

In the first few days of the war I was very busy helping around the community in any way I could. There was a lot to do here for people who wanted to help. I was also kind of involved in helping to set up the Situation Room. I helped Tammy Shlossberg, who was doing yeoman's labor in organizing people to work in different places and the various shifts.

Before the war started I helped a senior member of the kibbutz, Menucha Fastman, after she had some medical problems. A few days into the war Temy, her neighbor, told me that Menucha wasn't answering her door. She was concerned about her. Had she left? I forgot that I still had a key to her house, but that wouldn't matter if she was inside the house – the key would be in the lock. It turns out that she was home the whole time, but she was in her security room. I cooked a bit for her and got her food and other things at Alonit. Her air conditioning had broken down and she wasn't concerned that all she had to keep cool with was a fan.

Zvi

My name is Zvi Elkon and I am married to Aliza. I immigrated to Israel on April 14, 1948 where I lived on two other kibbutzim before becoming a part of Gesher Haziv.

On the second day of the war we went to Tel Aviv, but that was a planned trip. We were in Tel Aviv at our son Shimon's house, and since the war was going on, we stayed for another three days until we came to the conclusion that it was time to come home, which we did. Meanwhile we were watching the television every minute of the day like everyone else. We were very emotional. We assume that everyone had similar emotions to ours. Then we came home. But we found little or nothing to do, so we decided to go back to Tel Aviv.

A few days later, once the SMS messages started they became another factor for us while we were in Tel Aviv. It felt as if we were here, because we were quite well aware every time something went off or was going off or the warnings; we received everything.

Aliza

We came back to Gesher Haziv for around two days and there was nothing to do so we went back to Tel Aviv. Our children were driving us crazy to go back to Tel Aviv. We did go into the security room during the two nights that we were here and slept there.

M

I made a conscious decision to be here during the week. It didn't really matter for me because there was no work. But I felt it was important to help with the Situation Room because there were not that many people helping out and I thought that was the minimum I could do. Plus having people see others walking around maybe helped the morale a little bit.

There is a difference between people who grew up here and were going through something familiar (people who are used to Katyushas) and the people who never lived under a Katyusha barrage. People who grew up here reacted differently, even with this kind of intensity.

When the war kept on and the routine really became routine, I volunteered to sit in the Situation Room because after the second day of the war I had no patients coming. So at first I did one shift from 14:00 until 22:00 in the Hamal. But since people around me were becoming more hysterical, and I was pretty calm, it got hectic with the type of people who were there in that main shelter. There were many very nervous people there and it became difficult to work in the Situation Room. We were trying to answer phones – where did the Katyusha hit, find out if there were any fires or anything.

Evelyn

I attempted to make house calls to the senior people who stayed in the afternoons at least once every two or three days because it was extremely important that they see another person. So apart for bringing them things that they needed – whenever there was a "window of opportunity" (when the army thought it was safe for people to run errands outside security rooms or shelters) not every one was able to get down to the store to buy what they needed, so Ishai and I went for them. We even went to Faisel's for fruits and vegetables or to Nahariya to the supermarket to buy – we did this during the day.

Shanie

I returned to the kibbutz on Sunday, July 16th from the camp around 16:00 in the afternoon. I felt frightened because what I came back to was an abandoned community. It felt that there was no one left; it felt empty.

I tried to get into a routine throughout Monday and Tuesday, even though there was shelling throughout the day. In the late afternoon, during an easing-up of the shelling, I went to visit my grandfather, David, who was in Nahariya Hospital. He was recovering from a massive stroke that he suffered in May. My uncle, Yehiel, who also lives on Gesher Haziv and who stayed, drove me there. We were in the basement shelter where all the patients had been moved. The hospital had moved all the patients who couldn't be released into the basement where there was a built-in shelter. It had been built just for emergencies like this one. My grandfather was in a large room with many other people from his ward.

During my time at home I read the paper and listened to the radio, trying to keep up with what was happening. Anytime I read an article about the war my heart just jumped. I didn't do much for those two days, really. My poor dog, Skippy; I took him for short walks only because I didn't want to be outside. The cats didn't seem to notice that something had changed.

Tammy

My name is Tammy Shlossberg. I'm fifty-three years old. I am married to Yehuda who was born and raised on the kibbutz. Yehuda's parents live here as well as his two brothers and their families and his sister. We have four children.

We weren't here that first weekend of the war, so I only came into the picture from today. I'm the secretary of the executive director of the kibbutz, whose name is Shai Grossman. He and a few others (Effie and Micha to name two) took to organizing the Situation Room.

Shai had previous experience in situations such as these and he took it upon himself to organize the community. Because of this the committees and Situation Room were in place and working relatively quickly. Residents of the new neighborhood and the Municipal Committee were new to this kind of situation, and many of them weren't here as well, so they weren't even partners in all of this.

The Situation Room began almost immediately – with Ma'ayan, Niria and Lilach. At the beginning, Effie did the work duty roster for the Situation Room. After a day or two, Shai asked if I would be willing to do it and I said, "Okay." I know how to do the work roster, because I was in charge of the Early Childhood Education Department of the kibbutz for many years, and part of my duties was to manage a work roster, so I knew what to do and I had the experience. Again, I never thought the war would take so much time.

I also had to worry about the mail and getting someone to distribute whatever arrived. No one was around from the municipal offices to take care of the mail – when it arrived (and that became a *big* question) – that wasn't easy either. The job entails more than just distributing the letters – it also involves getting registered letters and writing them up properly to follow protocol.

Eugene

Carolyn and I usually do the food shopping together, usually at the Hypernetto (supermarket) in Nahariya. We did go once. Suddenly, they said: "Sorry the store is closing." We were at that time checking-out anyway. I wasn't panicked, but I remember that on the way home I felt a little tense. So now with the war and the risk of driving on the roads I said, "This doesn't make sense. We're going down to the Alonit, and I don't care if it means 500 shekels more till the end of the war." And that's where we shopped.

Monday, July 17 & Tuesday, July 18

SMS system set up on Gesher Haziv. Direct Katyusha rocket hits on Gesher Haziv, causing a fire; other hits in Sa'ar and the Western Galilee. Katyusha hits in Nahariya, Acco, Carmiel, Kiryat Shmona, and Hazor Haglilit. Safed, along the Northern Border, Emek Yizrael, and Afula; several missiles hit in Haifa with numerous casualties.

Helen

As the former director of Naot Kedumim and currently a member of the board of directors, there was a meeting scheduled at the reserve and I had to drive there. I said: "You really want me to come?" And they said they really wanted me to be there. So I drove. The road was empty; it was great. I take the back roads to Route 6 so I don't have to go through Haifa. But that's how I drive normally.

However, at no point during this time was there a change in my daily habits. I didn't have trouble falling asleep. The only real change was that at the beginning, the first week or so, I found myself constantly watching the news. I went off that relatively quickly. I watched the Hallmark Channel after a while because I said, I can't deal with this (the constant news) anymore. I just didn't want to know all the time, especially since they kept saying the same things over and over again. I just wanted to know where the Katyushas fell. And I was always up for the 7:00 news which has been a habit of mine for years, I guess it's something connected to my internal clock.

I also volunteered to help with the mail. Gesher Haziv receives its mail from the Mobile Post, which is a postal van that comes to the kibbutz once a day delivering and carrying mail to the main post office in Nahariya. Moran (the regular post office worker) wasn't coming to work at all. During the first few days there was little to no mail – outgoing or incoming, since the mailbags weren't being delivered like normal.

After the first week Zvi Baer or Zvi Elkin would drive to the Nahariya Post Office to get the mailbags for our community. I guess they would do a sort there at the main post office branch. But sometimes we would get a bag with stuff and sometimes it would be a bag of junk mail. However, if it's addressed to a certain person, even if you know it's junk mail, you can't throw it away, you just can't. Worse. none of us volunteers knew where other people's post office boxes were located – I know where mine is with difficulty. So we were working like the blind leading the deaf.

There were these rather antiquated lists that Moran had of people and offices. We couldn't even figure out how the order of the boxes went from the inside, because it's kind of weird. It took us something like four hours with three people working to do one sack of mail that first day.

Then we made a more organized list, which was composed in part from Aaron's SMS list and with phone and address lists that I compiled for the entire community, we just managed to combine them on the computer. Finally we got an updated master list.

Nonetheless it was a lot of work. So we started to divide up into categories. We took these whole huge piles of mail, which finally started being brought more or less regularly by one of the Zvis. And we would divide them according to boxes because otherwise we were running around crazily from one end of the room to the other. We weren't working according to a system, so we realized that's what we needed. And it became a daily work routine where different people were assigned: Iris, Aliza, Hannah Silver, Orli, and me sometimes when I wasn't in the Library.

Benny

I called the manager of the Shilav store back today and he said that his employee, who lives in Acco had a Katyusha fall on his house, and he didn't know who can open the store so I could get the things we bought for the baby. So he decided that if I could get to Nahariya in ten minutes he'd open the store for me. I was at the hospital, so of course I could get there in ten minutes. I said "yes," but when I went outside I found myself in the middle of a bombardment. It was unbelievably scary to leave the relative safety of the hospital to drive on the road to Nahariya. The store is on the Ga'aton Road where Katyushas had fallen. I put the things into the car as fast as possible, drove to Gesher Haziv where I put everything into the house, and then drove back to the hospital. I was on the road for too much time. It was frightening and unpleasant.

Judy

There were just too many things that were pressing, so I went up to work. A few rockets had fallen in the cities of Ma'alot and Carmiel, but it wasn't too terrible. The first day I left Mayzie, my Dalmatian dog, on a chain outside. She got herself all twisted up and one of the neighbors let her loose.

I went to work very early. I got up very early in the morning; I made sure I was up by 5:30, got dressed, walked the dog, gave her breakfast, and chained her up outside. Leah was home then so she let her loose later in the day. I left the house by 6:00 and was at work by 6:30. It was a safer feeling. It was usually quiet those hours – no Katyushas.

And it ended up that every day I went up to work I was the first person in the office. But what was neat was that on this day, whoever was at work was taken out to lunch at a restaurant because the regular place where we usually eat, the cafeteria, was closed.

We didn't hear any sirens in our office because I work on the far side of the building. We're also located on the far side of the industrial complex being the last building towards Carmiel, by the *wadi* (dry river bed), facing downhill. So occasionally we would see something falling in the wadi beyond us or on the hills across from us, which was further south. We had no sirens up there. The office across from us had someone call them from outside when an alarm sounded and they would tell us.

We discovered that the shelter in the building was down the back and cluttered and we couldn't get to it. So we had to think what other security measures were available. It turns out that on our floor there is a heavy security room, which is used for archives for the company that owns the building. They opened this room for us to use. So every time someone got notification that there were sirens in Kfar Haveradim nearby, people would go to it. Some of us would go more often, some of us less.

From my office into there was about a – ten to fifteen-second walk. Really close. But I strolled. I never ran. I didn't feel the need to run, because first of all I never run when I'm home anyway. But also because we sit with our back to the hill and almost anything that was happening was going over us. The only thing that really would have done anything would be a direct hit on the building and then it wouldn't matter where you were. It was a lot quieter where we were; we didn't hear most of what was happening in Kfar Haveradim or Ma'alot except by radio. It was quieter and calmer to work there than to be at home. So we got a lot of work done.

Coming home was a little more disconcerting. Occasionally there was some firing, occasionally there was some Katyushas, but not where I was; I was just very lucky.

Shai

It took about three days to get the SMS network off the ground. So starting from Monday, the SMS system began working, which was an extremely important tool in the community to pass on messages, like when to enter the shelters or when the supermarket, or clinic, or Library was open. The SMS also notified people where there had been hits in the community or fields, or if people have questions or crises or troubles who or where to contact, or if they're looking for a place to leave to, or anything like that, they could make contact through the SMS system. It was also used for all kinds of other messages – about performances that arrived here – it was a channel that was very, very important.

Lyn

We "lost" Oren on Monday, July 17th. Oren is a competitive swimmer and we got a phone call to say that the swimmers had been invited to Wingate. They had been training quite heavily up until then for the Israeli Championships – with morning as well as evening swimming sessions and they were training quite hard because it was supposed to be the end of July-beginning of August, and the competition did go ahead on those dates. So they invited all the swimming clubs in the North down to Wingate: Maccabi Nahariya, Kiryat Bialik, and Galil Elyon. The kids were put up in the dormitories at Wingate and they were well looked after. They were very happy there. Micha drove him down to Netanya.

It was a shock to us to see how empty the kibbutz really was. I think that sort of made an impression on the kids as well; it made an impression on me – just how quickly the community emptied out. You started to feel like a refugee in your own house. It just emptied out, it just really, really, did.

On Monday Rifi and others started the first activities for the kids in the shelter from first to sixth grades and from 9:00-12:00. It was really nice. The kids went and they had a good time.

Then Micha got a Tzav 8 to do the Situation Room. So then we knew we were here on the kibbutz. He couldn't leave and I didn't particularly fancy the idea of going somewhere and having him here worrying about what's going on with him. So we decided that we would stay. He was put in charge of organizing the Situation Room as well as finding places for people who wanted to evacuate from the kibbutz. The coordination among the families that wanted to leave, the places that were offering accommodation and what they were offering and who it was suitable for, and trying to match as many people as they could to places and get people out – the people who needed to get out. He also had to get a functioning staff for the Situation Room. So he really was not home a great deal that first week.

We did talk to the kids about it and ask them about how they felt. At that point the only one who actually voiced any concerns was Ela. I really think, if any of our children were disturbed in any way, it was probably Ela – it rocked her security a little bit. We had this discussion with them the first weekend, when families started evacuating the new neighborhood.

I think that when they first said that it would last about three weeks Micha and I turned to each other and said okay three weeks we can handle. We sort of mentally prepared ourselves for a three-week period.

Ela and Alon went to the shelter by the Laundry again Tuesday. I escorted them to the shelter and then back from the shelter. There was no freedom for them. And the organizers wouldn't let them go by themselves – the parents had to pick them up. I took Honey, our Labrador dog, with me when I went. Honey didn't like the booming so much, the heavy artillery, the constant artillery. She wasn't really thrilled with it.

Honey, was at home with us; being a Labrador she's usually very playful. Now, more often than not she was in the security room with the kids. She became quite glued to us, which was okay; we didn't mind that. Honey had her walks to take the kids to their activities and to bring the kids home from their activities and as I said, we did try to get out at least again in the evenings. She did not want to leave us, she was more than happy to stay with us. And of course the hamsters slept in the security room with Ela; she was not leaving the hamsters out of the security room.

But I didn't notice a great deal of difference with the cats. They were, "What are guys doing at home all the time" sort of thing. This is not normal, but they didn't seem to be overly affected by the constant noise.

Ilan

One day I was on my way to work in the Krayot and a barrage hit. And it was really close, somewhere in Kiryat Yam. I stopped the car and stood by the side of the road. I heard both the siren and the barrage. Miri was at her father's at the time. It was surreal, but routine. How absurd is that?

But on the kibbutz a shelter had been organized for the children so that they had something to do during the day. It was really comfortable, with TV and air conditioning and beverages. It was really fun to go there for an hour or two with Noa. It was also great to change environment and see people – different adults and parents, as well as children. It was really fun.

Miri

I remember my father's whole house was shaking from the intensity of the rockets hitting. I called Ilan on the mobile phone and asked, "Where are you?" And he said he was coming and would be there in a minute. I was looking out of the window of the mamad, which faces the road so I could see who was arriving. And I don't see Ilan and he said he would be here in a minute. So I called him again on the mobile phone: "Ilan, Ilan, where are you?" It turns out that he stopped the car and went into the stairwell of a building to wait until the barrage ended.

At the beginning I got mad at Ilan for driving to work. How do you know that the rocket won't fall on you when you're driving? Maybe it will fall on the road and not on you? So if you decided that you're driving– that's your decision! Who has the right to call him from the bank to tell him that he has to open a branch? I want to see that same individual come from Tel Aviv and open the branch!

Otherwise, the situation was really making me crazy – all day every day. I was alone with my daughter for a number of hours. How much can we do confined to the house? So I gave her long baths – how long could I draw that activity out? So, we started to take Noa to the organized activities in the shelter for a bit of a refresher and it was really great for us. But after a while we had to stop going because Noa was a bit younger than the other children, and without meaning to she sort of disturbed the others.

M

I decided that I would do the Situation Room shifts from 2:00-6:00 in the morning because it's quiet then. After doing two nights with my friend Avner, I decided that I really don't need him there because nothing really happens, and if something does then I can take care of it myself or wake him up and have him come down to the shelter. Basically I can get my peace and quiet.

At the end of the shift, at 6:00 in the morning I would go home to sleep in my security room, which is really not the strongest thing in the world, so I would sleep right very close to the wall. Ten to10:30 was when I would normally wake up and that was when the first Katyushas of the day would hit. Once there was a fire near the Artists' Workshops and Avner was doing some welding work close to where it hit. I got hold of him and by the time somebody got there, he had basically almost put out the fire by himself.

I'd work Monday, Tuesday, Wednesday nights and sometimes Thursday nights as well, depending on when I had a ride to Tel Aviv.

Carolyn

The fact that I didn't see my father much during this period wasn't nice. I talked to him three times a day and he was fine. He kept saying that everything's fine – but it wasn't fine. But nothing bothers my parents – they're crazy. And there were Katyushas falling very close to their apartment, which is on the Ga'aton near Bank Leumi (in Nahariya). They were maybe two blocks away from a building that got hit.

He said he had enough food. In the end it turned out that he didn't have cooked meals. He's ninety. But he walked around Nahariya like he usually does. He's one of those invincible people. He found places to eat and go shopping. He went to the Penguin Restaurant. All they had was schnitzel. They had no cook and nothing but schnitzel – the guy who owns it was the cook then, by the way. It was open. And I think they only had my father there and some newspaper reporters.

One day I went to work at the hospital as usual and a big Katyusha fell right next to the hospital parking lot. And after that they moved all the departments. All the wards were moved down to the basement shelter rather quickly except for mine. I think that was because our head nurse refused to go down. And we had mamadim on the floor. I didn't mind staying where we were and functioning almost normally.

We were lucky that Eugene and I didn't have to make many changes in our lives because of the war, since the security room is our bedroom. When the kids came home from the army they slept in their own rooms. But we would make everyone who was at home go into the security room when there were Katyushas falling. The kids weren't upset about the Katyushas either.

Noa

By now, I had already worked three or four days in the Situation Room. Sometime in the second week of the war I was paired to work with Niria Ziv. Niria worked every day in the Hamal, even before we got together as a pair – in fact so did I for much of the time, we just worked different hours. We just sort of hooked up one shift. The "click" between us happened there. We really connected.

Orit

I didn't have any problems with my place of work because I was on maternity leave. But if that weren't the case, I would have had problems because they were working. And I know there were people who had problems. At the beginning, during the first days of the war, the bank in Nahariya worked half days from 8:30 to 12:30 despite the bombardments.

Danit

The first week of the war we were very disciplined. Stav reacted well all the time, I must say, to her credit. She even got upset when I didn't react. Gilad was in the Situation Room so I didn't see how he reacted. However, it was very selective – when the goal was something good and tasty, it was acceptable to Stav for me to be out of the security room. When my being out of the security room was for other reasons, then it was more difficult for her to accept.

The war became a great time for me personally. I finally had the time to sew since I wasn't able to work. I really love to sew. I sewed a shirt and realized that I was missing purple thread. Within the entire radius of Gesher Haziv I couldn't find purple thread. I drove into Nahariya once and none of the traffic lights were working. I had to buy food and other things for the house, and so I went to all the sewing stores I know and everything was closed. It really annoyed me. I had this feeling of helplessness and that really concretized for me that the situation wasn't intact.

Tammy

The routine in our house changed a bit because of the war. We didn't sleep in our bedroom, but in the security room, which is a little more protected. I went to visit my mother-in-law, Devorah, more since she was stuck at home. She lives very close to me here on the kibbutz, but she was alone. I usually went in the late afternoons or early evenings. I also did all my shopping at the Alonit during the morning hours, which I usually do *not* do. I usually go shopping once a week to a larger supermarket, to the Mega for example.

But one thing that did not change was that Yehuda drove to work every day – he didn't give in – he works at Pizgad in Kibbutz Gadot (which is in the eastern part of Israel in the valley below the Golan Heights, about a one and a half hour drive each way). He drove there and back a lot. He also took responsibility for Polyziv, the plastics factory here on Gesher Haziv, even though he isn't exactly in charge there any more. So he was on the roads a lot, which was not so nice.

Most of the things I did at work were connected to the war; it was impossible to do other things. All the time there were "things" happening. In my daily routine the first thing I had to do was organize the duty roster, which wasn't easy. I had to call people and see who could do what, make the list, and make certain that there were always two people working. And it was impossible to arrange for more than one day at a time because people were always coming and going, leaving the community and then coming back, so there was nothing permanent.

I also had to make certain that there was food in the Situation Room for the people who were doing shifts. I would go down to the Alonit and buy what was needed there.

When I was at work, I was in my office upstairs where it is not protected. As long as there were no Katyushas I felt reasonable. The minute the Katyushas started flying I went downstairs. I'm not hysterical, but I am afraid. But not everyone was like me. Often Shai went up to the roof to see where the Katyushas fell. Not me, I went downstairs to where it was protected and safe.

I had no children at home, so I didn't have other people to worry about. But we were in telephone contact with our children all the time, all the time. I was really connected to them throughout this time, much more than usual.

I watched TV as usual, but the focus was on the Internet. Every morning I'd check the Internet and the TV to see what had happened, where it happened; I was a lot on the computer in order to check out the news. I went primarily to the Walla and Ynet sites. They weren't more informed than the TV or the radio. Years ago you could check out the Internet and get information way before it was on the news or radio. Now it's almost the same.

Micha

On Tuesday, July 18th, Steve called me asking if it was okay for me to accept a Tzav 8 to do Reserve Duty. Initially actually, he wanted me to start on Monday, but because I was driving Oren and two other kids from Gesher Haziv to Wingate, I actually started on Tuesday. Since I thought that Bermad, the factory where I work on Kibbutz Evron, wasn't going to be operating, that it would be closed, I thought it wasn't going to be a problem.

I think the Hamal started that weekend on the 13th or 14th – Effie, Steve, Ma'ayan Shlossberg and Niria Ziv started getting it going. Shai was very much involved in everything that was going on. Also it took a few days to realize that actually there was an emergency situation.

In the first few days I was working in the Situation Room or the Hamal as it's called here, to make sure that the shelters were all in operating condition, so we organized lists of shelters and what's missing, what's not working, what needs to be fixed, what needs to be cleaned. We were working the Situation Room around the clock, so obviously we tried to have two people there all the time. There is no need for two people as long as everything is okay, but once you had to pass on messages it was a lot of phone calls that needed to be made. We also tried to make lists of people who we knew were on the kibbutz and would help pass on information. So we would call one of these ten to fifteen people and then they would pass on the messages to another twenty to thirty each. That was a bit slow, and then there was a decision made to try to work with the SMSs, which was a very good idea. Aaron Sharif did a good job on that.

They wanted me mostly to help with the Situation Room – get it running and organized and help a couple of young women who had just finished the army; they wanted some adult to be there and help organize. So I was working on that – helping to set up the duty roster and the routine and how we do it. A big part of my time was actually like being a travel agency – setting up places for people who wanted to go down south and matching them up with places that were willing to host families. I was also helping with the work roster of the Situation Room – helping to set up routines of what happens if there is a Katyusha falling in the kibbutz.

And another thing we made was that only the two people who are on duty stay inside the Hamal, everyone else stays out because otherwise we would have four, five, six people sitting in a room that was 2 meters by 2 meters; it was a bit crowded and noisy and you couldn't get much done when you needed to get things done.

I was a bit more connected to the Internet and the television than usual, but that is also more because we were home more than usual and had the time to do it. When I was at home we went into the security room when we heard things happening. Before the sirens started, when we heard Katyushas fall in the area then we went straight into the security room and stayed there for a few minutes. In the first week or two they'd shoot a few Katyushas and then you'd know that for a few hours there probably would be no more.

I think that if the kids weren't around we probably wouldn't have run to the security room every time at home. But the security room is quite safe; we did feel safer there, more secure. Our security room is the old style, but it is a bit more protected because we built over it, and Ela's room is above it. We didn't believe that a direct hit wouldn't get into the security room, but it is more secure for shrapnel.

Paul

My name is Paul Smith. I spent a year on a Habonim Workshop in 1971-2. I went back to the States and got married to Kathy. We returned to Israel and to Gesher Haziv in January 1973 as volunteers, officially making aliya in September 1973. We have four children.

We (my family) were in Baltimore when the war broke out and only arrived on the morning of July 18th. While we were in the States we watched a lot of CNN. It was very difficult for me to be watching the news and seeing Nahariya in the state it was in. I also talked to a lot of people here – my phone bill was outrageous that month. I thought it would be like times before – a week or so and then it would be over. So I thought that we needed to hurry home before it ended!

We had left the car at the airport so we didn't have any problems with transportation North; we just drove home. We did stop at the supermarket near the Kiryon Mall – the Cosmos – because we didn't know what would be open further north than that. We'd heard that almost everything was closed, so we thought that we had better stock up here since we saw it was open for business.

So we started shopping. Then the store employees started telling people that we needed to go into the shelters. So we went into the cellar parking lot, which served as a shelter. That's how we first felt that we were home. We were there with everybody for about five minutes, then we finished our shopping and proceeded home.

We got to the kibbutz in the early afternoon. There were no Katyushas for the first few hours. I am in charge of the bananas and other tree crops on the kibbutz. That afternoon I had to meet the lychee advisor in the grove because it was almost time to begin picking the lychee harvest from the trees. So at 17:00 I met him out in the lychee grove and that's just when the Katyushas started falling. One fell very close. I hit the dirt because it was so close. The guy I was with is sixty-something and I think he doesn't hear very well actually. He looked at me down on the ground with this expression of wonder on his face as if asking: "What are you doing?" Almost immediately after that I began to smell the explosive so I knew it was somewhere close, but I didn't know exactly where because it was somewhere among the trees. The next morning I went out to see where it was, and it was about 70-80 meters from where we were standing. That's when I knew things were bad.

I also met with Yigal, my boss, in the office that afternoon. We decided that the most important thing at this point, since it had only been five or six days that the work crews hadn't been out to the fields, was to make sure that the irrigation was okay because there wasn't anyone really checking it. So, basically, for the first few days I had to make sure that the irrigation was working properly.

Kathy

My name is Kathy Smith and I am married to Paul. I worked as a caregiver in the Early Childhood Education centers of the kibbutz for many years.

When we returned from the States we decided that we weren't going to use the upstairs, where the master bedroom and bath are located. We had all our activity downstairs which I thought was a lot safer, and literally did not go upstairs for a month. Even so, Paul didn't sleep in the security room, he slept in our son Noam's room.

Hannah

I started to get up earlier and so went home earlier to take my shower and change clothes. Sometimes Giora woke up and when he started moving around I wasn't in such a deep sleep. Noga also went to her house earlier. I probably went home at sunrise every morning.

Sometimes there were people in the Hamal – like Niria and Noa – not that it really bothered us, but we did hear what was going on in the Hamal – they laughed and made noise sometimes. But considering the situation you forgive these disturbances. In the shelter I felt safe and that's why I went and stayed there. I wasn't calm at home.

Terry

I had already had a couple of days of not working. Teresa and I got into a routine of hanging around the house. We watched more news in Hebrew than we ever had in all the years we've lived in Israel. This was probably good for our command of the language. We were actually able to understand it. It wasn't worth putting the BBC on, which is the news channel we usually watch.

The news on the Israeli channels was so much better, so much more direct. We were in the middle of it. Something would land and a half hour later or less on the television there would be a report about the three, four or five rockets that had fallen in Nahariya. They stopped it very shortly after the first few days, obviously for security reasons. But initially you were like live in the war, on the television. We could also tell how far away they were from the booming sound, more or less. So that was a weird experience – being in the war and watching it live on the media.

After Paul and Kathy came back we got together. It helped break the monotony a bit. We sat around talking. Since I hadn't been working, and I was getting restless, I volunteered to help him. It's been years since I worked in the banana fields, but I wanted to work, feel useful, get back into a more productive routine.

Teresa

One of the real reasons that we stayed is that Terry really loves a war and the action. We could have stayed with family and friends, but we like our own routine.

For the first week or so of the war, we had a number of meals together with people. Each night someone else did the hosting, but we all brought something. But that stopped because we were eating too much. Even that became boring. We never made a formal decision to stop eating together – it just kind of fizzled out sometime.

Benny

When the first Katyushas hit, and throughout the entire war whenever there were bombs, what we'd usually do is first off we'd rush into the mamad, and if by chance one of the children was out of the mamad we'd call them to quickly enter the room. We did show some type of stress, but people kept asking us: "How is it that your children don't go nuts." The first thing we'd do in the mamad was turn on the TV – so if the kids were watching one of their programs we'd change the channel to the news and we'd quiet them down: "Quiet, quiet!" because we wanted to hear where the Katyushas hit. Our children reacted as if they were in another place. They understood what was going on – they heard the explosions. But throughout the entire war, not one of them, they didn't get panicked or hysterical or cry, as if they have lived their entire lives this way. The little one would hear a Katyusha and call the others into the mamad where they would all sit down.

Sometimes when we were in the mamad we would relinquish our need for the news and Orit would pull out a game for the children and play with them. I was more tense and needed to see the news, so she would stay and play with them or they would play among themselves. After the birth we would put the baby into the cradle in the mamad. The children kept each other busy. Sometimes they fought, but on the whole they got along well, almost as if they were three children of the same age.

Sharon

Ronny and I stayed together in the kibbutz part of the community for the first few days of that week, mostly in my apartment. We ran to the shelters a few times when we heard boomings. My entire apartment is supposed to be built according to the standards of a security room, but there are big windows in every room. They can shatter if an explosion occurs close by and that scared me.

When we went down to the shelter, we suddenly met some of our neighbors who we'd never met before like Sharon Sever and Simcha. We finally got to know more people in the community; people who we might have nodded to before on the path, but never had a conversation with. That was nice.

Once there was a loud noise and a Katyusha fell relatively close by. I remember I was talking on my cell phone at the time and the person I was speaking to didn't quite understand why I was shouting all of a sudden. I went down further into the shelter because I was afraid, but there was a lot of water on the floor. It was okay for use afterwards. I guess someone took care of the problem.

In the early days of the war the Tok-Toki (a coffee shop on the site of the gas station at the entrance to the kibbutz) was open. Ronny and I went down one day to drink a cup of coffee. Then all of a sudden we realized we were drinking coffee in a gas station. Definitely *not* the place to be when Katyushas are falling!

Ronny

We hung around outside the shelter, by the entrance, but we really didn't go down. So that if we heard a loud noise we'd be close enough to go down. This day, as we were standing there outside talking to our new friends, two Katyushas flew over our heads. We heard the whiz. These fell between Gesher Haziv and Sa'ar. Now, even though we heard Katyushas fall on Thursday, the week before, I guess we were still in shock. Now we realized what was happening. We heard the impact and immediately went down half a level into the shelter.

Evelyn

One day in the first days of the war, I went to throw out the garbage with my dog Bambi. We heard the whiz of the Katyusha over our heads. But a few moments before that, she started acting nervous – as if she felt the launch. When I got back to the house I asked Ishai if they had announced Katyushas in the area. He said yes. I said – on my word – it flew right over my head when I was at the garbage can. This happened to me twice. Bambi wanted to return home as quickly as possible when she was outside with me. We left her at home when we were out doing things, so she was at home a lot.

Wednesday, July 19

Direct hit on Gesher Haziv. Katyusha hits in Kiryat Shmona, Safed, Nahariya, the Krayot, Tivon, Carmiel, and the Western Galilee and all along the Northern Border; missile strike in Haifa.

Danit

We didn't make any real changes in our lives because of the war. Shlomi continued to go to work every day. Sometimes he left the house earlier than usual, not because he wanted to "miss" the time when Katyushas fell, but because his job demanded him to be there early. And sometimes he came home very late – again according to the demands of work. Sometimes he went in later to work because he had come home very late the evening before. Everything went according to what the army needed – it has its own rhythm. I don't know how much he was really "with" us during the whole ordeal except when he was home, but then he usually slept since he was so tired.

It turns out that we were really concerned about him. We had this practice that when he arrived at the base he would call home or he had to call us whenever Katyushas fell in his area to let us know that he was okay. Surprisingly, we didn't have to call him, not because he wasn't worried, but because we felt so safe here. We saw his situation as much more threatening than ours! This was a paradox since we are so close to the border. We had this feeling that our house was "untouchable." And that isn't a realistic feeling, I know that, but it kept us whole and satisfied.

However, during the war our garden stayed green and we worked outside when we could. When Shlomi was home on the weekends he mowed the lawn. We irrigated what needed to be watered, we collected the passion fruit that was ripe every day, organized the herbs, etc.

The second Wednesday of the war there was a very serious barrage. I was outside and I saw the Katyusha that flew in the direction of the houses on the kibbutz – near Naomi Ziv's – between the houses there. And I jumped backwards – I don't know if it was from fear or the shock wave – and I ran quickly to the security room. After a few minutes I received a telephone call asking if I was able to leave my house in order to give first aid psychological assistance to the people who were at the scene of the attack since I have a B.A. in Social Work and that is my profession. I've done this kind of work in so many wars already that it's like riding a bicycle.

So I left Stav with our neighbor. I was certain that Gilad was in the Hamal. And the one thing that really broke me during this event was that when I arrived at the scene, there was Gilad, who was supposed to be safe in the Situation Room, picking up pieces of broken glass in Naomi Ziv's house! On the one hand it was really nice that he did that, on the other hand he was supposed to be in a safe place and not walking around freely. And it gave me the feeling that we were at war and all kinds of values of good and bad are mixed up together during that specific moment. And of course I told him "*kol hakavod*" (roughly translated to: "What a great job you're doing") and I didn't let him know how tense I felt and what I was thinking at the moment. Then I turned to the task at hand – giving psychological assistance to the people who needed it. Afterwards I made certain that I checked out that he was where he said he was. However, that second Wednesday, when the heavy barrage hit houses inside Gesher Haziv, that's when I felt reality closing in for the first time.

Shanie

I left the kibbutz again on Wednesday with all the other teenagers and went south to Moshav Ramot Meir. They gave us shelter from the hostile situation we were under in the North. They were very nice and organized a party for us. They also had lots of activities to make us feel welcome and keep us busy.

Lyn

That first week Micha ended up doing guard duty a couple of nights when there was heavy shelling in Shlomi. The regular guy who guards is from Shlomi and his wife didn't want to be left at home alone. So Micha ended up filling guard duty at nighttime as well. So that first week we didn't see a lot of him.

By now we had all gotten into a routine – get up and organized, take the kids to the shelter for activities for three hours; I picked them up from the activities, we would come home; we would have something for lunch – either I would make sandwiches or whatever. Normally in our house we have something lightish for lunch and we have the family meal usually in the evenings so that we can all sit down together. And we tried to stick to that during the war. Micha was generally home in the evenings, and we would sit around the kitchen table and eat.

Having activities for the children from 9:00 to 12:00 every day in the shelter was wonderful. It kept them busy and it gave me that three-hour gap. I would allow myself to do things that I wouldn't do when the kids were home such as going out into the garden and mowing the lawn and things like that, which kept me sane. You either love gardening or you hate it. To me it's like a meditation – that's my way of relaxing, even if it's just pulling out weeds or whatever. So that was my time. It was only if the sirens went off in our area, did I go inside. More often than not I just went inside, and not into the security room.

The only time our dog Honey was really stressed was when Mocha (Anat Shani's dog) was killed. Because Mocha ran across our front lawn and all the blood was there, Honey smelled her blood and she really reacted badly. I had to go out and water our front lawn two days in a row just to take all the blood off. Every time Honey went out the front she started to shake when she smelled Mocha's blood. It was the only time she was really stressed.

Stav

Mocha, the dog that died, belonged to my Science teacher.

(Bethe – Mocha was a female Labrador. She was hit by shrapnel from the Katyusha rocket that hit the tree in the residential area. Although Motti rushed her to Dr. Tzafrir Volansky, the veterinarian nearby, and he worked on her for more than two hours, he was unable to save her. Fortunately, though, she was our only casualty in the community.)

Noa

I was paired once again with Niria on a shift in the Situation Room. Now, after we had worked once or twice together on shifts that we were given by chance, we asked Tammy, who did the work roster, to put us together permanently as a pair. Both of us were in fairly good control of what needed to be done in the Hamal. The hours that we worked were usually the critical hours – for the most part between 14:00 and 22:00 – the hours that really "burned." Our feeling was that it is better that someone who knows what they need to do and who can maintain self-control should be there during those hours and not necessarily someone who didn't know how to send an SMS, for example. For the most part we did what was needed to do – write the reports, pass on the information that needed to be passed on, etc. We also sang, talked, and laughed a lot. I didn't feel that it was difficult. You get to know the good parts of people in situations like these, especially of people who you didn't know beforehand.

There were also many times when it was difficult to find someone to work those hours. Also if the person/people who were changing with us weren't really prepared, we'd often stay on longer (sometimes as long as another hour or two) to help them get adjusted and organized. We knew what hours were ours, we'd arrive and the time we were in the Situation Room passed extremely fast. I worked with Niria a lot in the Situation Room during the war and we got along really well, but I didn't know her at all before this.

Aside from volunteering, I carried on as much as normal as I could, even though where I work in Nahariya was closed, so I was home on the kibbutz for the entire war. I worked in my garden and took care of my neighbor's cat and their garden while they were away. I helped out a bit in the Country Lodging as well – there were all kinds of little things to do like send or retrieve faxes and the like, so I walked down there when needed. I also fed the cats in the area of the Country Lodging. I did all the usual chores like laundry and clean the house. My parents also did their laundry here during the war. I didn't go for a leisurely walk, though. But I continued to do my usual things as much as possible.

There are always those people who can't deal with tense situations and break down, so for those people leaving the *meshek* (the kibbutz) was better. Take my sister, Rhona, who wasn't here, for example. Every time she heard something on the radio or got a SMS message or something like that we would immediately receive a hysterical phone call: "Where are you? Where did it fall?" The lack of knowledge, I think, brings a lot of unease. Knowledge and being in the situation and knowing that you have to deal with the situation that exists, puts a great deal of quiet and relaxation into that situation because you are there and you flow with what is happening around you. I think that the people who weren't here had a harder time of it than we did.

Tammy

One of the tasks that I took on during this period was in connection to the hosting of families from the community by people or other kibbutzim in safer areas. At the beginning Shai and Micha took care of it. Then they moved this task over to me.

I was really involved with trying to help residents of Gesher Haziv find accommodation elsewhere. There were a lot of telephone calls back and forth. Then people were calling me all the time: "I want here," or "I want there." It was just one big headache for me. Most of the people who called me were already off the kibbutz with their families. They were looking for a more permanent solution to their individual refugee problem. Most wanted to find a room in a kibbutz somewhere with good conditions, but there weren't many possibilities like that. Many didn't want to be hosted by an individual family.

All of the offers came through the United Kibbutz Movement offices. There were individual families who wanted to host and offered their homes. This whole "project" wasn't easy. There were a few families that went to Kibbutz Ein Hashofet for a while, but even there, there was some exchange of the families that were there. There were also some problems that developed such as how to write down the charges for food from the Dining Room. It still hasn't been settled, by the way, all the internal accounting. There were even some people who were being very picky about what they wanted. We offered them one thing and they wanted something else. A lot of telephone calls went on back and forth.

This wasn't what I usually do, but I realized that in this special time there was a need. There was no way that I could have done my regular work under these conditions. No one was available to take care of what we would normally do. Even Shai didn't take care of his regular things almost at all, only things that were connected with the war.

The Katyushas that fell inside the kibbutz were really scary, especially the one that fell near Hagit's house (the one that hit the tree). I was in my security room at the time. The noise from the rocket hit was so loud and so scary that I dropped onto the floor.

Terry

One day after Paul came back he phoned me up and I went to work around noon. This other guy and me were in charge of the water (irrigation systems, etc.) and other projects that needed doing in the avocado and banana groves.

Paul

Terry said that he didn't have anything to do. So I spoke with Yigal about taking Terry out to have him help me work on irrigation. Then he started to work with me. That was fun and we had our moments.

For the first week after our return we were getting together with friends and people in the area for dinner, barbecuing mostly. But after a while that was dragging on and we just ran out of energy for that. I don't know, but that wasn't much different from regular routine, except eating with friends during the week. We didn't usually have many Katyushas in the evenings; then we'd sit around, watch TV and go to bed.

Ishai

I continued my routine of distributing newspapers in the morning along with guard duty in the evenings; I was busy all the time. Almost every night I was on guard duty at the gate from 19:00 to 23:00.

When the SMS messages went out everyone who was on the list got them, including our other daughter, Rhona, who was in the center of the country. Then we would get a hysterical phone call from her: "What's happening there? What's happening?" We thought that was funny.

Judy

So basically, the routine was that any time there was an announcement I would go into the security room for a bit, and if it was quiet I would come out. When I wasn't working on the computer I was doing my regular things like watching TV and hanging around the house. I didn't sleep in the security room. I slept upstairs in my own bed on the second floor. I felt that I really wanted to sleep, and that even though there was background noise, I took the chance, just hoping that everything would be okay. I knew I wouldn't be able to sleep well on the mattress in the security room. We cleared the security room out of all the junk that was there at the beginning of the conflict. So we had a place to go any time we needed a more secure area. We went in when it was necessary. But I didn't want to sleep there.

The second Wednesday was really weird. I had worked from the house that day since there were too few people planning on going into the office. There had been very heavy fire in the area, which helped influence our decision. A little after 15:00 there was a barrage of Katyushas around us.

Naphtali, who had been home with Leah, was asked to come into work at 15:30 (he also works in the Tefen Industrial Park). But they weren't providing him with any transportation. So he came to borrow my car. They said they only wanted him for about three or four hours. He wasn't thrilled with going up there, but so, okay, I told him he could borrow the car. He got into the car, which was parked outside my house; this is about 15:15. He drove as far as the edge of the parking lot – heard the whistle of the rocket coming over and heard it fall. He turned around came in and told me that he was going to call work and tell them he wasn't coming in – there was no way. One Katyusha fell in Gesher Haziv among the houses, in Nissan Amitai's front yard and the dog died from a shrapnel wound.

I had gotten a call that day. There was a woman who was a reporter for NBC news I think (I forget) in New York. She was a correspondent and she wanted to interview a few people – former New Yorkers. I said fine. In the end the interview was that evening. It was me, Carolyn, Aaron and Iris up at their house. She interviewed all of us. We even went over to where the crater was, where the Katyusha had fallen that afternoon.

Carolyn

A journalist interviewed people from the kibbutz one evening – but only ex-New Yorkers – me, Judy K. and Iris (Aaron is not from New York), New York women living in Gesher Haziv during this war. Then she interviewed my dad – that was nice. There was a camera crew with one or two guys. The program was supposed to be aired on video, but I don't think it got aired. Wow, I can't remember any details! She must have been freelance. My father, who had a career in radio, thought she was pretty amateurish.

Eugene

One of the scariest moments I had was when the Katyusha fell near Naomi Ziv's house. I got on the floor and said to Carolyn: "Get on the floor!" You're not scared all the time, but you react to events. I say get on the floor because a Katyusha fell close by. Then you get up and life goes on. But you don't walk around freely. You just don't. Bombs are falling, common sense says don't go outside.

Sharon

After the Katyusha fell near Ronny's apartment; she decided to check out the damage. I told her to wait. We'd already learned that you don't go running after one Katyusha; you wait a few minutes because more can fall in the same area. That's what we didn't really know at the beginning, that they fire Katyushas in barrages and not singly.

Ronny

After I realized that the Katyusha had fallen somewhere close to my apartment, I called Tzvika, my landlord. He said, "Come quickly." I waited one, two, three minutes and ran fast. A window in my bathroom broke and some plaster fell off the walls from the explosion in the tree, but nothing major. That was close – only 25 meters from my house, but most of my place is behind where the rocket fell, so it was less exposed to the shock waves. And since the Katyusha exploded at the top of the tree most of the damage was higher than ground level, at least that's what was explained to me afterwards.

Orit

When the Katyusha fell close by we were in our bedroom, lying on the bed with the baby. Our other three children were in the mamad. Then suddenly we heard the *boom*. It sounded as if it fell right on top of us.

Because of the danger posed by the Katyusha rockets, we had to change our daily routine. We could no longer allow the children to watch TV in the living room. We had them play and sleep in the mamad during this period. At nights we slept well because there weren't any rockets being fired and we slept in our room. The mamad just wasn't big enough for all of us.

Miri

I went up to a meeting of the community concerning early childhood education. No one knew what was going to develop and what to do. Everyone thought at the beginning that this war would last a week. And then, when it didn't end, and it didn't end, and it still didn't end… Rifi and others wanted to have a meeting to think of a solution about what to do with the kindergartens and nursery schools. I said: "Okay. I'll participate in the meeting. I'm here and it is important to me." So I said to Ilan: "Let's take Noa and let her play in the playground while I'm at the meeting."

However, it seemed that the new playground (between stage one and two of the new neighborhood) was a little dangerous because it is in the open air. So we thought about taking her to the old playground above (near the Dining Room and the Moadon, which is the general activity room for the community) because there, if Katyushas start falling, there's a shelter close by. The meeting was to be held in the Office

Building where Shai sits, but downstairs in the sheltered area. So I said to Ilan: "You go with Noa to the playground and I'll go to the meeting."

Suddenly, while the discussion was underway, I hear a whistle right over our heads; I mean really ("*mamash*")! I jumped up and ran outside. I wanted to see where Ilan and Noa were. I ran up the path and arrived at the playground and saw that it was totally empty. Then I became hysterical. I was running screaming, "Ilan, Ilan, Ilan, Ilan." Then I thought maybe they went to hide in the Synagogue area – in the shelter of the Dining Room. So I ran down the stairs to the niche and he wasn't there. I'm still screaming, "Ilan, Ilan, Ilan, Ilan." So I continued down the stairs and pushed open the metal door to the shelter proper. I see two older ladies sitting and watching television. And there's no Ilan. I ran back up to the surface and I'm screaming, "Ilan, Ilan, Ilan, Ilan." And there's no Ilan. Then I saw a young woman who was standing outside. She said: "Don't worry. A Katyusha passed overhead." So I told her I wasn't worried about the Katyusha, I was worried about my family – where were Ilan and Noa? And then I see them coming towards me. They had gone to see where the Katyusha fell. It was the one that fell near Leah and Naphtali's house.

So then we found ourselves outside. I decided that I wasn't going back to the meeting. Then Kobi arrived to do a shift in the Hamal, and then someone else arrived and we're all standing there outside on the patio and the Katyushas are continuing to fall. We're watching the Katyushas fall and the mushroom clouds appear near Shlomi, for example. Katyushas falling had become routine for us. I can't explain it, but almost from the very beginning I didn't get scared by the rockets. I said: "Okay, that's the situation, but I won't let it ruin my life."

Ilan

I had just finished playing with Noa in the playground and I said to myself: "Until Miri finishes in the meeting I'll take Noa in my arms down to where the Katyusha fell." Just as we were walking I heard the whistle from another Katyusha, which must have fallen in the fields. So I took Noa and decided to go into the shelter near the Dining Room. There we met up with Miri. And then we continued standing outside the entrance on the big patio between the Clubroom and the Dining Room. Other people arrived as well. And here we were standing outside watching Katyushas fall in the few kilometer vicinity of Gesher Haziv. Normal people would have entered a shelter and emerged after only two hours or so.

Otherwise, when I was driving on the roads to work, I really tried not to think too much. The radio was on and the window was open a bit, so that I could hear a siren or something else happening outside if the need arose. And I drove; I drove as if everything was normal. I arrived and went to work – but it wasn't normal – there were sirens in Carmiel and Katyushas that fell near us. But in the shelter we felt fairly safe. We heard some of the hits, but not all of them. When I drove home I just drove – I didn't think too much about what I was doing or what could happen. The instructions we received about what to do during a siren are really correct – to stop the car, lie down on the ground, to decrease the possibility of being hurt. But you say, "Nothing is going to happen to me," and continue according to your normal way. But things can definitely occur, and they did!

Micha

The second Katyusha that fell was also not far from our house. And like the first one, I was not at home, but at Effie's house. However, we were also only about 30 meters from the Katyusha. I remember we heard it; we ducked down, waited a few seconds but didn't hear anything more, so we ran out, Effie and I started looking for where it fell because we knew it was very close. First we thought it was further south, but then I saw smoke and dust coming from a bit north.

We started running in that direction to see if anyone was hurt. The people who live right next to the house, were already outside, so I knew they were okay. Then we started looking around, going from house to house, checking to see if everybody is okay. Lucky for us, no one was hurt, except for the dog. What I remember also from there is that I could hear a gas leak from somewhere because one of the bits of shrapnel hit the gas cylinder at Haggai and Ruti Givon's house. I went to turn it off. Then we split up and we did a round of the houses close by and knocked on doors to check that everyone was okay and not in shock, quite a few elderly people live in the area and we wanted to make sure that everyone was okay.

Hannah

Carmela, an older member of the kibbutz, was also in the Dining Room shelter at the beginning. But she is limited physically; it's difficult for her to walk up the stairs. So she couldn't hurry if she had to, which means that going home to shower could be a difficulty. And Aubry (her husband) was at home; he didn't want to come to the shelter. So her daughter, Irit, would bring her food all the time. Carmela has other family in the country so she went there after about ten days or two weeks, but I really don't remember exactly. And that was good for them to leave. Helen went to stay with some friends of hers. She had a ride. Afterwards, when she returned she said that if she didn't have that ride she wouldn't have gone. I think Carmela and Helen left on the same day.

I was in the kibbutz shelter the entire war, but so was Noga. Noga has a dog she needed to take care of. Every day she had to go home to let it out and feed it. So she couldn't leave because of her dog. For me it was an experience.

Helen

I regularly volunteer in the Library on the kibbutz. After we saw that the war was dragging on, it became a point of honor, so to speak, to keep the Library open. People did come and it was very rewarding. Even more so because a lot of people from the new neighborhood came who we hadn't seen that much in the past.

You get tired of looking at the news and watching TV shows and you want a book, especially for children. So the fact that we were able to keep the Library open was very nice. And Temy Goldwasser (who has been running the Library at Gesher Haziv on a volunteer basis for many, many years) was wonderful. But somebody had to spell her. That was the other thing that I was doing.

Kathy

I was in much more contact with people in the States during this period. I had lots of phone calls from my family: "Why are you…," or "Why don't you come …?" When we were still in Baltimore, my whole family kept calling me up because they knew we were flying out to come home and they kept saying, "Why don't you stay, why don't you stay?" But Paul had to get back. He had to be where the action is. He couldn't leave his bananas under Katyusha fire without him being there. So we came back.

Actually we had to come back anyway, because Noam had to go into the army and we couldn't send him home to go into the army on his own. We had to come back.

Thursday, July 20

Nothing eventful on Gesher Haziv. Katyusha hits in Tiberias, Amiad Junction, Rosh Pina, the Upper Galilee region, Safed, Acco, Carmiel, and the Western Galilee.

Judy

Again we weren't working in the office (the second Thursday in a row) and I didn't have an awful lot of work to do. A little more than a week had passed since the beginning of the conflict and there was no end in sight. I had my routine, Leah and her family had hers, although we were together quite often. However, Leah and Naphtali have two little children and there weren't that many activities organized for the kids on the kibbutz. It was rather difficult to keep the kids busy and happy all day, every day, especially when you can't let them play outside or go for walks. So we decided to go down to my mother's in Netanya. And I suggested to Leah that she pack enough for at least a week. At least there it would be easier to take care of the kids.

Aliza

We came back here again because after several days in Tel Aviv where we could really relax so to speak, we could do anything – we had an ideal situation – a beautiful apartment. But that's the interesting thing – we had conversations with people on the kibbutz all the time, we kept calling our friends daily to be in touch. All of a sudden it just happened to the two of us, we just couldn't – home is home – we just couldn't stay at Shimon's anymore, we had to be where we live. It just hit us – we have to come back. And we had to bluntly tell our kids: "We're adults. We're responsible for ourselves and this is what we're doing!" And by that time they had cooled down and they had accepted the thing.

So we got into the car and we came. The day we came back the roads were pretty empty – this was the second Thursday of the war – then we decided that we had to stop off at Faisel's, the vegetable place, to get some things. Faisel's is usually crowded with all kinds of people and you have to wait in line to get to the cashier. That day there were very few people, and while we were inside and all of a sudden right across the road a Katyusha fell with a *boom* and all of a sudden you jumped, and we said: "Well, we're back!"

Zvi

Many people ran out to see where the Katyusha had fallen at Faisel's and some were ducking under the tables. When you've seen a Katyusha fall before, and once you've heard it and if you're still there, so you know that everything is okay.

The first time anybody goes through this kind of shelling it's very upsetting. It's hard to say, but you become practically immune. You learn how to continue.

Tammy

At the end of the second week the mail routine changed a bit. Aliza and Zvi are a senior couple who left the kibbutz after the first couple of days. They called me a few times to see whether it was worth their while to return to the kibbutz or not. At the beginning I told them: "Don't come back. People are still leaving the kibbutz and there isn't anything to do." But after a while, they called once more and again wanted to do something to help. Then I realized that I needed someone to take charge of the mail and that this was something that Aliza could do. So they came back and I gave her the task of the mail. Zvi became the driver and went into Nahariya or wherever we needed him to go. And so for the both of them, and for us (the rest of the community), it was good that they returned.

And for me personally, a weight was removed from my shoulders since I didn't have to worry about the mail all the time anymore. Aliza took care of most of it. I helped her find people to work when she needed it to help her. But the bottom line is that the mail became her responsibility and that was good.

We didn't always receive the mail and that was a story as well. We had to send someone into Nahariya to the Central Post Office in order to get the bags of mail, when usually the Mobile Post van would come once a day and deliver the mail bags as well as process what needed to be done. Now we were cut off. I would have to call the Central Post Office in Nahariya to see if we could send someone to get the mailbags. And they didn't always answer the phone – sometimes they were in the shelter because of a barrage or a siren. They didn't really function well during this period.

Nurit, who is the manager of the Gesher Haziv Municipality, only came once a week or so to the community to speak with Shai a bit – but the bottom line was that all the operational running of the community was on Shai, not Nurit where it should have been. Even with the problem that I faced with the mail, when I asked her what I should do, she said, "I'll think about it," and in the end it was me who came up with the workable solution, not her. The kibbutz functioned here, not the municipality.

At the beginning, I also did all the shopping for the Situation Room. I drove down to the Alonit and bought what was needed. Later, I got other people to do it because I decided it was way too much for me – all that running around. So Yehuda or Effie or people from the Situation Room itself – those were the others who I asked to do it.

Micha

In the first few days in the Situation Room we tried to get people to call when they left and call when they came back, but it was too much to try to keep track of everybody. Basically the idea was that whoever was here, in time of need, try and call.

At least we did try every night to make a list of what we call the *kitat konnanut* – Response Unit. That was one thing actually, that every evening one of the jobs in the Situation Room, was to call around to a few of these people who were listed as part of the Response Unit to see who was here and who was not, so in case they were needed during the night, to call them.

I had to go out the Situation Room a lot. When I was on Reserve Duty I used to walk around a lot, quite a bit. I would come home and then go back to the Situation Room, then be with the family a bit, be in the Situation Room, go to the offices, do some work in the offices there with Tammy who helped a lot doing and organizing things. Tammy also worked from her office, which is not protected. She did a lot. Then I remember an incident that happened when I was about halfway through my reserve duty, the third or fourth day that I was doing this travel agency work; the first week or ten days of the war. I was sitting in the office making phone calls to different families and to different places to start trying to match families and places with hosts down south. Sharon Yosef walked in. She's from the new neighborhood and had been helping out with the activities in the children's shelter during the mornings. She came to get some supplies that came from the Regional Council – all kinds of toys and equipment for the activities for the children.

So I just started talking to her and asking her how's she doing. She told me that her husband wasn't home, and I think she was almost alone at home with her children. And she told me that her mother had been hurt in one of the first Katyushas that fell in Nahariya and she was lying in Nahariya Hospital injured. And while we were talking all of a sudden she burst into tears, and broke down a bit. I realized that we needed to get her out of here. So I asked her if she's interested and she said yes. And I think that same day we managed to find a place for her in Kibbutz Ma'ayan Zvi, a kibbutz just south of Haifa. Afterwards it turned out that she went to stay with this family that had another unit after extending their house; and she was living in that unit. She got into a very good relationship with them and I think she stayed there until the end of the war. I think she's still keeping in touch until this day. I know she was very, very happy and very pleased.

And that was one of my rewards for working hard was managing to find a place for her when I felt that she tried to stay and tried to continue with her life and she realized that she really needed to get away and find a place. It was really nice to actually find a place during this war.

It was starting to get kind of frustrating because some families were kind of picky – oh, we don't want something like this, we want toilets in the room; we don't want shared toilets for a few rooms; we want to be with our friends. It was a bit annoying to be working hard for the families that were a bit picky, so it was nice to know that I had done at least one good deed in this situation.

Carolyn

I usually like to go for walks around the kibbutz. During the war I only went for one short walk and it was not comfortable. I didn't feel like I could do what I wanted to do.

Terry

Once I started working I got up at 6:00 and drove to the Haga office. I usually started work by 6:30 and continued until about 10:00. I took the *tractoron* (ATV) from the office to the fields.

It wasn't always 10:00 when we finished. I was sort of working with another person, but he didn't want to work past 10:00 because that was when the Katyushas started falling. However, most of the days I didn't get home until half 11-12 (11.30 or 12 o'clock). I'd come up to the office at 10:00 with the other guy. He didn't know how to work the computer, so I would check all the water systems on the computer. But most days I'd go back down to the fields because Paul was still working. And then I'd mess around with him for another hour or two. We'd buy beers from the Super, if it was still open, and end the workday that way.

Then I'd go home. The first thing I'd do is take a shower. It was always scary that there'd be an attack while you were in the shower. Then I'd eat a late breakfast-lunch with Teresa. The rest of the afternoon was taken up with running in and out of the security room. In between we'd watch the news to see where the Katyushas had fallen. At night we'd usually get together with our friends who lived on the kibbutz.

Teresa

Every morning I'd get up early with Terry. Then I'd putter around the house tidying up. I'd usually just about finished when he arrived from the fields. It was the same every day – eating a late breakfast, running in and out of the security room, noshing, watching the news, etc.

Kathy

There were some definite changes in our normal life. One was that we slept in. Another was that now we were having this round of dinners in the neighborhood. Every night, someone else would host. The number of people eating varied, but there were often ten people or more. So I was busy cooking, we'd go shopping.

Sharon

When my father, Menno, left for the States Ronny and I moved into his and Joyce's house in the new neighborhood. Then our lives changed a bit. There it was really empty. The house opposite ours still had people, but that was about it, we were fairly alone on the street. That second weekend a few more people in the area left as well. And even if people were around, they were inside their houses – total quiet and this really made us feel weird as if we didn't know what was going on – were Katyushas falling on us or not? We weren't listed on the SMS contact list at this point so we really felt out of the loop.

We were into all the media, a lot of media. I was in greater contact with people via e-mail daily than I had been before this all started. We suddenly had a lot to write as well as finally being near a computer every day. Here part of the routine was to go outside and use your eyes – you could see that the people were okay and that the kibbutz was undamaged, that the surroundings were okay.

I found it difficult to be in the center of the country because I didn't know what was going on. If there haven't been any deaths, the news doesn't always tell you what really happened, and not even then. It was calming for me to be here, even though that probably sounds weird.

Ronny

Sharon and I heard the loudspeaker from the kibbutz from Menno and Joyce's house, but not very clearly. We had to go outside to hear what was being said. We also heard the sirens from Nahariya and Shlomi, so we knew when to go into the security room or the mamad.

We'd get up in the morning when we wanted to, get something to eat, turn on the computer, turn on the TV, listen to what had happened that night and watch what had happened early that morning, as well as get opinions from people in Israel and the world about the situation. We'd tune into CNN for the most part, or the news from Ynet and a pirate site that put up information immediately – Rotter – where people who had the password were able to write in information as it occurred. Someone would hear the booming and three or four minutes later there would be an item about how many Katyushas fell and where. And this was way before the info was on the TV news.

You know, it was calming to be here. You know exactly what's happening around you. The Hizbullah also got into somewhat of a daily cycle. Katyusha attacks occurred at a certain time in the morning and then again at a certain time in the afternoon.

One day we got an SMS saying that volunteers were needed to work shifts in the Situation Room. We called Tammy Shlossburg who put us on the roster right away. There were two weeks or so when Sharon and I worked shifts four or five times a week.

M

I once went down to the shelter next to my house, but there was this couple living there. It was maybe ten to eleven days since the war started and they were so nervous that after twenty minutes I walked out of the shelter.

I have a scooter, not a car, and I went out on the scooter. I wasn't more apprehensive than usual driving around. I was going fast and zooming through intersections. It was actually pretty good.

Kupat Holim, the HMO-type of health insurance company I work for, was basically closed. The Kiryon Mall and shopping area was open, but I told them at Kupat Holim that I wasn't going there. I'd have to take my scooter to Kibbutz Evron (east of Nahariya) and from there take public transportation. And I felt that was not a smart thing. Plus, we were living okay – over there they had bigger Katyushas – and I didn't think it was necessary. For the time of the war, I got paid back, though. It was very quiet here, like a vacation.

Nothing interrupted my daily life during the week when I was on Gesher Haziv – with sirens, with anything; I'd go to the bathroom, take a shower. At some point I'd check the *sidur avoda* or work roster of the Situation Room. I would go in the evenings to my parents, as I usually do. My father – nothing changed with him. Sometimes he would walk from the living room to the bedroom, if it was really noisy.

I was up all night from 2:00-6:00 in the morning, then slept till 10:30, have coffee with friends, maybe go swimming, come back, eat, go visit the parents, watch TV, watch the news. I watched a little more news than normal on television. Not really many more e-mails than usual though. And basically by 21:00 I'd be sleeping before the night shift, wake up fifteen minutes to 2 A.M. and hopefully catch a movie on my shift. It was better to be by myself; that way I wouldn't have to be polite or talk to somebody. One time I came to the Situation Room and there was this woman from the new neighborhood and she was told that she should come for that shift and I told her that there was no need, and sent her home. I really didn't want anyone to bother me. At 5 o'clock in the morning or so when Noga woke up and walked in, I shut the door so she didn't bother me.

I would spend my weekends in Tel Aviv. So basically on Thursdays I would wait and try to catch a ride from Gesher Haziv south – there was almost no public transportation – and I didn't really feel like waiting on the road for a taxi or something and basically there were enough people going. I got into a habit of getting hold of Kobi Georgel on Thursday afternoon to see when he was driving south to be with his family. Kobi's kids were not here, and it was hard for him that they weren't here.

When I went North, I could feel that I was going back into a war zone a little bit. Driving in the car between Haifa and the kibbutz you felt like you were a little bit on edge because I feel that was the worst place to be – the Acco area, the Krayot area. We drove around via Yokneam. Coming through Nahariya could be a little tense. Driving out was a little bit iffy until you got out of the risky zone.

I would probably have acted differently if I were married and had children because you're not worried about the same things. That's what I see with my married friends. They had their kids to worry about. It can be really frightening because you have to worry about somebody else.

Then I'd go to Tel Aviv and on Sunday try to find a ride back home to the kibbutz.

Hannah

When I was home taking a shower I didn't feel tense, but I did the minimum. Chava usually cooks for me, but she doesn't cook every day. So sometimes I eat the same food for a few days. I don't mind. She asked me once if I didn't want to take food with me to the shelter. So I told her that I didn't want to be bothered heating up food and then waiting for it to be hot to eat because I didn't have "a quiet soul" and eating at her house did give me peace of mind. Since she was working we didn't always know when she would get home. I told her that when they eat to call me and I'll come from the shelter. So I went home for just enough time to shower and change, and the same thing when I went to Chava's.

Helen

I normally volunteer at the Nahariya Hospital once a week, although now I was there more often than normal, whenever I was needed. Now the hospital was very busy – of course as a hospital, but in other ways as well. The particular volunteer work I do there normally is in the International Liaison Office. The woman with whom I volunteer, Judy Jackovitz, was suddenly inundated by dozens, maybe even hundreds of foreign letters and other types of correspondence. And this was even before the hospital was hit (which was later, on Friday July 28th).

One day Judy called me up frantic. She had fourteen teams arriving at the same time. We would be running around like when the underground hospital opened and the first casualties were coming in from Acco and Nahariya. This was before Haifa became the point of attraction, which was mostly in August towards the end of the war, when the Hizbullah got the beam more on Haifa than here, even though things did fall here. But throughout the whole time there was endless activity at the hospital. I thought it was a bit ghoulish. The minute everybody and their beeper got a message or notice that ambulances are coming in, all the hordes run over in order to get a bloody picture. It bothered me.

Shai

Later on we sent an SMS message out asking for volunteers to staff the Situation Room. We also personally asked certain people to volunteer. It wasn't always that easy to find volunteers, but somehow we managed. There were certain people who became permanent workers. Later on we expanded and also tried to improve the functioning and service given.

Orit

I was on maternity leave, so being at home became normal. And I had it easier than usual because both Benny and my mother-in-law were here with me. If I was alone I would have had to organize four children by myself in the mornings. I would also have had to get up more in the nights, because when Benny goes to work I get up at night more for the children. Now we both got up when needed, so for me the war made my life a little bit easier.

I felt that it was important to be informed and I found the information on Ynet site, the Internet site, was more up-to-date than the television reports. They also reported more on the Katyushas that hit in our area, especially when the TV didn't report a lot of them. In our area they would say that the Katyushas landed in open areas, at least that's what it sounded like to us. We would hear the rockets hitting and the TV didn't report it, but the Ynet would say where they fell, especially when they fell here on Gesher Haziv. So we felt more informed.

Benny

We took the children to the activities in the shelter from 9:00 to 12:00 every day – also knowing that we were taking an unbelievable risk. Often there were Katyusha barrages at that time. At 9:00 the activity began – the SMS would say to enter the mamad. After ten minutes or so, when I would see that it was calm, I would simply take them to the shelter where they could be in a larger space than the mamad.

We drove in the car all the time; I drove quickly with my eyes to the sky. I left the children there – they can manage by themselves – but there were days when I got caught and had to stay in the shelter for a while because there were Katyushas falling. I would feel the entire shelter shake. When I could, I left. They were supposed to finish the activity at 12:00, but it happened a few times that I had to stay with them there. There were some people who had left before us and managed to get back to their homes. So we stayed until I felt, and heard, that it was quiet outside.

Evelyn

Since I am the chairperson for the Seniors Committee I was considered a part of Tzachi, the Emergency Committee. Every day we would have a meeting to discuss the things that we needed to do and what happened that day. The meetings were usually between 17:30 or 18:30, so it was a summary of the day. At the beginning of the war there was quiet during those hours, so it was good to have the meeting then.

Noa

In my house the TV is always on, but as "wallpaper" in the background. This is normal in my house – I don't usually actually sit down and watch programs. Now, during the war, though, that changed a bit. It was only when I heard something that interested me, like when something fell close by, did I actually "tune-in" to what was being said or watch the screen. There weren't a lot of options because whenever anything "happened" then all the stations reported it.

Then my new routine continued. I would go to sleep at 4:00 or 5:00 in the morning and then get up at 8:00 or 9:00 in the morning. It was usually quiet in the mornings, so I hung out in my own room with my computer and things. What I usually do around the house after a day's work, I now did in the mornings.

Danit

There was a period of a couple of days when I just couldn't manage to wash the floors. Every time I got organized to wash the floors in the house there was an announcement over the loudspeaker or a siren. It became a family joke that in this house we don't wash the floors because Nasrallah doesn't agree! We used a lot of humor as a means of coping with the situation.

Another way of coping – surprisingly – came from the books of J.K. Rowlings – *Harry Potter*. You know there are the Guards from

Azkaban – chocolate helped us deal with them. So every time we had to be in the security room because of Katyushas that fell around us, we ate chocolate. Now we need to lose all those kilograms and a few months later we still haven't succeeded! But then it really helped us to deal with those tense situations. I guess that there are ingredients in chocolate that help overcome Nasrallah.

One of the things that happened to us was some type of event that caused a gradual lessening of our senses. For example, I can remember myself outside hanging up the laundry and there was the noise of booming from rockets landing nearby. I heard the loudspeaker from Nahariya as well as hearing my son Gilad make an announcement over the loudspeaker here on Gesher Haziv from the Situation Room. And I continued to hang up the laundry out of some sort of apathy, all the way to even idiocy, and I thought to myself: "This time they (the Hizbullah) aren't going to disturb me from finishing this task of hanging up the laundry."

This was a bubble of reality inside reality. And I can say that it's a cliché – but we became accustomed to normalcy inside an abnormal reality – we reacted normally to an abnormal reality.

Stav

Oh – I have a story to tell – Every time my mother went out of my room to cook or clean, a Katyusha fell or there was a siren. But, when my mother made pasta with pink sauce she was allowed to be out of the security room!

Gilad

I wasn't around the house that often when my family was in the security room, so I didn't eat that much chocolate with them when the Guards of Azkaban were around.

Friday, July 21 & Saturday, July 22

Numerous Katyusha hits on Gesher Haziv; fires started, but no casualties. Katyusha hits on Kiryat Shmona, Migdal Ha'emek, Tiberias, Upper Galilee, Safed, Nahariya, Haifa, the Krayot, Acco, Ma'alot, Carmiel, and Shlomi. On Friday, numerous direct missile hits in Haifa with many casualties. Sixty rockets shot into Israel by 13:25 on Saturday with many casualties.

Bethe

Wednesday, July 12, until late Thursday, July 20 ~ My name is Bethe Schoenfeld and I am forty-nine years old. I have a PhD, MA and BA in English Literature and I was educated in the UK, Israel, and the U.S. respectively. I met Asher Coren in 1980 when I was a volunteer on the kibbutz and then officially immigrated in 1981. We have three children: Lavie, Shanie, and Meshi and numerous animals. This is our prologue since we (Asher, Meshi, and I) weren't on the kibbutz or in Israel for the beginning of the conflict. We were in the States on a planned visit when it all began. That was a weird story in itself that I want to relate.

We were flying from Los Angeles to Baltimore. The plane made a scheduled stop in Dallas to change the crew and clean the plane. It was supposed to be a short thirty-minute stop that stretched into one and a half hours.

During the time that we were sitting in the terminal, Meshi heard something about Israel and the Northern Border on the CNN broadcast on the screen in the lounge, but she wasn't certain what she heard. Asher went closer to the screen in an attempt to clarify the information. He asked me to listen since my English is better than theirs. When I was able to glean what had actually occurred, we realized the seriousness of the situation. We had left our son, Lavie, who is serving in the Israeli military, stationed on the Northern Border and our sixteen-year-old daughter, Shanie, was at home on the kibbutz, alone, taking care of the house and our numerous animals.

We tried to call both of them from our cellular phone, but the time difference and the situation didn't allow us to make contact. Needless to say we were quite concerned.

We arrived at the Baltimore-Washington International Airport late. We retrieved the rental car that we had arranged for in advance and drove to Chevy Chase where we were going to spend the night with my oldest friend, Robin Land-Stein (we've been friends since the sixth grade), and her family. She had invited a few other friends over for dinner and everyone was waiting for us. It turned out that Shanie had called Robin at 4:30 A.M. (D.C. time) when the conflict began. She was quite upset (a normal reaction) and had miscalculated the time difference. Robin understood. Later that evening, Asher managed to make contact with Shanie, his father and sister, Tamar.

We actually thought about returning to Israel in the next day or two. In the end we stayed and kept to our original plans, but we were virtually glued to any TV set or Internet screen we could find to keep abreast of the developments.

Our flight out of JFK (New York) was a few hours late, so we missed our connecting flight from London to Tel Aviv. We managed to get seats on an El Al flight to Israel, but we also knew that there was a high probability that our luggage wouldn't make the connection from Heathrow to Israel, and it didn't.

Friday, July 21 ~ Shanie met us at the airport in Tel Aviv when we arrived, accompanied by Asher's sister, Ruthi, and her husband, Elnatan, as well as his other sister, Tamar. We had originally planned on taking the train, which runs from the airport to Nahariya (the closest town to our home). But because a long-range rocket launched by Hizbullah hit a train station near Haifa (killing eight people), all train services north had been discontinued. In addition, all bus services had been discontinued to Nahariya. So there we were in the center of the country, in the middle of the night, with relatively limited options for transportation North. We opted for a large sherut taxi north, and so Asher, Shanie, Meshi, and I were on our way home.

I can't begin to describe how great it was to return home when we finally arrived. It was in the wee hours of the morning and of course it took time to unwind enough to even think about sleep. Skippy, our golden retriever mix, needed a walk and so he got one, despite the hour.

From the very next day we started to get into a routine – the routine of war. However, none of us in our wildest dreams thought that this conflict would last as long as it did, and that our community would be under fire for so long.

So, we had just arrived from the airport very early that Friday morning. I needed to organize and clean the house. Shanie had done her best to keep it clean, but I needed to have it my way. So, even in the middle of the night, I started sweeping and dusting and putting away. Those actions helped me to adjust. At least there weren't any rocket attacks that night. That kind of welcome was the last thing we needed! I was up until 4:00, slept for a few hours and then drove north to pick up our son, Lavie.

Lavie, who was stationed on the Northern border called to tell us that he was allowed to come home for the weekend. However, since there was no transportation from where he was I volunteered to go and pick him up. Without really thinking about any danger, I got into the car and drove off. In reality I should have taken someone with me for comfort. There was a war on and I was driving alone on the Northern Road. I got to the area of Avivim and found five or six tanks on the road at the intersection shooting into Lebanon periodically. That was weird. I made it to Lavie's base and he was waiting for me at the gate. At least on the drive back to the kibbutz I had company. Lavie and I exchanged information and experiences after not seeing each other for three weeks or so.

That evening we were a family united, albeit under rocket fire. We conducted our usual Kabbalat Shabbat with song, wine, and good food. Even our dog, Skippy, came to the table when we started to singing, as is his usual habit.

Late Saturday morning, Lavie and his friend Shelley (Eugene and Carolyn's daughter) were going to visit some of their friends from their garin (his group from his year of community service) who were also home. Lavie borrowed Asher's car and off they went. They must have been gone for only a minute or two when there was a Katyusha attack on Gesher Haziv. I remember calling him on his cell phone and telling him that they should come home. He said no that they were all right and continuing. When he returned later he told me that he saw a Katyusha fall right in front of him. He was quite unnerved, but hit the gas and sped away from the area.

At the same time that Asher was off fighting the fire in the afternoon, I received a phone call from my good friend, P.J. (Col. Dermer, U.S. Army), who's currently the military attaché at the US Embassy in Tel Aviv. He was in the area with a group from the U.S. Congress. They wanted to see a settlement in the war zone, so Shanie, Meshi and I met them at Polyziv. Asher was on the other side of the factory fighting the fire. If I had known then that the fire was so large we would have probably gone to see it. Only later did I discover how much area had been burned.

They had come in two cars. I got in one while Meshi and Shanie got in the other. We took them to see a house that had been damaged on the perimeter security road in the gimel area of the new neighborhood. It was easy to reach. Along the way we answered any questions they posed.

Luckily the house that had gotten hit was still under construction so no one was hurt. There was damage though, easily visible from the road. Then we drove into the kibbutz and showed them a shelter. All along they asked us questions about the kibbutz, about choosing to live in this kind of society, how we felt about the war, etc. Some of the delegates were really knowledgeable about kibbutz and the Israeli military. I was extremely impressed.

Shanie

At the beginning I wasn't around much, I was also quite scared since I was alone at home with the animals. After my family returned from the States my attitude changed and I felt much calmer and able to deal with the situation better.

That weekend, after my parents had returned, I volunteered for the 22:00 to 2:00 shift in the Situation Room. If people from the community called I answered the phone and gave them what information I had. If the army called on the radio we had to answer them and had to alert the Emergency Squad. I passed the time by playing on the Internet and watching TV. I ate a lot of chocolate because we had received *tons* of donations from the Israeli chocolate company, Elite.

On a day-to-day basis I was at home most of the time not doing much of anything. It was pretty boring. I didn't have much chance to experience anything exciting when I was walking around the kibbutz. That was a bit of bummer since I was looking forward to some action. The war became something that I stopped fearing because it became so long. To tell you the truth, I wasn't really afraid to leave my house after I started volunteering in the Hamal at nights. I realized that there really wasn't any reason to get scared. Every time I heard bombing I went into a security room or I ran, more or less.

Asher

My name is Asher Coren. I am fifty-one years old and I was born and raised on Gesher Haziv. My father still lives here as well as my eldest sister, Tamar, and her husband. I am a computer analyst by profession.

Before the war, I would visit my father, David, in the hospital every morning and then go to work at Tadiad – Information, Technology, and Service, which is south of Acco. My father, who is now eighty-nine, suffered a massive stroke in May. I decided to continue doing this despite the war. Every morning I went to the hospital. I helped feed him, shaved him. Most importantly, I conversed with him. On most mornings I was able to speak with one of the doctors about his condition. He used to be on the first floor of the new building where the Rehabilitation Ward is located. He was in a double room, but most of the time he had the room to himself. Now all patients were moved to the shelter in the basement. When I arrived this morning I saw that although the basement shelter wasn't like the ward, he had relatively "decent" conditions. All the patients in his ward were in one large room, but there was a bit of space and a bit of privacy for some of the patients, like my father.

Our luggage hadn't arrived because of the plane change in London and we were waiting for it to come. Around 11:00 on Saturday we received a phone call from a driver who worked for El Al and in a hysterical voice he tells me, "I have your suitcase from El Al. I am going to throw it at the gate to the settlement and flee." (He was supposed to bring it to us at our home.) He told me that while driving to Gesher Haziv a Katyusha had just fallen not far from his car. When I got to the gate I saw him from afar trying to stop any car that entered the road to see if it was me so that he could get rid of the suitcase. He gave me the suitcase and said that he had never been as scared as he was right now.

Saturday afternoon ~ At least two Katyushas had fallen in the late morning in an open area near the factory and caused a fire. Since it was July, the bush was dry and caught fire quickly.

It was around 14:00. I had just eaten lunch and thought about going to rest since I was still suffering from jet lag. Also, during the nights there had been a lot of artillery fire (mostly ours), which kept me awake or in a light state of sleep. I had also woken up early that morning so I could go visit my father in the hospital. The Situation Room phoned and asked if I could help fight the fire. I got dressed in long pants, high boots, T-shirt and a hat – I'd fought fires in the past and knew what to expect.

When I arrived at the location of the fire, a large group of people were already working hard. There were at least three points of fire raging. The fire fighters were working in the west. There was a group in the area of Polyziv, because there was a fear that the factory would burn. This is the group that I joined. Paul Smith and some Thai workers were fighting the fire near the avocado groves. Two minutes or so after I arrived, a light-engined plane arrived (usually used for crop-dusting, but now used to help extinguish fires) and spread a red chemical substance onto the fire, and us. The red drops spread with the breeze and covered the volunteers. But it worked. It had a good response in stopping the fire, at least that's what others told me, since I hadn't really gotten a grasp of what the situation was.

I ran directly to the end of the water hose where the nozzle is, because I saw that people holding the hose were really tired and in need of assistance. I held the hose along with Yuval Gaon and pulled it while Baruch aimed. Then I changed places with Baruch so he could rest – now he pulled while I aimed. I fought this part of the fire for thirty minutes or so.

When the flames calmed down and we thought we had finished, I went east in the direction of the avocado groves and realized that help was still needed there in fighting the fire. We lengthened the hose we used on the hill so that it became a very long hose. The water source was the hydrant near the factory. The Thai workers had managed to extinguish the fire in the first row of avocado trees.

But there was still fire in the undergrowth on the slope of the hill leading west and up to the factory. The people there didn't know that hot spot existed. So I focused my work there along with Assaf Louis, two Thais, and Paul. We were joined by a man not from our community. I recognized him as someone who works in one of the factories connected to the kibbutz conglomerate, from Milouz. He had seen the fire while driving on the main road and came to help. It took twenty minutes or so to fight this fire. Then we discovered that there was another spot behind the factory where the cypress trees are. It was very difficult work to move the hoses from where we were using them in the east to this area. The fire tractor that belongs to the kibbutz arrived then with Assaf and Yuval Gaon on the tractor.

Late Saturday afternoon ~ I returned home from fighting the fires exhausted. Fire fighting is physically demanding work. I still had to cut the grass even though I was totally wiped out. A few days before we went abroad we had some landscaping done. New grass was planted which received irrigation three times a day for three weeks. The grass had grown to almost 60 cm high and I *had* to mow it. Areas of grass hadn't received irrigation because of the height of the grass, so it was really important to cut the lawn that day. So even though I was wiped out, I mowed the grass. Luckily, no rockets were fired while I was working.

Bethe & Asher

As parents we projected or tried to project calmness. We knew that by acting scared, we would only scare our children more. This is how we had chosen to react for all the years that this kibbutz has been bombed and we've been together. This attitude has been especially true since we've had children to care for and raise. We tried to make the best of a nasty situation for however long it lasted. But we never thought that this round of conflict and hostilities would last so long!

Even at the best of times Skippy reacts badly to loud noises. Now he was really unnerved. Since the beginning of the conflict Shanie hadn't been home all that much and he had been alone in the house with the cats and the shelling. Now that we were home he was like glue. He followed us from room to room and stayed right next to our legs. When we sat down at the computer to work, he pushed himself against our legs so that we would move to make space for him under the table that held the computer equipment. He also took to sleeping in the hallway that leads to our room.

Sharon & Ronny

We met so many new people when we did shifts in the Situation Room. It was wonderful. We usually worked shifts at night like 22:00 to 2:00 and in the afternoons 14:00-18:00. Those were the problematic hours when it was difficult to find people to work. And we also got to know the people who were living in the central shelter. That was interesting.

At the beginning, when we started volunteering in the Situation Room, there wasn't a list of volunteers for the Fire Fighting Brigade. On that shift, I remember, we had some action – fires in the fields and rockets at Polyziv, and we needed to alert the right people. And there was no list! We told the person in charge and he was supposed to get the list together. Luckily we didn't need that list at any other time we were in the Situation Room, so I don't know if it ever made it to the computer as promised.

However, we quickly learned that not everyone, those not in this specific situation, has an idea what our lives were like, almost as if we were living on two different planets. When I would speak with my friends from Tel Aviv or Hod Hasharon, I found it difficult to believe that we lived in the same country.

Our daily routine was much easier. You don't have to worry about what you wear or how you look; there was no one to see what you wear. Except that my life sort of disappeared. That was weird.

Evelyn

We received phone calls every day from our family in the Center asking how we were and what was going on. And we had to calm them down, telling them that we were fine and all was well considering the situation. We also had phone calls from the States every day from our son asking questions about how we were – and we were the ones who had to calm them down. It's not as if they didn't know what we were going through then; they had been through similar situations in the past with Katyusha barrages on Gesher Haziv, so they knew.

Tammy

Part of my day was devoted to doing the work roster for the Hamal. I thought it would be something I'd do for a week or two, but the war continued and continued. And it wasn't easy to do this job. There were people who volunteered a lot, and then there were people who volunteered less. And it was especially difficult to organize the night shifts. I found that a large majority of the people who stayed had a desire to help and they volunteered whenever they could. The youth were very willing to help. But in addition there were all sorts of social issues and personality types that needed to be taken into consideration when organizing the work roster. I really needed to maneuver – who to pair with whom and who couldn't be paired together.

We went to visit my sister twice for the weekends, but that was difficult because it means being in her house and all the cooking. She doesn't have a dishwasher, so there were a lot of dishes. So each time we said, "Enough, we'll stay at home." But then after a time it was hard to hear the Katyushas falling all the time, so we left. Then, when we were out, we'd do some shopping on the way. We always returned Saturday evenings.

Aliza

What we did around the house changed somewhat. We spent more time in the security room. I worked on my Klimt puzzle there. We're fortunate because we have the television and the computer there normally. We're the only house in Gesher Haziv that doesn't have a television in the living room – and I'm so proud of that! – except for the people who don't have television on principle, which I don't know how they live in this day and age without it. But living in that room, I was able to work on a puzzle – I do picture puzzles, and that helps me; that is the focus for me in all the insanity, surrealism, and absurdity. I mean concentrating on reading was not easy because you live in a sort of state of apprehension. It's not fear, it's an apprehension.

Our jobs were different, mine and Zvi's. I was in the Mail Room – it took quite a few days to get it organized – and there were all kinds of volunteers. Sometimes there were even too many volunteers and I had to send people away without hurting their feelings because they, too, wanted to help.

The situation was that the Mail Room, where the mail comes, wasn't a secure room; it wasn't safe. But right across the hallway was the municipal secretary's office, the conference room, whatever you want to call it, and that was very safe, supposedly, so every time they kept saying that something's coming – at the beginning we would run to that room and take the mail to sort it out there and then come back to the Mail Room and give it out.

But that stage passed and you became immune to what was going on. You just kept on with your work to keep yourself busy. That was the most important thing – to keep yourself busy – although we did go into the safe room for a few minutes when we felt we needed to.

Getting hysterical is not going to help, not help you or help the people around you; it's not good for your health, especially at our age. And when we got back I refused to sleep in the security room. The bed is terrible there and I wanted my own bed; they (Hizbullah) were not very noisy at night, so I slept in my bed – whatever will be, will be.

Television was too much. You wanted to know what was going on, but you had to learn how to regulate it, otherwise you could just sit there all day. And, oh yes, we have cable. Thank God for cable. We watched stupid movies. In the end we watched more television than usual, though. I was on the Internet more than usual. I was reading *The New York Times* and *The Forward* on line. I also play Solitaire on the Internet. I had to distract myself.

I was lucky Zvi was driving so we could get food. Otherwise we went to the "super" here on the kibbutz.

Ilan

During the day, when we could we wandered around the house. We didn't stay in the mamad all the time. We just went into the mamad when we hear the exit sound of the rocket leaving the launcher or the siren. Then we'd sit there for a few minutes and then return to whatever activity we were involved in before the mess began. We did sleep in the mamad though. And of course Noa took her morning and afternoon naps there as well as sleeping there at night.

Benny

This period was definitely different for me since I'm not usually home during the days, and now I was – all day, every day! We woke up later than usual – we slept a lot more than usual. We woke up at 8:00 – the whole house woke up then. I have to say that our baby was such a good girl, even until today, she hardly cried, she slept a lot, and was up relatively little, so the amount of time we had to take care of her was minimal which really helped us out a lot. She was like a little doll.

So in reality we only had three children who we had to keep occupied. So we woke up in the morning, had breakfast – the children ate in the mamad while we had our coffee here in the living area. In reality, we were walking around outside of the mamad most of the time. Then we'd check out to see what had happened throughout the night, watch the news on the television. Then around 8:30-9:00 the first Katyushas would be fired.

Finally I said: "Okay, I have to do something with myself." The grass was getting high – so I said: "I'm going to mow the lawn!" I'd do two rows with the mower and hear rockets hitting, close enough not only to hear them, but as if they were going to fall directly on me. I ran to the mamad, waited five minutes, went back outside to continue; again Katyushas were shot, again I ran inside – it was crazy, but I said to myself: "I have to finish this project, first of all." It was important to me that if I started something then I had to complete the work. I didn't think about the risk, I didn't say to myself: "It won't happen to me." But it was dangerous, so it should be forbidden to say that.

Paul

I went out to the fields today. That might sound strange since it's Saturday and it's during a war. But I always go out to check the situation in the fields on Saturdays. That's normal for me.

Eugene

Normally, when the kids have leave from the army, they come home. Now, that changed. When they got leave I would beg them: "Please don't come home, its dangerous here!" But they wanted to come home.

Shelley was home one weekend and the garin was getting together. There were bombs falling outside and she said: "I have to go, I have to go visit Navo (her boyfriend)," and I said, "What do you mean you have to visit Navo? Don't you hear the bombs? They're bombing Nahariya and Acco!" What could I do, lock her in her room to stop her – she's twenty years old and in the army!

A lot of us didn't leave the house during this time – in terms of going out to look at the sunrise or the sunset, we just didn't do it, that's all. I took a walk at 5 o'clock in the morning because I figured it would be okay, and then you were in the house. That was it. But you're not scared all the time. You're just aware, you really are. If you're scared all the time then you shouldn't be on the meshek– you should be down south somewhere.

Terry & Teresa

This weekend we drove to Migdal Ha'emek to visit our daughter, Gabi, who was staying with her boyfriend Nir and his family. Once we left the kibbutz it was a bit tense on the road. We usually took the back roads to minimize the danger. When we got to Nesher, on the northwest side of Haifa, we would suddenly feel relieved. However, on our way home the feeling was just the opposite. When we got to Nesher then we started getting tense and listening for loud noises and looking more at the sky.

This evening, while driving through Kfar Yasif, there was a bombardment on Nahariya. So when we reached the town we went looking for where the Katyushas had fallen. We were chasing the police cars and fire trucks looking for "action." At one point they told us to go away, so we drove back to the kibbutz.

Lyn

We did go away a couple of weekends – more to see Oren – because he was quite stressed about us being here on the kibbutz and him not being here. The news played a big factor in these kids' lives – I'm talking about ten- to fourteen-year-olds – that was the age of his group and they were away. They felt quite stressed about their parents, what was happening to them, where they were, what was going on.

Shai

Between this and that there were all kinds of occurrences, like Katyushas falling, that kept us busy. Throughout the war we managed to staff and improve the Fire Brigade that was forced to confront quite a few fires throughout the war. We weren't ready or organized at all for this kind of event. The first fire, the one that broke out at the factory, was extremely dangerous.

Meshi

My name is Meshi Coren. I'm Bethe and Asher's youngest daughter. I'm thirteen years old now (I was twelve during the summer of the war).

I wanted to stay on the kibbutz, so my parents' decision to stay was fine with me. It was my choice also. I could have gone to my aunt Ruti's house if I wanted to, but I wanted to stay here. The last days we were in the States, when we were in Baltimore, we really heard a lot about the war. I wanted to go home. I asked my mother if we could get an earlier flight. But since my mother hadn't seen her family or her friends, we stayed.

I missed my brother. When we were in the States at the beginning of the trip people asked us about him because he's in the army and we'd say: "Oh, no, he's on the Lebanese Border; it's okay. He's fine," because there were problems with Gaza at that time. And then the war started and we said to ourselves: "He's on the Northern Border, oh no!"

Danit

Normally, we drive from one place to another with no fears. However, during the war we tried not to drive too often on the roads as a family, even though the roads were all open. But when we did, Stav asked questions about whether we had gotten into the range where we could be a target, or if we had left the critical range of fire. Justifiably, she needed to know.

We weren't more media oriented than usual during this time, though. Stav watched children's shows most of the time on TV. As for us, we didn't have a computer for a while. During the second day of the war there was an electrical blackout and as a result our computer was damaged. Gilad was able to sort out the problem after a while and get the computer working again.

We tried not to listen to news, because there is something worrying and pressurizing in listening to the news. In the evenings when Shlomi arrived home we did listen, but we tried to turn it on in a room where the whole family wasn't gathered. At the beginning of the war we found that listening to the news was quite disturbing, so we stopped. If something happened that was physically close to us we'd know it; if something happened far away there was nothing we could have done to help anyway.

Stav

We were traveling on the roads pretty regularly. When we traveled on the road we were kings! All the other people were tense and were in their houses, so we drove like kings.

Kathy

I spent all my time in the house; it felt secure. We did go outside to barbecue sometimes in the evenings. For some reason we thought it was safer then. We kept trying to figure out what time the Hizbullah were going to send the Katyushas – well we haven't had Katyushas at that time of day, so let's have the BBQ then! I think there was some rumor going around that they don't like to shoot at night because they become more visible to the army. But there were some at night. But it was during the day and daylight hours when we were really bombarded.

Helen

Did I go into the mamad when there were announcements or sirens? You want to hear the truth – no! There was one night when it was really noisy when I slept in the mamad though. Later I realized that the "really noisy" was our outgoing artillery and not Hizbullah incoming. But to be perfectly honest my two cats weren't happy about me being in the mamad.

Noa

In the evenings the first thing I'd do when I got home from working in the Situation Room was to take a shower, but then I always do that. If it was quiet, which it usually was in the evenings and night, I'd sit outside and enjoy the quiet. But for the most part I'd have hours-long conversations with a friend on the telephone. But that is also part of my normal practice. We'd speak until 2:00 or 3:00 in the mornings usually, and during the war as well.

Sunday, July 23; Monday, July 24; & Tuesday, July 25

Numerous Katyusha hits on Gesher Haziv and the Western Galilee. Abundant Katyusha hits against Rosh Pina, Hazor Haglilit, Safed, Tiberias, Carmiel, the Golan Heights, the Finger of the Galilee, Kiryat Shmona, Tiberias, Carmiel, Mj'ar village, Nahariya, Acco, the Krayot, and Haifa; many fires raging and casualties. By 21:10 on Tuesday it is reported that 104 rockets have been shot into Israel; thirty in the area of Ma'alot, twenty-two in Safed, sixteen in Nahariya, and fifteen in Kiryat Shmona with casualties.

Benny

The mamad was quite crowded, and although the room isn't so small, with so many people and things in it, it was crowded. But the children stayed there – for two and a half weeks until our trip to Eilat, they almost didn't leave the room except for going to the toilet or taking a bath, and the few times they "escaped." We wanted them to stay in the mamad because there were constant Katyusha attacks.

We knew that we were taking a risk by continuing to sleep in our own bedroom and not in the mamad, and to have the baby sleep there with us as well. At night we quickly realized that there weren't any rockets, so we continued to sleep in our room. My mother was here also and she slept in one of the children's rooms. I personally wasn't able to stay in the mamad. There were many instances when there were barrages and we all went into the mamad. But after two or three minutes I had to leave. My mother also had to leave quite quickly and she usually left a few minutes after me, but Orit stayed with the children.

Another project I allowed myself to do during this time was to paint the wooden deck outside. I would manage to paint two or three rows, and there was a Katyusha barrage. My mother shouted at me all the time to come inside, since we clearly heard the whistle of the Katyushas that passed over Gesher Haziv or the hits that were close by. It should have taken me half a day to paint the deck. This time it took me a few days to paint it. Some days I had to surrender, raise my hands, and say that I would continue the following day. I did do things outside during the day when I needed to, like mow the lawn or paint the deck. But on the whole I tried not to be outside when I thought there might be shooting.

We were seven people living in the house, so we had to clean rather often during everything else that was happening. However, the house was organized – tip-top – all the time. We always made certain that the daily routine was normal. My mother cooked lunch and dinner every day, I helped her. We had cooked food every day the entire month of the war. That helped a lot – to eat something good every day.

Terry

As usual I went to Haga at sixish this morning. I found that the tractoron wasn't working. So Paul took me down and dropped me off near one of the blocks of bananas. He gave me a bunch of things to do there. He went off and said he'd be back in a minute. Then shortly after, I heard a Katyusha fall but not too close. I thought then that I should find a safe position for myself, just in case they fell closer. I was in an open grove with no real shelter to protect me! So I kind of scrunched up next to this tree and bent over to fix the pipe on the ground, which had been damaged the day before by a hit from a rocket. I had purposely picked that tree to fix at that point because I just knew there would be another rocket shortly.

It was a place that seemed somewhat shielded from the north (the direction the rockets are fired from) and because of the way the tree was growing, I could get behind it. I was bending down trying to fix the pipe when I heard the *whoosh* of the Katyusha. It sounded just like it was coming straight at me. All I could think to do was to dive into the mud with my hands over my head. That is what you are supposed to do in this kind of situation. This bloody thing, I could have sworn was going to come straight at my head. It sounded like I was hearing it until the very last minute. And it landed actually not as close as I thought (which was right next to me), when in fact it had landed probably two blocks away, about a couple of hundred meters. But the noise that it made was worse than the actual fall.

I got up and got my cell phone out and called Paul to find out where he was. My hands were shaking like a leaf. I couldn't even press the button to call. So I walked out onto the roadway to calm down a little bit and phone him. And he was doing his usual "bit": "Ahhh, don't worry. I'll be back in a minute." I said, "Get your ass here now!" So he came quickly. It really shook me up; not so much the bang when it landed, but the noise of hearing it coming.

The next day having *The Sun* reporters around was a nice break. We took them to the place where the Katyusha fell near me the day before. They only wanted a picture of us Brits – Paul was kept out. I felt weird posing in the banana grove and they were telling us to pose here and pose there, don't smile, look like you're worried, or miserable. I wasn't happy with the whole thing. It's like you're putting on an act for the idiots back in England who don't know what's going on. I wasn't happy putting on the show for the camera kind of thing because it was unnecessary. There was enough that had been done already and people who were suffering from the conflict without making us pose in front of a camera. But we did it.

The truth of it is that Paul and I could have been standing there with a beer in our hands, which is what we were doing anyway. It was that time of day. We had finished work and Paul had gone and gotten some beers. I could just imagine my family and friends in England saying, "Oh look, he's got a beer in his hands!"

Teresa

Today I was famous! Terry and I were interviewed by reporters from the British newspaper, *The Sun*. When I had gone to Alonit Monday morning, one of the workers there said something to these two guys who were in the store that "Teresa is from England." I spoke to them there in the Alonit a bit, and then they asked me if they could come and take some pictures of me and Terry. They also wanted a photo that I had of my entire family. I went home and sorted through photos in the house. Then we met up with them later in the afternoon. They wanted to take photos of us in the fields. After we did that we brought them back to our home. It was exciting to have a day without the mundane routine of every other day. The article was printed in the newspaper on Tuesday. It reads:

Hezbollah attack left us shaking
By Oliver Harvey

Brits Terry and Teresa Hills emigrated to Israel for a better life.

But their village Gesher Haziv — just a couple of miles from fighting on the Lebanese border — has been peppered by 20 Katyusha rockets in the last fortnight.

Standing at the scorched earth caused by an explosion, Terry, 48, said: "I was working in the fields when I heard this enormous bang a few feet away. I saw a flash of smoke and flames. It was a Hezbollah rocket. I came home to Teresa and I was shaking like a leaf. A woman was killed by a rocket nearby last week. I admit I was terrified."

Terry was a building contractor in Ruislip, West London, before he and Teresa moved to Israel 18 years ago with their kids Joseph, 26, and Gabi, 20. Hairdresser Teresa, 46, said: "We thought it would be a better place to bring up children. And it was nice. Now I'm terrified Joseph will be called up. He has served as a paratrooper. Gabi has served in the air force. She is staying away from the fighting."

Then Terry and I had the same experience together on Monday as Terry had in the banana groves when a Katyusha rocket landed very close to him. We were home in the security room that afternoon because there had been a number of boomings. A few rockets sounded as if they had landed close. And we were lying in bed in the security room. We were hugging each other out of fear and for comfort. This one sounded like it was coming straight through the wall of our security room, it was so loud. The head of our bed is against the north wall. We were just waiting for it to come through the wall. It turns out that it was a Katyusha that fell south of us.

Bethe

I went to sleep last night at 3 A.M. I stayed up alone watching stupid American sit-com reruns. They weren't even funny. I was just "vegging" out in front of the TV. It is quiet in the nights. The Hizbullah don't usually shoot at night. All of the liquor I bought in the duty free shops has been put to good use. I guess the few drinks I had were what were helping me to relax from the tensions of the day.

I woke up late to the sound of explosions in the distance. I didn't even bother to get up and go into a security room. I just lay in bed for a while. I didn't have to go to work because the Summer Semester at the Western Galilee College where I teach English (EAP or English for Academic Purposes) wasn't beginning. Can you imagine that – not opening a semester because of a war! We had come home a few days ago specifically because I would have to begin teaching today. And now I don't. No one knows what will happen, since no one knows how long this conflict is going to last. There might not be a Summer Semester at all this year.

My daughters were still sleeping when I finally did get out of bed. Asher had gone to work since the computer software firm where he has been employed since 1985 is open. I poured myself a glass of cold coffee and read the newspaper. I unloaded the dishwasher. I swept the floor and tidied up. I need to take our dog, Skippy, out for a walk. It's always a question when might be a good time – meaning no rockets falling. I plan my walk with him around the kibbutz in such a way that I am never far from a shelter. Thus, if I suddenly hear rockets falling I can run to safety. He has to go out and I think he's more scared than I am. In the house he sticks close to us, whereas outside he seems to feel a little better, less skittish.

Around 10:00 I heard the sound of a rocket. So I walked into Meshi's room (she was still sleeping), which is a security room. Skippy comes to know the routine too; he comes with me and plops down on the floor. We believe it will protect us if a rocket lands nearby. I hear the rocket fall. It wasn't a very loud boom, so I knew it wasn't close. I wait a few minutes and then quietly leave the room. I continue doing chores around the house. Fifteen minutes later I hear rockets again and once more move quietly into Meshi's room with Skippy. The cats aren't bothered at all by the noises and continue their cat routine undisturbed.

On Monday I realized that I needed cat food. I called one of my usual suppliers to see if the business was open. Asaf at Hippopatum answered the phone and told me that not only were they open every day, as usual, but they were still delivering. He said that they were even delivering to places really being targeted like Gesher Haziv – after all, the animals had to eat! And they did deliver the animal food just as promised!

I function best when I have a set routine. In uncertain situations such as this it was even more important for me to get into a rhythm. I basically just continued as normal – get up, drink coffee, read the newspaper, empty the dishwasher, sweep the floor, tidy the house, do the laundry, etc. Then I'd turn the computer on and deal with any e-mails I'd received throughout the night.

The only problem is that my computer is not in a security room. It's in a room facing east and what used to be the fields, but is now the new neighborhood. So if a Katyusha fell, I was relatively unsafe. When I started to hear booming, especially if they were close, I'd go into the security room.

This afternoon the rockets landed close. We could hear the loud boom as they landed. A short while later we received an SMS from the Situation Room that there was a fire where one of the Katyushas landed in an open area on the southwest side of the kibbutz. I decided that I could help fight a fire so I put on long pants, a T-shirt, and hiking boots and rode my bicycle to the site.

It must have been a small fire since I passed some people on the way going home. When I arrived a few people were trying to hook up the hoses to the closest hydrant. There was a problem opening the bolt. A special key was needed that no one had since it was a new hydrant, so someone had to go get it. The light-engined plane came and dropped the red chemical. People were just standing around. Paul then attached the hose and began squirting the water on the fire. The fire truck arrived and took up position near the small grove of trees. I decided that I could help carrying the hose and pulling it to where it was needed.

Then out of the blue Meshi showed up. I had told her to wait at home, but she didn't hear me or didn't want to hear me. So she was with me out in the open. We saw that where the fire company truck had worked there was still a hot spot, but they had already folded up their hose and wanted to get out of the area. Eli Dinur had taken over from Paul and so he sprayed water in that direction.

And then another barrage of Katyusha rockets started. We had no place to go for cover – we were out in the open. So I told Meshi to lie down on the ground. The Katyushas flew right over us and landed about 50 meters away. We heard people behind us who had taken cover in a concrete construction for infrastructure – of electricity, water, etc. As soon as we could we ran there where we crouched down and waited. A security officer from the Regional Council drove by and started yelling at us: "Why are you out in the open!" What is a kid doing here?!" "Get home!" he shouted at us. I sent Meshi home at a run because it really was no place for her to be. Then he kept yelling at me to go. I shouted back at him that I could help extinguish a fire. He just told me to go home quickly. At that point I realized that there was no point fighting, so I got on my bicycle and pedaled home.

Meshi was already home when I arrived. I asked her if she was scared and she said yes. I told her it was perfectly all right to be afraid. After all we had just been in a scary and dangerous situation.

At this point in the war my morning routine changed a bit. I'd still get up, have cold coffee, empty the dishwasher, take the dog for a walk, sweep the floor (or even wash it), and do a load or two of laundry. But now I started to get some serious work for the college done from home.

My colleague, Yehudit Lahav, lives at Kibbutz Shomerat. It's relatively close to Gesher Haziv and also in the Western Galilee. However, her kibbutz is closer to Acco, which used to be (emphasis on the past tense) out of the Katyusha rocket range. So she doesn't have a security room in her house. During this war the Hizbullah were able to fire rockets that not only reached her area, but went much further south as well. Yehudit also decided to stay home during the war.

We spoke on the phone quite often checking up on each other. At some point we realized that we both have the Skype program set up on our computers. We had planned on reworking the Advanced Level textbook for our classes at the Western Galilee College where we lecture. We thought we would do it in September after teaching the Summer Semester course. But now we had the time since we weren't teaching. So we decided to try to work together using Skype. That way we kept the phone lines free.

The new morning routine would go like this: One of us would call the other on the land phone line to see if we were available for working. Then we'd both pull the file up onto the screen in front of us and discuss changes that we wanted to make while actually working on the texts together. It worked relatively well. Sometimes the program crashed and we'd have to reboot the computer to get it working well again. Every once in a while we'd hear a loud galloping sound over the speakers that was pretty annoying.

This evening, as on many evenings, I went to the hospital around 18:00 to be with Asher's father, David and help him through dinner. We spoke about the news and the problems of politics. We spoke about my children, especially Lavie in the army. Then I would get him organized for dinner and help him eat the prepared food.

I wasn't happy at all with the arrangements in the basement shelter. It was clean, well organized and run like any other hospital. But he was underground. There was no natural lighting. And it was crowded. I wanted to get him out of there. Unfortunately, the rest of the family didn't concur. So I continued to visit him as often as possible.

Earlier, in the late afternoon, I had received a phone message from Yulia, a woman I know who is heavily into animal rescue in the area, something about cat food. I immediately thought that she needed some food, so I called her back. Yulia told me that a lot of donations of dog and cat food had arrived and that she had set up a central distribution center in her village at Nes Amim (a few kilometers south of Nahariya). Many people in the North had abandoned their animals when they fled and the trash cats no longer had a food supply since the cities and villages were less populated than usual. It was late evening then, so Asher and I went for a fifteen-minute drive to Nes Amim. Yulia gave us a few 18 kg-bags of dog and cat food. I then distributed this food to others on Gesher Haziv who were feeding the abandoned animals or those left behind in the care of others who needed more food.

After we returned from Nes Amim I walked up to the Laundry to feed the cats that live there. I saw a female golden retriever sitting in the road near the apartment she lives in. I said hello and petted her. She was really happy to get a little attention.

Then I drove down to the gas station at the entrance to the kibbutz to fill up my car. The station wasn't manned, but you could fill up using a credit card. There was this man standing next to the pump island, but he wasn't filling up his van. It was kind of eerie since there weren't any other people around. I asked him if he needed help. He said yes, that he didn't have a credit card, so he couldn't fill up. I told him I'd help him out and I ran my card through the machine on his side of the island. He paid me in cash for the gas he pumped and drove away. I'm glad I could help, but it was a very weird scene.

For a number of months I'd been running into references to the author Thomas Friedman's work. I'd never read any of his books, so while I was in the States I went into a bookstore to buy one. The only book they had was *From Beirut to Jerusalem*. It sounded interesting. I started reading it there and I continued reading it here after we returned. But suddenly I was having trouble reading his accounts – they were too close to home and what we were experiencing now. I had to stop. Almost nothing had changed in the Lebanese situation since 1982, although the players and their names have changed. It was too close for comfort. It took me two months after the end of the war to return to the book and finish reading it.

Asher

Tadiad was open so I decided to go to work. It is located south of Acco and businesses in this area were allowed to remain open. It is usually a twenty-minute or so drive from Gesher Haziv to Tadiad. However, now the situation was totally different. So many people had fled the North that there was no traffic. The feeling while driving on the road was fun because there was no one on the road. There were also no police, so you could drive as fast as you wanted. But on the other hand, driving was a risk; I could be hit by a Katyusha at any time. And that feeling sits on the back of your neck at all times while driving.

The routine was that if there was a rocket attack or if you heard a siren (only later did the Nahariya area have sirens before imminent attacks) you stop the car and find a place to lie down on the side of the road for two to three minutes. Then you could continue on your journey.

At work, about half of the employees were there. It was also July-August when people normally take vacations, so in total the activity at Tadiad wasn't affected much by the war. A certain area in the building was designated as "safe" and every time there was a siren people went to that area and waited five minutes or so. During this first day, I didn't go to the designated area at all. I ridiculed the entire drill. I just stayed in my office.

I learned that on the second day of the war Tadiad decided to close the new northern branch of the company, Tadiad Development Center or TDC, which is located in Kibbutz Sa'ar (right next to Gesher Haziv to the south) and bring the employees to work at Tadiad because it was a bit safer. That first Sunday of the war, the TDC employees were already working at Tadiad, so when I arrived they had settled into their new routine. I also learned that Yehuda Brook, the CEO of Tadiad, had organized places to stay on his kibbutz, Hasolelim, for people who worked at Tadiad and who lived in the Nahariya area, the Krayot, or other places in the north. Hasolelim is out of range of Katyusha fire. Moshe Zohar, for example, was at Hasolelim for over a month instead of at his home in Nahariya and he was really happy.

At the beginning, the Dining Room was open for lunch as usual at Miluot Industries where Tadiad is located. So upon my return from the States, I walked to the Dining Room for lunch around noon. It was a nice break from the routine we'd gotten into of work-sirens-work-sirens, etc.

I worked regularly and then went for a walk with Skippy after 18:00. When we got to the area where Bethe and others had fought the fire earlier, I saw that there were still some hot spots in the area of the fire. I tried to put the flames out by kicking dirt and sand onto the flames, but wasn't able to. When I got back to the house I called the

Situation Room and let them know so that the fire would be extinguished by volunteers or the Fire Fighters.

Today I decided to go to the designated "safe" area at Tadiad when the siren sounded. Not because I thought it was safer than my office, but because it was a social gathering. You spent the five minutes or so in the company of others. There were also light refreshments available, other than the standard coffee and tea.

The sirens interrupt my concentration. While I do manage to get work done, I can't seem to get deep into a problem I'm working on with all the interruptions.

The consideration of whether to stay at home or drive somewhere is based on risk management. When we drive on the road in a regular situation we know that there is a risk that there will be an accident. We don't stay at home fearful of what might be.

In the same manner and with the same attitude, Bethe and I decided to stay and sleep at home, on Gesher Haziv, and not flee to safer areas in the center of Israel during this conflict. (We had also just returned from a three-week vacation to the States where we traveled to a new location every few days and just wanted to be at home – safe or not). When the rockets were launched (and we could often hear the sound of the shell leaving the rocket launcher, even though it was in Lebanon) or the rockets were falling, in order to minimize risk my family and I would go into one of the two security rooms in our house.

It could be that if we had major rocket barrages falling on us like those in Nahariya or Kiryat Shmona, I would have thought differently. Although Gesher Haziv suffered twenty-four hits, we were lucky. The only casualty was a dog that died from a shrapnel wound. Yes, there was damage to property, but that can be fixed. Also having my father in the hospital was another reason to stay.

So we lived our lives as "normally" as possible considering the situations and risks. Skippy needed to go for a walk in the evenings, which was part of his routine. I didn't mind taking him out. I felt safer walking than in a car because my response time is quicker. And Skippy seemed calmer when we were outside, whereas he was quite jumpy in the house.

Danit

The second Sunday of the war I had to go to Jerusalem for a meeting. It was the one work-related meeting that I had during this period. I left the children with relatives in Haifa, on the safe side of the mountain.

That was amazing – the bubble within the bubble. I arrived in Jerusalem and there was nothing out of the ordinary there – everything was normal – no war or tension because of it. And even more than that, my colleagues reacted as if it was extremely normal that I managed to arrive on time for the meeting! I had driven with Shlomi until Haifa and from Haifa I took the train, because the trains didn't go any further north. I got to Jerusalem and it was totally different! The people there just didn't understand what was going on in the north of the country. From the comments they made like, "Okay, so let's begin running it tomorrow," I realized they didn't understand that that option didn't exist because nothing was working in the north! They didn't understand that something simple like going out to buy writing paper was a problem. Or the difficulties involved in organizing a support group when the people are scattered all over the country. Or even to arrange a meeting in a coffee shop, which was an idea that arose at that meeting in Jerusalem – it just wasn't clear, and it wasn't understood, a type of disconnection between one world and another.

And when I arrived at the train station in Haifa in order to collect my children, there was a siren. People were acting hysterically in the designated "safe area" there. And their hysteria didn't connect to me. That was the strongest impression I had during this time – a bubble inside a bubble.

I wasn't working during the war, so in the house it was like vacation time. I didn't do much except for going up to the Mail Room and volunteering to distribute the mail that did arrive, which was some sort of contribution to the community that I felt I wanted to give. I also fed some of the animals that had been abandoned, and other things that were more community-oriented. In a paradoxical way the atmosphere here in the community was quite relaxing. In the final analysis I think we managed very well staying at home. We handled the war very well.

One event might not be connected to another, but somehow they do become connected in our minds. For example, a Katyusha fell once and then a few seconds later a part of Stav's bed broke. I know it was coincidence, but the day-to-day situation and the booming from outside suddenly came together as if the events were connected in some way.

Normally, my children eat a heavy meal in the middle of the day and a lighter meal in the evenings. We continued doing that throughout the war as well. The entire family only eats together on the weekends, since Shlomi is at work during the daytime. However, the food that I prepared was of a lesser quality than usual, I must admit. This occurred because of a lack of certain ingredients – I couldn't get what I needed. On the other hand, since I had more time available I put more into cooking.

The only real change in our eating routine was that sometimes we had to eat in the security room. This change happened because a few times we would start to eat and then there would be a Katyusha barrage. Since it's more worthwhile to continue eating hot food, we improvised. So then we sat on the floor in the security room cross-legged using an untable-table (a large board that I wrapped in plastic so that it would be easy to clean) and that became our dining table – on the pillows, in Bedouin style.

Once, Stav and I stayed with Carmela Bartal, our neighbor, for a while and they made alligators from beads. It took a lot of time and we all had a lot of time, so it was possible to make very small and intricate things. And suddenly, and I mean suddenly, a heavy barrage of Katyushas began – massive, serious. We left all the things where they were because the rockets were landing really close to us and we went into their security room.

In the middle of the barrage I left the security room in order to get chocolate because the Guards from Azkaban eat chocolate! My actions were totally irrational. If someone else had done that I would immediately check their normal mental state, because it was a really weird disconnection.

When I returned everyone was sitting in the security room hugging each other and very tense. Somehow, going out to find some chocolate gave me strength. It was a feeling, an illusion that I was in charge of the situation. It doesn't matter that things were falling and blowing up around me from the sky – the fact that I went out, made me feel as if I was in charge. And it is perfectly clear that it was illusion (or delusion), but at that moment it was what I needed. And by the way, the chocolate really did its work and helped us relax.

Stav

When my mother came to pick us up at the train station in Haifa I had this really bad stomach ache. And I was uncomfortable. We had been staying with our cousins in Haifa when my mother went to Jerusalem.

When we needed to eat in the security room my mother took a type of bulletin board and covered it in a large plastic bag so we had a movable table. There was a time when all we ate was pasta and sauce because that was all there was in the refrigerator.

Micha

I was on reserve duty for one week, I think until the 23rd and then on the 23rd and 24th we went away with the whole family to Kfar Vitkin which is close to where Oren was, at Wingate, so we could spend some time with him. He wanted to come home with us. It was difficult to leave him behind, but we did. At least one child was in a safe place, although when they starting shooting the long-distance missiles, then Wingate became a bit more of a worry.

When I was home in the afternoons, since it was summer, we would have liked to go down to the beach or to the pool, but we couldn't. We mostly stayed inside the house, but occasionally we tried to let the kids play outside, mostly on the south side of the house because it is a bit more protected, and because it is behind a security room. And we told them that as soon as they hear a loud bang just duck or run into the security room. I had to go through the whole routine with them – if they were walking to their activities in the mornings, what to do in case they get caught. Not just running in panic.

I was replaced during my reserve duty by someone else because I needed to go back to work. My colleague had a scheduled trip overseas, so I wanted to go back to make sure that everything was running properly because Bermad got permission to keep operating despite the war, despite the Katyushas. There was a Katyusha that fell very close to Bermad itself. It was on the first Saturday of the war when one fell about 15 meters from the office where I work. That was the only Katyusha that fell within the boundaries of Evron. A few fell in the fields, but nothing else inside the kibbutz.

At the beginning, in Bermad, they set up a security room next to my office, with computers and a whole network there for whoever wanted to work there. I continued to work in the office, but whenever we heard or thought we heard something, before the sirens started, we just went into the security room and waited a while and then went back to work. They kept working on the floor in Installation, but only with people who agreed to come to work. I think the army gave them a license for up to thirty people in Installation. So they worked on a twenty-four-hour basis, people worked a morning shift, night shift. Basically Bermad continued working throughout the whole war. I continued working as usual.

But the normal routine at Bermad was disrupted. There is a Dining Room at Kibbutz Evron, and on regular days we eat there. But it was closed during the war. So for breakfast someone would come around and give us sandwiches. Between about noon and 13:00 you were allowed to go to the Dining Room to take food in take-away dishes, go back to your office or to the security room to eat your lunch. One other thing they did nice at work, spoiling us, was that every day after lunch, at about 14:00, the same guy who walked around in the morning with the sandwiches would walk around with ice cream.

I don't have organized transportation to work, so I was driving. I drove home during the busy hours for the Katyushas in the afternoons, between 15:00 and 17:00. So that was always the most frightening time of the day, because I had to drive through northern Nahariya where they had a lot of Katyushas falling.

Helen

Even as the conflict continued, I found this a very positive experience. I was very happy that those people who felt that they wanted to leave left. I was happy for them and happy because it reduced the pressure on those who were here. When you have to deal with hysterical people, it doesn't help one's own state of mind.

I lazed around much more. And it was nice to have the inner moral sanction to be utterly lazy. You don't have to clean the house if you don't want to. But I wasn't obsessing about cleaning at all. There was gardening work to do, which actually I enjoyed doing. I would often wonder: "Do I really need to pay attention when the rockets fall?" I would stand hesitating and ask myself: "Should I at least go into the house?" which I usually did.

I also drove into Nahariya to get prescription drugs for whoever needed it. Zvi Baer and Zvi Elkin did most of it, but a couple of times the kibbutz nurse, Tzofit, asked me if I could go in. And often there were individual requests from residents who needed things. For example, Olga had a lot of medical problems at the beginning of the war and she doesn't drive. She was also very stressed. So I kept taking her in for things she needed. There was a shortage of drivers. I suddenly thought, "Maybe people need things," so that's what I did.

I went down to the Alonit market and brought up deliveries whenever there was a window of opportunity, which didn't really mean anything because a window could be announced and if a Katyusha falls there goes the window. But more or less whenever the people of Alonit opened up I went. And by the way those people were incredible. Can you imagine working in a gas station when Katyushas are falling? Definitely not the preferred place to be! So whenever I could help I did – if I was there or somebody asked me to go down, I would do that and do deliveries of the items.

Meanwhile, in addition to all the reporters swarming the hospital, there were all the delegations from abroad. And it was the job of the International Liaison Office to arrange for and escort all those brave souls who were coming from the federations to see. They seemed to feel that they had to see the situation with their own eyes. So I had more work to do at the hospital.

At the hospital a lot of stuff was happening that started to accumulate. Money was literally pouring in and it doesn't matter if it was $18 or $50,000. First of all it took some time to adjust to this burst of activity that had never existed before. And suddenly Judy Jackovitz, the woman in whose office I volunteer, ended up being the center not only for all of the delegations and reporters, but for money as well. For every contribution we had to write letters of thanks, and just doing the physical part of taking care of all the checks – literally bags full –

that were coming in. So that was one thing I kept saying: "I'm here if you need help."

One of the most important things for me was the fact that once we connected everyone with SMS on the kibbutz, I felt easier about going out – even to the hospital, because I knew people could get me if needed.

Paul

That Sunday marked two weeks that nothing had been done at all in the fields – there were bananas to be picked and stuff like that and we had to decide what we were going to do. There is a certain amount of time that you can just irrigate and that's it. There are certain things you have to do to take care of the trees, pick the fruit, and that sort of thing.

About a week after I got back, we started to look for workers because we couldn't use our Thai workers any longer. The Thai Embassy had forbidden the farmers in the North to use Thai workers out in the fields during this period. So first of all I sent all our Thais out of the area so that they wouldn't have to sit in a shelter all day and could make money elsewhere.

Then I brought in a contractor with workers to do the work that had to be done. A lot of the contractors in the area weren't interested and those who were had difficulty finding people who would agree to work. The one that we work with was actually able to find workers and we started slowly at first and then more and more workers were brought in to help do what had to be done. But it was very difficult because they would work from 6:00 in the morning until the Katyushas started falling which was somewhere between 10:00 and 11:00 o'clock. And then they'd leave. So we didn't really get a lot done. And we had to pay them for a full day, even though they weren't working a full day. At that point we were only picking bananas and lychee. When I started bringing in workers, I would get up as usual around 5:00-5:30 and be out in the fields by 6:00 when the workers arrived.

In the evenings, when we weren't having a meal with friends, I'd just sit and watch TV. I only went into the security room a few times when there were sirens, I think, not really, and if we did it was for a minute. Not usually, actually.

Judy

Sunday evening I drove back to Gesher Haziv alone. It was a very funny feeling because the roads coming north got emptier and emptier. But I basically had to get to work the next day. I started getting back into my normal life.

I kept going to work early and working until 15:00 or so. I got a lot done at work even though we were only working Sunday to Wednesdays instead of our usual five-day week, which included Thursdays. Coming home was less routine. I usually took a shortcut through the Ragum neighborhood instead of turning north at the traffic light at Nahariya. One afternoon I went through there and apparently ten minutes later a Katyusha fell there and killed a man right in front of a shelter. However, that didn't stop me from using that shortcut.

Last week I was talking to the man I share an office with about my dilemma with Mayzie. Since Leah wasn't around now (being in Netanya), I was concerned about leaving the dog alone all day. The booming really scared her. I said: "What am I going to do with my dog, she's crazy?" He said: "Don't worry – bring the dog to work." So, since he's a dog person I figured it would be okay.

So Monday morning I was up by 5:30, took Mayzie for a walk, gave her breakfast, and by 6:00 we were on the road. I had her leash with me, a blanket for her, and I actually took one of the chains so that if someone insisted I could chain her up downstairs. And we went up to work in Tefen. She was very well behaved.

I kept taking Mayzie with me to work. She knew the routine as well as anyone, especially when it concerned what to do during a siren. The security room at work wasn't really big enough for all of us to squeeze into (even if we wanted to). The entrance to this room was opposite the stairwell, which backed onto the elevator shaft in the building. And you know that an elevator shaft is super poured concrete. So we went into the stairwell behind the elevator shaft figuring we were just about as safe as being in the security room. I didn't feel the need to go running into the security room. And I wasn't the only one. Mayzie came with me at all times. She had the routine down pat.

Much of what I did in the evenings, especially once Leah was in Netanya, was determined by what I could or couldn't do that included Mayzie. I didn't want to leave her alone, either at home or on a chain outside the house; she was disturbed enough already by the noises. So I usually stayed home with her, or went to visit at houses where I knew she could come in, too.

Miri

My father, who lives in the Krayot, acted as if everything was normal, but too much. He walked around and drove where he wanted to. He said: "I've been through all the wars in this country. What is this? Who is this Nasrallah who is going to make us captive or enforce a strike on the entire country? What kind of behavior is this? Putting the citizens into a situation where they have to flee or protect themselves by sitting in a shelter for days on end? We have to show him that we are continuing to live our lives as normal as possible." So he refused to go into any mamad or shelter or anything. So I stopped arguing with him.

Noa was in the bath once when I received an SMS message to go into the mamad. Now what was I supposed to do? Take her out of the bath wrapped in a towel and make her hysterical and run to the mamad? Or when she's sitting in her high chair eating lunch – what am I going to do? So I left her doing what she was doing. It's really sad to say it, but the whole situation simply turned into a routine.

The rockets were falling all over the North. I'd rather be at home where it is at least comfortable. How long can you sleep in a strange bed – every time to drag things around and laundry and it's an uncomfortable situation. Everyone was wonderful hosting us and doing things for us, but it's not your house and you don't feel totally at ease. In Tel Aviv it was good because we did things, but I was really happy to return home, really happy.

The television was on non-stop, all the time. We felt that it allowed us to know where we were standing – what was happening. I was tuned in to Nasrallah's broadcasts – he's a real dog – but what he said happened, so I felt that it was important to listen to him. I found it very difficult watching the television. I'm a very sensitive person to begin with. And then to see the pictures being broadcast on the television – there were many evenings that I would just sit there crying while I watched. It was difficult, very difficult. I found the decisions that were made for us very difficult. I would just sit and cry. But I felt that it was important to know what's going on.

Zvi

Part of my job during the week was to go into Nahariya and take care of things for the kibbutz and individuals – the bank, the post office, and the medical facility of Kupat Holim.

I went to the Post Office where we collected the mail. Everything was going on normally there, more than normal. It was a very active place. There was much more activity to take care of all of the people who had come in from God knows where – the villages. The Post Office was open for regular people, of whom there were few. It was now open to serve the villages which had their mobile mail cancelled. There was an atmosphere of complete understanding and cooperation and helpfulness on their part. You could park where you wanted to park – even where it is forbidden. As soon as they know who you are they immediately gave you service to the best of their ability and I couldn't have asked for anything better. The atmosphere was one of understanding and cooperation.

The same thing occurred in Kupat Holim, which was my other main station. Kupat Holim, to the extent that they could, were very quick. I usually took the prescriptions from the Clinic on the kibbutz to the main building in Nahariya where there is a pharmacy. They received them and it took them maybe ten or fifteen minutes to have them filled. The area of the building where the pharmacy is located was considered a safe place, so I felt all right being there

My last stop was Bank Discount, which had moved its offices to the basement of the Carleton Hotel. The bank was in operation there and soldiers had been given a resting place down there. So the three places that we had to get service from took care of us very well.

Things at home changed a bit, but not much, during the war. I slept in the security room; one of us had to survive.

I wasn't scared driving on the roads. It's like being here in the house. You don't sit here in fear waiting for the next bomb to come. You just go on and do whatever you're doing and if you hear a bomb coming you go to a safe place. If I was on the road and I heard something coming I drove faster, just like everyone else was doing. There were no speed limits, and definitely you were going to drive as fast as you could knowing that wherever you were going there was a safe place. Fortunately I had no flat tires!

Lyn

I escorted my kids to the shelter and then back from the shelter every day. There was no freedom for them. The organizers wouldn't let them go by themselves – the parents had to pick them up. At the beginning it was in the shelter by the Laundry and it was there for a good week or so. More often than not the activities were run by Rifi or Irit Ziv, which was really nice.

A few times I used the three-hour gap to mow the lawns. I have to admit mowing the lawns was very nice because you didn't hear the artillery, which was a constant background sound – boom, boom, boom – constant all the daylight hours; it started at sun-up and stopped at sundown. When I had the lawnmower going it nearly drowned it all out – it was nice. I was wary when I was outside, but I wasn't afraid. But I only allowed myself to do those sorts of things when the kids weren't home, because I felt responsible when the kids were here, that I couldn't tell them to do something and then do something different myself. I had to set an example. Those three hours allowed me to do things I wouldn't have done with the children at home.

And I really think that it preserved my sanity, because for me, after getting up in morning, making sure they had their breakfast, taking them over to the activities, then I had a little bit of my time. I'm not saying that I was in the garden every morning; sometimes I just came out and sat on the step for a cup of coffee and sat in the sun and read a book.

Our feeling is that this is our home and we chose to live here and this is part of living here. Where are the people going to go when they start dropping the bombs on Tel Aviv? We took all this into account.

We had family calling us. My mother was calling us from Australia offering plane tickets every day: "Please come, please come, I'll send you the tickets!" We had relatives in safer areas of Israel who offered to put us up or give us their apartment when they went overseas. For basically all of August we had an apartment available for us in Ramat Gan. It is just not something that we thought seriously about doing – leaving.

When some families started coming back to the kibbutz, families with little kids, they started activities with the younger kids as well, those of nursery school age. They realized that they couldn't have the two groups together. So the older kids moved over to the shelter near the twenty units, Rifi's house. And they actually had a nice time. They did all sorts of things. But I still had to take them to the shelter and pick them up – every day.

The kids were watching more television – yeah, oh yeah! Not so much the first couple of weeks because there was so much about the war on TV and we don't have cable, just public stations, and they watched a little bit of the children's programs that they had on.

Micha went back to work at Bermad today. I was very stressed every day when Micha was coming home from work. He would finish work every day between four and five – Katyusha time. He would phone me and say: "I'm leaving" and until he got home I was physically tense. He said there were no speed limits – the traffic signs are just decorations on the sides of the road; he just goes straight through.

I had the news on in the background. Or I would turn it on on the hour when they had the short five minutes of serious news bulletin about what was happening and where, and then turn it off again, because I found that after a few times all the news was just too much, although I couldn't go without any news.

Hannah

I don't know how, but with all the tension, the time passed – every hour there's a news broadcast. Sometimes I had a newspaper to read, but rarely. When the TV's on I can't concentrate to read. Theoretically there was a lot of time, but in reality it felt as if there wasn't. And the time passed.

Meshi

I got bored just sitting in the house and watching TV all day. I saw so many reruns! Half of the things I saw on TV I had already seen and I still wanted the Animal Planet channel in our home, but my mother wouldn't get it! I didn't read books, but I played on the computer a few times. I didn't ICQ or Messenger any of my friends, either, because no one was at home. Sometimes, when my mother needed me to do stuff, like take the garbage out, or walk Skippy, I did it. I usually tried to hurry.

During the whole war I wasn't really scared by the Katyushas, I was more excited, I'd say. But all the constant noise worried me.

My friend, Shoshan, was in the country, but she was at her aunt's or relatives' and Noa was on a planned vacation with her family abroad. So I didn't have anyone to be with. So it wasn't like I had somewhere to go and chose not to; I didn't really have somewhere to go.

I got up, ate, watched TV, I ate, watched TV, and watched more TV. I stayed up very late at night – the earliest I went to sleep was midnight, more like one or two around that time. I got up around noon, maybe later. This isn't very different from what I normally do on vacation; but this time I was alone. That's the thing – none of my friends were around.

There was a Katyusha barrage in the middle of the afternoon. My mother went out of the house. About twenty minutes later I didn't have anything to do in the house; it was pretty boring, so I decided to go find her. I didn't hear any Katyushas falling and it wasn't an hour that I remember anything usually fell. So, spontaneously, I put my shoes on, I think I changed my pants and went.

I started walking and when I came my mother wasn't angry or anything, so I thought: "How can I help?" So I took the hoses and helped move them around and I tried to spot potential fires. I felt helpful.

But then Katyushas started falling and I didn't really know how to react. I started hearing the *whoosh* whistle sound and *boom*. A few Katyushas fell in Sa'ar, which is about 50 meters away. My mother grabbed me and pushed me onto the ground, there was a little hill there. And then when there was a short break in the shelling, we ran to a cement box. Then some man came, maybe he was a security officer, and he started shouting: "Why is there a kid here?" And I said to myself: "Oops!" So I went home. I can't remember if I took my mother's bicycle back, but no I think I ran because she rode it. I wasn't scared, just nervous. The whole time my mother pushed me to the ground she was more scared than I. I was like: "Katyushas!" I said I was scared when my mother came home, but I wasn't really scared.

Evelyn

The husband of one of the caregivers in the old age home used to bring her to work. But when the shelling became more intense, they closed the husband's place of work because they couldn't get anything done having to run into the shelters every five minutes or so. So now we had to provide transportation for this lady as well.

One day we received a donation from a dairy that was owned by an Arab person in our area. Suddenly Ishai and I were called to distribute the products; eighty percent of the population wasn't around, but we went from house to house and anyone who was there we gave containers to. It was a real experience to do the distribution. We loaded all the boxes into the car and started driving. The responses of people were so funny. But one thing that was really nice is that later Mel Grossman searched for the owner of the dairy and went there to thank him. That was really nice. He came to me one day and said "Milkmaid, I want to tell you something." And I laughed. "Milkmaid!" he called me. In the middle of all that was happening we're out there driving the car to distribute the dairy products. It took us two to three hours to distribute all the containers.

When I had collected a large list of products that the seniors needed, we went out to buy what was lacking. In the next war this is something that needs to be more organized – the whole issue of provisions needs to be addressed.

After a few loud boomings our dog, Bambi, decided that she didn't want to be outside any more. She was under our bed whenever she could be. She was attached to me if I was in the house. She followed me around from room to room. Since then she sleeps under our bed. She really felt unsettled.

Kathy

We took our son Noam to the army on July 24th. He had to be at the Hof Hacarmel bus station where there was an organized pick-up to take them to the induction center. The streets were empty in Haifa, it was amazing. Haifa was a ghost town. We drove through Haifa all the way to the southern end and there was no one on the streets; it was so weird.

M

I hadn't been connected to the fire brigade on Gesher Haziv team in the past. I got an SMS that day when the Katyushas fell in the southwestern area of the kibbutz. I came down and basically people were just standing around. But then we got organized and I kind of enjoyed doing it. If I was already standing around why not help out. I wasn't here when the area near Polyziv was burning on that Saturday otherwise I would have helped out then as well.

I'm a beach person and I surfed and swam a few times during the war, up to a certain point when it stopped being okay. I felt it was a little bit unsafe to go down to the beach because even being a 100 meters or a few hundred meters out in the ocean, there were Katyushas that hit the ocean. Then I started going to the Kfar Hanofesh Achziv (just a kilometer or so north of Gesher Haziv on the main road) where my friends are running the place and we would swim in the small pool there. We did it once when suddenly we saw all the crows flying up into the air and we said, "Oops!" and walked very fast into the mamad they had. That was pretty close.

I didn't really interrupt my normal activities; I think more or less everyone joined *my* routine. I worked as a volunteer in the Hamal. In the evenings I did a little bit less. We would gather at Assaf Louis' house. The best way is to turn the music up when the bombs start – we had a few BBQs there. We were getting together more often with friends than we usually do – there was not much else to do – Shahar, Kobi, Avner, Assaf, basically whoever was here, most of those guys were here most of the time. Shahar was working at Cabri with the horses, Avner was working at the metal shop and rode his bicycle 50 kilometers every day. Assaf was here until they called him to the Army Reserves. Shahar was called to the reserves afterward.

Shai

For the second fire we were a bit more organized – we had people and equipment – this was the one in the area of the carob trees between gimel and daled. With time we kept getting more efficient so that we knew what each person was supposed to do and what were his/her responsibilities. We also organized a rescue committee so that if needed, if someone was trapped in their homes, we could rescue them if something needed to be broken or cut, or if we needed to get someplace with a vehicle, So we prepared a vehicle with an electric saw, ropes, first aid kit, etc. We were prepared for any challenge such as that. When a Katyusha fell we went to locate it and if it was inside the kibbutz we would mark where it hit. That's basically what I did from the standpoint of my job.

In my house the security room is normally used as the bedroom for two out of my three children – the two smaller children (our eldest daughter has a room of her own). That first Thursday we took the children to their grandparents at Kibbutz Gan Shmuel (north of Tel Aviv, but south of Haifa). When the children were here they always slept in the security room. And Tzofit also usually slept with them there. I didn't sleep in the security room; it was my own choice.

Each of our children had something else going on. The middle child, who is eleven years old, was seventy percent away from the kibbutz staying with family either at Gan Shmuel or Jerusalem or Kfar Saba, so he was here only a small part of the war. Our younger daughter, who was eight, during the first few days she was off the kibbutz, but after that she returned because she didn't want to be away from us, so she was here sixty to seventy percent of the war. For Shaked, who is fourteen, she had activities with the youth movement when she wasn't on Gesher Haziv and part of the time she was in Jerusalem. She chose where she wanted to be. It was harder for our daughters to be away from the kibbutz and the family for an extended time.

Sometime in the middle, when it was really tense around here and there were Katyusha hits close by, Tzofit went down to sleep in the shelter with the children. This happened for three or four nights.

When the children were here, during the days, they went to the organized activities. Tzofit was either with the children or fulfilling her duties as nurse in the Clinic. One of the primary reasons that she didn't go away more was because of her job as nurse. She was here most of the time; she hardly left. But when she did leave for a short time she organized a substitute to take over her duties in the clinic.

We ate at our dining-room table which is located only a few steps away from the security room. Yuval, our youngest, had some difficult days when she didn't want to leave the security room, so it's possible that on a few occasions she took her plate to eat there, but most of the time she ate with us. However, she spent nearly all of her time in the security room, especially during the really tense days. We don't usually have a television in their bedroom, but for this period we organized one. If the Katyusha hits were very close then she stayed more in the security room.

I hardly went into the security room, even when the rest of my family did. First of all, I was at home relatively little. I'd get home for half an hour in the middle of day and wouldn't return again before 20:00 or 21:00 at night. And when I was at home, I was sitting around the television in the living room most of the time. If there were Katyushas that fell, I'd leave the house immediately in order to look for it in whatever direction I was told to go. If I was at work during a Katyusha hit, I would attempt to go up to the roof to see where it hit. And if we saw where it landed then we needed to inform the authorities of its location. And if it hit inside the kibbutz we'd go and make sure that nothing had happened.

Carolyn

My father was here once and I went to Nahariya once to see him. And my mother came back the second week and we all went to Tel Aviv together for one night.

Ilan

The second week of the war we went to Eilat for a vacation that we had planned two to three months before the war and we decided not to cancel. It was a family gathering with my parents, my brother and his family, but it wasn't really relaxing because the newspapers arrived all the time; the news seemed to pursue us, and the casualties made us feel really bad. So it wasn't really a vacation. We felt great – it was comfortable and we were together – and we were out of the target range; but it wasn't what we had planned, it wasn't a relaxing vacation. Not a real vacation.

Back at work in Carmiel, the shelter in the mall was organized for our bank to work in. So from that point on I went to work fairly regularly. Once, when I was leaving the mall and on my way to the parking lot at the end of the workday to come home a siren went off. A Katyusha fell *very* close to where I was and I went back inside the mall to the shelter. I waited ten, fifteen, twenty minutes until the situation relaxed, then I went back to the car and drove home.

At home in Gesher Haziv we got caught by Katyusha rockets twice when we went outside for a stroll around the neighborhood on the road – on the internal road, not the main road, because that was something we would not do. Once it was fine – it passed peacefully. The second time we got caught on the road by a siren very close to our home, just a few houses away. Now if you're an adult and you get caught by a siren, you run home in the fifteen seconds it might take you. But with our little daughter it was different, especially since we had her little bicycle with us. We heard rockets landing in the area. I got a bit upset at Miri when she said: "Ilan let's get out of here?" And I said "Go where. We won't manage to get home safely?" We realized that in a few of the houses still being constructed in this area, and where people still haven't begun living there are mamadim all ready for us. So we ran inside the building and into the mamad and flattened ourselves onto the corner of the far wall of the mamad since there wasn't a window. But it was still a safe place to be at the time. We waited there for about fifteen minutes for the danger to pass.

Noa

The second time that I was driving on the road was when I had to get to the Emergency Room at the hospital. So we drove and there were some Katyushas that fell when we on the road. Then more fell when I was in the Emergency Room.

On the way home I decided that I wanted to go on a tour of where the Katyushas had already fallen in Nahariya. I work in Nahariya and know the exact places in town such as where all the streets are located. So I took my mother into town to locate where the rockets had fallen and where damage had been done.

When you hear the Katyusha whiz and land from afar it sounds much worse than it actually is. In reality, when you see the house that was hit on the fourth floor as well as the electrical pole that was hit on Me'assdim Street and the building that was on fire where that triangular area got smacked a lot on TV – it stops your breath. But seeing it for yourself in the place where it occurred, the reality is a bit different – it's less dramatic. But it also crystallizes how easy it is to penetrate our homes, our privacy and our own small world. If it's a burglar who invades our home or a rocket, the easy invasion of your own private world is intolerable.

Ronny

The SMS messages really helped to minimize the level of stress, especially when you were outside of Gesher Haziv. It kept you in the loop when you knew what was going on.

Sharon and I got organized extremely quickly into our war routine. The only real topic of discussion was whether to go shopping or not to do anything all day. We were inside the house or out on the porch most of the time. We worked in the garden as well. Sharon is a chef, but we didn't make fancy meals. We ate relatively simply – vegetables or yoghurt for example. We didn't have much of an appetite – we never said, "Let's have a feast!" Once every four or five days we got ourselves organized and drove to the Sabri market to get stuff.

I used the pet food I got from Bethe to feed cats around the kibbutz, which I usually did in the late afternoon or early evening. This was not something I'd done before. Suddenly cats came to the house where we were staying. Then, when I'd go back to my apartment to feed my cat, other cats from the neighborhood would be there crying and want to come into my house. I knew there were at least two people on the kibbutz who feed trash cats. I used to distribute the food when I walked around – that was a good excuse to walk around a bit. We also fed some dogs that were wandering around.

Sharon

A lot of people used to call the Situation Room looking for information or answers to questions. We were there to try to help. As Ronny said before, the SMS messages really helped to release some of the tensions people had. Once someone called because he thought there were enemy drones in the sky above his house. We couldn't give him an answer about what they were. He didn't realize that we were "just the neighbors from across the street" who had taken charge of the phones. He wanted more from us.

We did call Effie, who was in charge, and he said that he had heard that question before and told us to have the man call the Central Situation Room. And that's what we told the caller. He was insulted. We tried to tell him not to take it personally that we're doing the best we can!

The most important function of our work there was organization – writing down the names of people who wanted to participate in one of the trips out of the area, for general information, and so on.

We really didn't do much throughout this period except for sitting outside on the porch a lot. We saw everything. People should have paid us for being spotters. We watched all activity to the east and north. We saw all the Israeli activity here on the border. There were two artillery batteries to the east of the sewage treatment plant where we could see what the Israeli military was up to. We heard all the noise all the time, both ours and theirs. We'd see *yitziot* (the rocket leaving the launcher) from Lebanon. For a time, between 19:00-20:00 the Israeli military got into a routine, so there was usually a lot of our activity then, and we'd watch that.

With so many people gone the animals didn't have enough food. There were a lot of cats and a few dogs wandering around. They looked hungry and lonely. We got some pet food from Bethe to feed the abandoned cats and the trash cats in certain areas of the community. She had gotten hold of donations of cat and dog food that businesses sent North during the war. We also found Victor, or he found us. He's a big black and white male cat. One day he just showed up at Menno and Joyce's house. We fed him and he stayed. So I guess Victor (that's his name now) found us.

Tammy

Most days during the war, the main office building was empty except for me and Shai. But when people happened to enter the building for some reason, they were happy to see us there and that not everything was closed up or that there was someone to speak to.

Was I scared? When there were Katyushas falling I was scared, I won't say that I wasn't, because you can die from being struck.

My husband, Yehuda, was on the roads a lot and I didn't really like that. It was Russian roulette in every place. In the kibbutz it wasn't safe and on the roads it wasn't safe. We're always in telephone contact, so during this time we were a bit more in contact than usual, but we didn't get into any new habits where Yehuda would call me when he arrived at where he was going or anything like that.

From the second week of the war I waited for the end. And it kept getting longer and longer and farther and farther away.

Aliza

Talk about absurd stories. I go out one afternoon to put out the garbage and *boom*, out in the fields something falls and I ran back into the house. That's surrealism, emptying garbage and having a Katyusha fall not too far from you.

CHAPTER TWO
The Middle

Wednesday, July 26 & Thursday, July 27

Numerous Katyusha hits on Gesher Haziv and in the Western Galilee; fires started, no casualties, water supply interrupted. Numerous Katyusha hits in Tiberias, Safed, Kiryat Shmona, Nahariya, Acco, Haifa, Carmiel, Ma'alot, Mag'd El'Krum, Hazor Haglilit, Rosh Pina. In the Krayot there are both fires and casualties. As of 18:52 on Monday, 130 rockets have been fired into Israel: twenty-seven near Ma'alot, ten near Nahariya, six near Carmiel, and two near Acco. By 20:51 on Thursday, eighty rockets have been fired with forty casualties.

Judy

On Wednesday I had a "normal" day at work– busy as usual. However, there were so few people intending to come into work the next day (the third Thursday we didn't work at the office!) that they decided not to open the offices. If you had something to do from home, fine, if not then don't.

Since I wasn't going to be working on Thursday I decided to drive to Netanya for the weekend and on the way I had this strange experience. Just as I got to Nahariya a siren went off. I wasn't sure what I wanted to do – pull over or keep going, fast. First one car pulled over then another car pulled over. There were these people across the street saying: "Come in, come in" (to their house). The young guys from one of the other cars went running across the street. And I said to myself: "They're saying come in, there's a siren and I really should go into their security room." I thought that maybe I could get to the underground tunnel nearby instead of going to their house, but I couldn't find the entrance. I left Mayzie in the car, poor dog.

So I went over to this house. They were very nice and gave me not only shelter but something sickly sweet to drink as well. As soon as there was an all clear I was thankful to these people, but I felt stupid for stopping because nothing fell near there. The instructions are to stop your car and get out and lie down, but I never know where to lie down, and I always feel so stupid. I think it would be better just to gun the engine and get out of the area. "Who cares if it's a 60 km zone in Nahariya. There are no cars on the road, the police aren't giving tickets, I'm going 90 and I'm getting out of here. I'm getting the hell out of Dodge!" If the Katyusha has your name on it then it has your name on it. If it hasn't, you'll be okay.

M

During the first two weeks or so, whenever there were fires, I got called to help put them out. Once there was a Katyusha around 13:00 and it hit very close. So Avner and I got in his parents' car to find out where it hit on the kibbutz.

Then we thought it might have hit near the beach, across from Gesher Haziv, so we went there and found out that it had hit behind Moller's factory and a fire had started there. So we went into the Achziv beach area, where there was a guard, and asked him to get ready so that if the fire spread to help pull out hoses. As we're talking, the fire was spreading closer to the gate/fence on Moller's side, but it could have easily leaped over the road, where it would have caused greater damage. There's thatch on the roof of the restaurant at the beach and there was a southern wind that day which would have helped the fire spread.

It was Avner and me and the same fire crew that had attended the southwest fire we had on the kibbutz a few days earlier, and they weren't really functioning. I was holding a hose and then all of a sudden I see that there is nobody on the other side. And I started yelling: "Is there anybody on the other side and is it okay for me to walk away?" I called Moller and asked him what happened to the fire brigade and he said they got a call and were told there's another barrage coming, so they all went to the shelter. And I was left holding the hose on the other side like an idiot.

Bethe

Besides taking care of cats on Gesher Haziv, I also take care of the cats at the Western Galilee College where I lecture. We have about twenty cats there now that are taken care of by lecturers, regular staff, proctors, and students, among others. I feed them every day when I'm there and in the last year or two I try to go at least once, maybe twice a week when classes aren't in session to make sure they have water and some food. So now, even in this surreal situation, but especially since it's summer, I decided to drive to the college one morning when my daughters were still sleeping to see how they were. I figured that since Acco is also getting bombed now (the city had been out of range before) there wouldn't be anyone around, but I was pleasantly surprised. There was a skeleton staff working at the college – centers had been set up in the security rooms and shelters. People were also taking care of the cats – giving them food and water. The cafeteria made lunch for the people every day. So in addition to the dry food that some people had brought for them, all the leftovers were given to the cats as well. I don't think they've eaten so well in a long time!

After I left the Western Galilee College I drove south to the Krayot. Since our luggage had been damaged on the flight from New York to London to Tel Aviv, El Al Airlines took responsibility for fixing or replacing the damaged bags. I was told to go to a store in the Krayot. So I called and got directions drove there to take care of the bags.

Now this store is located close to Hippopatum, the pet store I deal with, so I decided that while I'm in that area I'll go to Hippopatum as well. My car was standing in the left-hand turn lane at a red light waiting to turn left, when I suddenly noticed that in the car ahead of me was Aviram (an ex-student, current friend, who also happens to live in Gesher Haziv). He's a police officer in *Magav* or the National Guard. He got out of his car and came to mine to see how I was. We spoke for a few seconds and then he returned to his car. Then all of a sudden a siren sounded. I really didn't know what to do. I was still at the red light. No one around me was getting out of their cars or running to a "safe" area, including Aviram in the car ahead of me. Now he's usually a very responsible person, but I didn't see him reacting to the siren. He didn't get out of his car, didn't do anything. I felt kind of strange, but I knew that I would look and feel ridiculous if I got out of my car and I was the only one doing so. So I just stayed where I was waiting for the light to change and hoping that nothing fell close.

Aviram and I were in the pet store together and then parted. I drove down the block to the luggage store and took care of my business there. But then another siren wailed. There was no security room or safe area there, but I decided that being inside the store was better than being out on the roads. I waited for a minute or two after the siren stopped and then continued on my way. Luckily I had no more excitement on my way home that day.

Later that day, Shanie and I volunteered to work in the Situation Room for a four-hour shift. Shanie did the first half from 14:00 to

16:00 and then I took over until 18:00. An SMS was sent announcing the possibility of having free accommodation at Kibbutz Sdot Yam for the weekend. There were a limited number of rooms available and it was on a first-come first-served basis. I was put in charge of the registration. That's an easy thing for me to do. I gave the callers what information I had and registered the families.

That evening, when I went up to the Laundry to feed the cats, I saw the golden retriever again. I gave her some food because I didn't know if anyone was feeding or taking care of her. The next morning I found her sleeping on my front porch. Sometime during the day I called Judy and asked her if she knew anything about the dog. The story was that the dog's name is Nicky. Her owner left the kibbutz with his son because of the rockets and left Nicky under Yael's care. Then Yael left the kibbutz and asked Judy to feed the dog and the cat (yes, there's also a cat). Judy said that she'd feed the animals, but couldn't be responsible for walking the dog on a leash. So she just let Nicky run loose. Nicky decided to accompany Skippy (and me) on our morning walk. She doesn't seem to be upset about the noises around us.

The following day I noticed that Nicky has taken up residence on our front porch. So I feed her there as well. Then I found the cat that lives with Nicky on our front porch too! He's come to be with his dog. We don't know the cat's name, and neither does Judy, so we just call him "Nicky's cat."

Meshi and I also got into a routine of driving around the kibbutz around 18:30 every evening, or later, to feed the trash cats and those whose owners had abandoned them. First we started in the new neighborhood where we gave food to a mother cat and her four kittens. Meshi loved to play with the kittens. Then we went to feed and take care of Tiger, a wounded cat. We had to give him penicillin and clean the wound every day. He belongs to a family in the neighborhood, but they'd left because of the war and poor Tiger was alone, longing for company and care. Then we'd drive around to some of the different communal trashcans and leave food for the cats that lived in that area. After a few days they were waiting for us to come each evening.

This is an e-mail I sent to family and friends at 12:21 today:

Shalom family and friends,

After a lovely visit to you all we've returned to a different reality.

We spoke with Lavie briefly 2 nights ago. He was very uncommunicative - so basically I have little information. He's still in the same area, but we don't know what he's been up to.

A few more Katyushas hit us today. The nights seem quiet.

I'm finally able to get some work done during the days - the article for publication needs a bit more editing and then I have to update the textbook/workbook for the next academic year at the college. I've begun working with Yehudit on Skype doing that to keep the phone lines clear.

Asher's at Tadiad. Meshi is with me watching TV mostly. Shanie is around and has been doing "*toranut*" (a voluntary shift) in the "war room" for a few hours almost every day.

There are many abandoned dogs running around and the cats don't have their regular food sources since so many people have gone south. Through my connections I've managed to get some bags of cat and dog food as donations and that's helping a bit.

We'll keep you posted.
bethe

Meshi

I went to a performance this afternoon in the shelter where the activities for the kids are held. It was Diane and Ada who had performed at the Jacob's Ladder Folk Festival, but we hadn't seen them there. I went before the end, but it was pretty much the end, because my mother came home a few minutes later. There were tons of little kids there and it was annoying; the performance wasn't much fun, which was a shame because the performers are good.

I took Skippy for a walk and I was around the large, central lawn. I don't remember hearing the noise, but I do remember hearing the boom. It was just really loud, I mean really loud! I went down to the Situation room in the Dining Room shelter, which was close by. I was with Skippy so I felt a little uncomfortable. I felt weird to go down there just like that. I had been there a few times before when I went to take snacks to Shanie, but now I kept Skippy on a short leash. I stayed there for just a few minutes. Then I kind of ran home. I guess I was a bit scared, but it's not like I thought a Katyusha is going to fall again any second, I just don't want to be outside during the boomings, it was too noisy.

I used to go with my mother in the evenings to feed the cats. I wanted to do it because it got me out of the house and because I like cats. Most of the cats didn't come to me, but some of them did. I wasn't scared going around to feed them.

Paul

I'm one of the few people whose "normal" life wasn't really interrupted by the war. But even my schedule was a little different than normal, though it was still basically going to work.

Kathy

Normally I would be out and about during the day working, doing errands, or working in my garden. But throughout this period my life had changed and I was always in the house. I wasn't scared or living in fear or so distraught that I had to ask to get out or to go down south or anything like that. And I don't have little kids so it doesn't matter – it's not like they were driving me crazy and we couldn't go outside. On the one hand it doesn't bother me not to go outside for days at a time. On the other hand, this is surreal.

Terry & Teresa

Once the sirens started it changed things a lot. Before the sirens you probably wouldn't know when an attack was imminent, so you just went about your business. When a Katyusha did fall you'd react and then get on with your business. When we started to have the warning sirens, they would go off every ten minutes or so on some days. Then, we were in and out of the security room all the time. I don't know which situation was better. Also, even when the sirens *did* go off, they didn't always pinpoint the area where the Katyusha would land. Often we felt that we were just reacting because that is how we had been programmed to react.

Aliza

This is your surrealistic, absurd situation on the one hand, but on the other hand you have this feeling of bonding with people outside the kibbutz and inside the kibbutz that you don't usually have or it's not always there. But in times of stress it's there. There are a few hysterical people around. But I couldn't blame anybody who picked up and went. I'm not ready to put the blame on people, especially those with younger children who had to get out! People react differently. I was glad that they organized it so that families were able to get away sometimes, like to Sdot Yam. That was wonderful. But we didn't go away on the outings.

We went to visit the neighbors across the way during the weeks of the war. Our closest friends don't live on the kibbutz anymore, but some of the people we do hang out with weren't here and some we just didn't speak to a lot. We tried to get to see people here and there. But we didn't go to any of the performances that came. I don't know why I didn't go.

Asher

I've stopped going to the "safe" area at Tadiad when a siren sounds, even for the social aspect. Now I just stay in my office and continue working to the best of my capabilities.

Shanie

At a certain point, I don't know when exactly, because each day was the same as the next, we had alarms to alert us when we had to enter the shelters or security because an attack was imminent. And that is what we did basically throughout the rest of the war.

My personal habit was to wake up at noon or 13:00, if my mother didn't wake me up beforehand. Then I basically did nothing for the rest of day besides the normal hygiene thing (brush your teeth, wash your face, etc.). I read the paper, watched TV and news on the Internet. I also volunteered a lot in the Situation Room; that kept me busy and I felt like I helping others.

Miri

I had this "event" occur once when I was at my father's. A relative of ours who lives in the States called. I guess the way that events were presented there were as if the situation was really bad and she was worried. Just as the call began there was a siren. And my father turns the phone in the direction of the sound and says: "Can you hear the siren?" And I say to him: "Dad, there's a siren, shouldn't we go into the mamad?" And I hear rockets hitting not too far away and the house is shaking. And then he says into the phone: "Do you hear. The rockets are hitting just now!" He's not even in the mamad. And then I shouted at him so that he finally listened. I think that this was the first time that Noa actually got scared. I really shouted at him, and then unfortunately Noa got scared more from my shouting than from the Katyushas landing nearby. "Dad, come into the mamad already, what is it with you?" He's communicating on-line with the States saying, "Do you hear? Do you hear?" But then he's the type of person who believes that if your time has come then nothing can change that.

Tammy

At the beginning we thought it would take a few days and be finished. We never thought that the war would last so long! At this point my schedule changed a bit. I worked in the office in the mornings and then at home in the afternoons and evenings. This was in contrast to my normal day when I finish working in the office and that's it! During the war my day's work didn't end and it even continued through the weekends. At the beginning I would come home and then go back to the office. But afterwards I decided that since the afternoon hours were difficult hours, from the standpoint of Katyusha rockets being launched, I attempted to finish what I was working on in the office and then tried not to return but to continue working from my home. Then I would bring the work roster for the next day to the Situation Room to hang up there.

I always drive from my home to the main kibbutz office building. And I continued to do so during the war. I got caught a couple of times when I was on the internal road and a siren began to screech. So I drove home very quickly and went inside. But it never happened that a Katyusha fell in our area while I was on the road.

Micha

At the end of July, when the sirens started everywhere (*shahar adom,* warning system), it made things more frightening. Before, if you didn't hear the Katyushas, you didn't know about them. Now every time there was a siren, even if they were Katyushas that were just going to fall in Acco, the sirens made us jump and we felt that we had to go to the security room and it was a bit more of an interruption to day-to-day life. And also at work, every time there was a siren we knew we had a short time to get to the security room because then the Katyusha falls.

I worked my usual hours, which are from 6:00 to 16:00 or 17:00. So I continued through the whole time; I was working, but I wasn't. It was surreal. You're trying to concentrate and all of a sudden you're listening for the Katyushas falling and then you're ready to jump under the table if it's very close, or run to the security room.

I remember driving to work at 6:00 in the morning and the road was empty. Nobody was paying attention to speed limits; the limit was 60 km and people were driving 100-120 km. You felt safer and it was known that the police weren't dealing with speeding, especially not on empty roads.

Benny

I work at the Electric Company, and I was surprised that few people called. I was totally disconnected from work for weeks, so I called. But since I didn't want to speak with my immediate manager, I called Human Resources instead and asked them: "Do you know that

I'm here at home in Gesher Haziv under siege?" I made this call in response to an order that the Electric Company employees received to return to work. Even after all the rockets that fell in Haifa, the CEO decided to return all employees to active work. So I received a phone call in the middle of the war to return to work. And I said to them: "What are you talking about? I can't leave; I can't abandon my family. We're here under bombardment. You obviously have no idea what's going on around here (in the North)."

Hannah

Sometimes towards the middle of the war, Iris started coming to the shelter to give an exercise class for the seniors. She brought other people with her who weren't normally in the shelters, who usually take this exercise class with her. She came three times a week and we exercised for thirty minutes.

Ishai

There were a few nights when the regular guard was unable to arrive so I guarded all night. It was okay. The quietest place on the kibbutz was the guardhouse – no one came in and no one left. And if something happened I would report to the Situation Room, if I heard something fly overhead or something like that. If I didn't hear an explosion, then I knew it went far. If I did hear an explosion, then I knew it landed somewhere nearby.

Noa

I had many soul-searching conversations with my friend who I always talk to. We spoke many nights after I returned from my shift in the Hamal. We'd often speak for a few hours in the early hours of the morning. Our conversations highlighted the parts of how I was coping with being totally alone in the "field" and that my child is not around. And nonetheless I was at home alone and I heard a loud boom and you don't know where it fell. And the fear of the first few minutes when you pick up the phone and call your parents, and you can't wait for them to answer already so that you know they're all right. And things like that.

Carolyn

I worked fewer night shifts during this period than I usually work; I really hated night shifts then. But that meant that I worked day and evening shifts. The road was the worst part perhaps. It's all scary, so you're nervous, but I wasn't petrified or anything and everything worked out fine and hopefully my luck won't run out. There are certain levels of scary – one is a little adrenaline, another is really scared like one you don't want to feel often in your lifetime.

I found the war very depressing much more than frightening. The frightening comes and goes, you get scared and then you're not scared. So you drive to work and get there and it's fine.

Danit

And at one point, finishing the purple shirt became an obsession with me. I couldn't finish this garment because I didn't have the thread.

In the end I took the children on a day out in Tel Aviv. There we went into a store in order to buy this thread. And we discovered by chance that the family who were running the store were related to the child who sat next to Stav in class throughout the entire year. For these people, our being in their store had a very positive effect, more than for us, because they had been hearing what was going on from the news and now they were able to hear it from us first-hand. They became less worried and more optimistic; our words gave them strength.

What's funny is that I did find the purple thread in that store in Tel Aviv, but up till now I haven't finished the shirt! The minute I had the thread, it was as if everything was normal. I usually don't have obsessions like this – this was something unique to the war.

Friday, July 28 & Saturday, July 29

Numerous Katyusha hits on Gesher Haziv and in the Western Galilee; Katyusha hits in Haifa, Acco, Safed, Rosh Pina, Ma'alot, Carmiel, Kiryat Shmona, Hazor Haglilit, Tiberias, Upper Galilee, Emek Yizrael, the Krayot; two rockets hit Nahariya Hospital, some with casualties. By 20:22 on Saturday, ninety rockets have been fired into Israel.

Carolyn

So far a few Katyushas had fallen in and around the hospital grounds and in Josephtal, which is not too far away. Friday a Katyusha went right through the fourth floor of the new building of Nahariya Hospital. It went in and exploded inside. If you could get around to the north side of the building you could see the damage. It did a lot of damage to the fourth floor, to the Ophthalmology Department. But nobody was there. But I think, by the way, even if you were in the mamad and if the doors weren't totally shut, and we didn't always close them totally, you would have been wounded.

They moved my ward down to the basement shelter sometime about three weeks into the war. I found being in the basement shelter very uncomfortable. Other people didn't find it quite as uncomfortable, perhaps, but I found I did. It was very crowded and disgusting. When I first went down there, to me it just looked like something out of a Civil War movie. I said: "God this is gross, who ever thought I would be nursing like in a Civil War movie?" There were only a few partitions up in the big room. There are some walls, and then they used the movable screens to try to separate between women and men here and there. But basically it was one big room. They would put women on one side and men on the other. There are three built-in nurses' stations at least in the big, big room. But there were eleven different departments down there by the end of the war and only three built-in nursing stations. And there was only one major, big bathroom that David's first room was on the route to, and then a few other bathrooms at the beginning of it. We finally came down and got some better conditions.

I was disappointed in the nurses in Nahariya Hospital for their attitude of not demanding better conditions – for patients and staff. The staff had horrendous conditions. When we came down there, I don't know if it was my head nurse or what – but the other wards had been down there for over two weeks and didn't have any drinking water – all sorts of little things, little things that the administration could have done. I remember that when I worked at Rambam, they couldn't do enough for you during the war, that was the nice thing at least about nursing in a war that at least everyone wanted to help and everyone volunteered and all the good equipment came out – there were telephones all of a sudden, and that was not the situation in Nahariya Hospital.

Bethe

A few light bulbs had blown out in the house. When I looked in the closet for replacements I noticed that we were out of a number of different types of light bulbs. At first I was at a loss about where I would be able to buy replacements – as far as I knew most of the stores in Nahariya were closed, although I hadn't gone into town to check out the situation. As I was thinking over this problem, it suddenly occurred to me that since it was morning, I could make a few phone calls first to see which, if any, hardware stores were open.

First I called Shilling Hardware, the store that I usually buy from. And lo-and-behold not only did they answer, but they were open. I identified myself as I normally do: "Hello, this is Bethe from Gesher

Haziv." My American accent and where I live, as well as the fact that I am a frequent customer of certain businesses and banks, always helps people identify me. They said that they would be open until 11:00; it was 10:00 at the time. I told them that I was on my way. I parked behind the store, on a side street as was my custom so I don't have to pay for parking on the main street, never even thinking about the fact that most of Nahariya was a ghost town and that I could probably have parked wherever I wanted. I bought what I needed, thanked the owners for being open and drove home.

But it was weird. A city that is normally bustling with people and action at mid-morning was almost totally deserted. I found out later that Piccolo, the music store I buy my CDs from, was open the entire war as well. If I had known that I would have gone in to give Avi my business and support.

Later that afternoon Asher and I were sitting in the security room with Shanie and Meshi after a siren sounded. We heard some rockets land and they sounded close. A few minutes later the phone rang. It was David. A rocket had hit the fourth floor of the Nahariya Hospital, in what was once the Ophthalmology Ward. But since all the patients had been moved to the basement shelter, there was no loss of life and only property damage. But to hit a hospital! David didn't want us to come to the hospital to visit him that afternoon if it was dangerous on the roads.

Asher and I invited some friends over for the Sabbath meal. Since we'd been in the States when the war broke out, we hadn't really seen them since our return. It was not only an occasion to get together but a way to break the monotony of the week. The Hills (Terry and Teresa) and the Smiths (Paul, Kathy, Timna, and Noam) came. Everyone made something, so we had a wide variety of foods. We sat around our large dining room table eating and drinking. At some point someone's mobile phone received an SMS message from the Situation Room telling us to go into the shelters. Then slowly everyone else's mobile received the same message. We hadn't heard any loud noises outside, and so chose to ignore the warning.

For some reason on Saturday I decided to go into *The Guardian* (the British newspaper) on-line. I found this article written by a *Guardian* correspondent about how he had sat with a Hizbullah soldier in a private house in southern Lebanon with stockpiles of weaponry. The writer spoke about how the Hizbullah soldier bragged that he and his comrades have patience and are just waiting for the Israeli soldiers to come looking for them. But then he said that Israel is just a small part of the problem. As soon as the Hizbullah finish with the Israelis, they'll turn to the Sunni Muslims and fight them. Wonderful! That really gave me a feeling of security. I'm certain that most people who read that article in Britain and around the world didn't take the wider ramifications of what this Hizbullah soldier said into consideration!

Lavie called this evening. When he called Friday night I didn't get to speak with him, so tonight he spoke only with me. He also wanted to tell me that "the party begins tonight." I knew that he meant his unit was moving into Lebanon to fight. I'm glad he called to let me know what was happening. But after reading that article in *The Guardian* earlier that day I told him to be careful, that they were just waiting for the Israelis.

Before the war some of the twenty-something members, most of whom were born and raised on the kibbutz, decided to create a club for people of the community to gather in, called the Ekonomia. They were allocated the basement of the building that once housed the kibbutz Dining Room. Now, during the war, it became a safe place to meet in the evenings. Adar Sharif set up a screen with a DVD system and speakers so we could watch movies, listen to music, or just gather together.

Later that night, I took the DVD copy of Monty Python's *Life of Brian* I had bought in the States, to be shown in the *Ekonomia,* the community's social club. Terry and Teresa were there as well as Sharon and Ronny and a few others. At one point Terry went outside to smoke a cigarette. When he came back he said that the sky over the border into Lebanon was awash with light. So Teresa and I went out to take a look. The sky was so bright that it looked as though there were projectors stationed all along the border. After what Lavie had told me earlier in the day, I knew that the light show was caused by Israeli artillery and airpower.

Asher

At some point, the hospital decided to move my father and the other patients from his ward into another area. They were moved into a larger, more general space where each ward was separated by temporary partitions. Soldiers who had been wounded at the front were put in the room that David was originally in. In essence, the entire hospital was in one huge room.

Danit

I drove alone a lot on the roads during the war and I got caught a number of times when a siren sounded. It's not nice to say, but I turned up the volume on the radio so I wouldn't hear the siren and I continued to drive. I didn't drive any faster, I just kept going. I didn't feel any safer or any more vulnerable by turning up the volume. I simply disconnected. It is difficult to explain, but I disconnected emotionally from what was happening around me. People were stopping by the side of the road and lying down in ditches, and I thought that if a Katyusha falls in the ditch nothing can help them. What I thought about at that moment were the whereabouts of Gilad and Stav. If they were in the places they were supposed to be in or not? And that was that more or less. I decided that I wasn't going to worry about insignificant things, as much as I could. It is very unnerving not to know whether your child is where he or she is supposed to be, especially when Gilad had already given me a few examples of not being in a safe place. So I increased the volume of the music and strived to get into the music. On the one hand I was worried about my children, on the other hand I had an emotional disconnection through the music.

One day, in order to refresh ourselves, we went to visit friends in Emek Yizrael and it was really quiet there. We arrived and we started to eat dinner. And suddenly there was a siren. Stav, without thinking twice, took their two children and went into their security room. And then we heard the booming of the rockets landing. In our personal experience the Katyushas followed us. Wherever we went there was boomings.

Stav

The Katyushas followed us from Gesher Haziv to Emek Yizrael – except in Tel Aviv and Jerusalem. In Tel Aviv people told me that they weren't opening their stores in the afternoons because Nasrallah could bomb them then.

Eugene

I didn't always go into the security room when bombs fell or sirens wailed. Sometimes I would stay in the living room and watch TV. When I thought it was necessary I would go into the security room, even if it was after Carolyn had been on a night shift and was sleeping there. Bombs were falling between us and Nahariya, and to me that's close.

Orit

The area that we live in – its true that we heard a lot of Katyushas – they passed right over us and we heard the heavy Israeli artillery, but the bottom line is that this area is relatively safe, and I say it again relatively. We felt much better here than if we were living in Nahariya. Nahariya was heavily targeted this time.

Sometimes we would go outside at 19:00 in the evening and it was so quiet. The Hizbullah didn't usually launch rockets then, so we went outside to get a breath of fresh air. There were almost no people around. So even if you went outside in pajamas no one would see you. I felt as if I really had a private house!

I remember that throughout all of my childhood there were periodic Katyusha barrages. Once during my birthday I had a party in a shelter. All the children brought me presents. Then there was a siren and everyone had to go home. At least I got the presents that they had brought! I remember that until today. I also remember barbecuing outside the shelters. But I don't remember it being a traumatic experience as a child. I also wasn't traumatized by this recent war, although it did continue *way* too long!

Meshi

During the days I watched TV, a lot of TV. But, I remember when my friend Noa came back, I tried to call her just to see if she had come that day – it was probably the late middle to the end of the war. She said she was a bit tired, but she did want to see me. So I walked to her house, but I wasn't afraid walking there. I was just like: "Yeah! I can see someone again!" because all my friends were away.

Terry & Teresa

On Saturday, this weekend, which turned out to be the third weekend of the war, we went to Migdal Ha'emek during the day to visit Gabi again. It seems that this had become our Saturday routine. Just like last week, as were driving through Kfar Yasif there were rockets landing in the Nahariya area. We were just a few minutes away from Nahariya again. This is becoming weird – every weekend when we return to the Western Galilee there's a rocket attack.

We saw *The Life of Brian* one evening. That was strange. When I (Terry) went outside in the middle to have a cigarette I saw the sky over the entire border with Lebanon lit up almost as if it were daytime. There were lots of boomings as well. Something was up.

Paul

As usual I went out to the fields today. All was well except for the damage caused by the Katyushas that landed all around.

Kathy

I'm not afraid of the rockets and this isn't the first time I've been under fire. But I usually felt the need to go into the security room in my house because I have a responsibility to be an example for my kids and the rest of the family. Timna, our daughter, and I were always in there together. We also slept there. Teresa used to run over from her house nearby. For some reason she felt safer in my security room than in hers. When I thought it was necessary I went into the security room, but if I was involved in something, like watching a TV program, I'd stay on the couch, except there were times when it did sound close, so I'd go in.

Sharon

I stayed here alone one Saturday and that was pretty scary. I had a cell phone, but it wasn't mine since I don't have a cell phone of my own, and I didn't know how to use it very well. And there was lots of activity and booming that day. I felt like I needed to know what's going on all the time. Even if I was in the security room and I heard my phone beep in another room, I'd go check the message even though I knew that it would probably say to get into the security room. And that's not really in my personality; I needed to know and once I knew, I felt okay. It also didn't automatically erase the SMS messages so that the memory got clogged up. Then I wasn't receiving the SMS messages and I felt like I was in a total blackout.

Ilan

We "jumped" to Tel Aviv a few times to refresh ourselves. But even there the feeling we had wasn't one of relaxation. We were glued to the TV screen, for example. We did get out and do things – like walk along the boardwalk or go to the playground. We felt more relaxed because we were in Tel Aviv. However, we did feel that we were on a different planet when we were there. When I went to sleep at night, I had this undercurrent of fear that Nasrallah was holding something back that might reach Tel Aviv.

We wanted to return home from Tel Aviv because we felt safest at home. The unknown was more difficult to handle than the known, which is why we watched TV all the time.

When we were coming home after being away for a weekend, by the time we reached the area of Zichron Ya'akov (south of Haifa), we already started to feel some sort of apprehension. When we got to the Krayot we didn't hear sirens, but we saw people standing by the side of the road and under bridges. So we rolled down the window and asked someone if there had been a siren. They replied that yes, there had been, but it was already okay to continue driving. Like, how did they know? Ten to fifteen minutes had passed since the siren, so it was assumed to be safe.

Miri

Each time we went to visit Ilan's parents in Acco, we had a dilemma because Katyushas were falling there as well – when to drive there? Go now, okay, Nasrallah doesn't shoot Katyushas in the evening. And at the beginning they didn't shoot in the evening. But afterwards they did shoot during those hours. Then each time you ask yourself when it is safe to go. Go now? No wait. Wait for what? Yes. No.

Once we were visiting Ilan's parents and I was speaking to a cousin of Ilan's on the phone, when suddenly there was a siren. She says: "What's that I hear?" And I said "Na'ama, that's a siren." So then she asked: "Are you serious? What are you going to do?" And I replied: "Nothing." So then she said again: "Are you serious?" What am I going to do, run down five flights of stairs with Noa to get to the shelter? She couldn't believe my reaction. She was watching television as if the events were happening somewhere else. That was the first time she had actually heard a siren, because in Tel Aviv you don't hear them. People who don't have children in the army or live in areas not affected by the war were disconnected from our experience – as if they were living in another country.

Sunday, July 30 & Monday, July 31

Nothing eventful on Gesher Haziv; Katyusha hits in Acco, Ma'alot, Kiryat Shmona, Metula, Hazor Haglilit, the Krayot, Nahariya, some with casualties. By 20:05 on Sunday, 148 rockets shot into Israel. In Kiryat Shmona alone ninety-one rockets hit the city causing seventeen casualties and damage to ninety-eight apartments. On Monday the IDF decreased aerial attack for forty-eight hours after the Kfar Kana tragedy, except for targets that attack Israel. A few rockets launched at Kiryat Shmona.

Hannah

The interpersonal relations among the different people in the shelter were fairly good. At the beginning there was some tension, because in reality everyone was a bit stressed. Noga had a problem since she also had to worry about her daughter, Lilach, for food and everything. And Lilach was always doing things that Noga didn't want her to do like going outside. They also don't hold the same opinions.

But their relationship didn't really have any effect on me. Noga had a cell phone, so each time there was an alert we got a message. Once Noga shouted at me, and I didn't know where it came from, except maybe her stress because of the situation. She was also concerned about her other daughter, Amalia, who also works in the

Laundry and went to work. So Noga would call Amalia on the phone, and when there was no answer she would start to worry.

I was in one room with people who aren't part of my family and I live alone. We didn't have many problems though. We didn't dress or undress in the shelter. We stayed in the same clothes. In the mornings when I went home I showered and changed into the fresh clothes I wanted to wear for that day. We slept in our clothes.

The war continued and continued. Everyone in the shelter wanted to return home. Of course! But it (the shelter) wasn't something extremely terrible. We had air conditioning, beverages, television, and that also has an influence – the conditions there were fine. Also, the fact that the Situation Room was connected in this central shelter kept us from being totally disconnected.

Paul

The contractor has been able to bring more and more workers in to help do what had to be done. There were days when we had about thirty workers out in the fields working very inefficiently. It was also very costly since they only worked maybe four or five hours a day. They really didn't get a whole lot done. But that was the only solution I had at the time. We started doing other work that needed to be done in the bananas – like cutting the dead leaves off the trees, tying up the bunches, taking care of the weeds, and all that sort of stuff. The banana pick (*katif*) was a disaster. There were guys there who had never done it before and the banana bunches were very large. I had to be there constantly because they didn't know what to pick or how to pick or how to carry the bunch or how to put it in the boxes. But we got it done. I was still getting up and going to work, but my day was that instead of doing what I was supposed to do – I was basically babysitting. I was out there every day with them from early morning until way after they'd left, regardless of the shelling.

Bethe

At dinner Friday night we decided that we would get together for dinner at someone else's house the following week. If we couldn't go to work, then at least we could stuff ourselves with good food as well as being in the company of good friends. Today was Sunday and Terry and Teresa were the hosts. Shanie decided not to come for some reason, so it was just Asher, Meshi and I. As always there was too much food. Terry barbecued hamburgers and kebabs and there was an array of salads on the table to choose from – a veritable feast!

I have an organic garden where I grow a variety of vegetables. The entire time we were in the States the automatic irrigation system watered the plot. No one picked them while I was gone, so there were lots of vegetables ready to be eaten or used. I distributed as many as I could to my friends. I had given a few eggplants to Kathy and Teresa on Friday night when they were at our house. So Kathy got creative and made slices of eggplant Parmesan – that was delicious!

There are a bunch of "trash cats" at the Country Lodging rooms near Teresa's house. Since the B&B rooms were empty because of the war, and so many people had left the kibbutz, the trashcans that the cats ate from were relatively empty. So I took some cat food with me and went over to that area before dinner to see which cats were around. I found the usual eight to ten and gave them food. I even saw a sweet gray male with different colored eyes that I feared was injured. He was fine and welcomed the food. I gave all the extra meat to the cats, so they were content.

On Monday evening we had dinner at the Smiths'. Paul barbecued and Kathy made some really delicious baked vegetables. With all the salads and other varieties of food on the table, once again we rolled home. While this routine of eating with friends every night is pleasant, it's getting to be a bit much. Because we can't really move around much in the open since we never know when a rocket attack will occur, most of us aren't doing any physical activity. Eating a huge meal every evening without exercising has one result – putting on weight.

A "strange" habit that I have is to park on the street when I go to the hospital to visit David. There is a large parking lot connected to the hospital, but I don't like to use it. It's very crowded and I don't like the way other people park there; it also costs money. So I prefer to walk a short distance and park on the street.

That has always been my habit and I didn't change it now. What was so absurd about my decision is that I could have been taking undue risks by walking the extra distance. The parking lot was relatively empty during the war so that wasn't an "excuse." What's even more absurd about my behavior is that there is an area closer to the hospital on the road where many people park. It is designated with red and white colors on the curb, which indicates a no-parking zone, but normally people park there, and I rarely see the police giving out tickets. I just couldn't bring myself to park there during the war, even though I knew it was "safe" to do so.

Ilan

The SMS messages from the Situation Room were really good for me. When I was at work in Carmiel I would get the same SMS message that Miri received here on Gesher Haziv to her cell phone.

At the beginning we were the target. The first Katyusha fell right here on the road. But then when Regba and Shavei Zion were hit I felt safer. "We're out of range," I said. We still hadn't reached the realization that this feeling wasn't true. We were still in danger.

What was different than normal was that Miri and I were home a lot more with Noa than usual. The nursery didn't open and she only had some time together with her friends when we took her to the organized activities in the shelter.

Miri

I felt good here, even though Katyushas fell very close to us. I felt that Gesher Haziv is my home. I feel safe, even though it is more north than Acco, or closer to the border. It also helped me that there were no sirens here at the beginning. In Acco there were sirens and the sirens really made me feel bad. Just to hear them, it wasn't good for me.

I tried to remain as cool and calm as possible for our daughter, Noa. I said: "Okay I'm normally a calm person, I won't let this situation upset me." And Noa responded really well – I never saw any signs of distress, panic, fear, or that something was unusual. We just ignored what was going on around us. We acted as if everything was normal. And we stayed.

However, that doesn't mean that we weren't in danger, just in denial. I was driving on the road one day and I saw a Katyusha fall directly in front of me – I think it was at Moshav Liman – I really saw it fall. Then, just as I took the curve into the kibbutz another Katyusha fell in a grove of cypress trees. I also saw that one! But then I got home, stopped the car and opened the car as if nothing out of the ordinary had just happened. I didn't feel anything different than normal, which is strange when you think about it. I just refused to believe that anything bad was going to happen to me.

Another day when we went to visit Ilan's parents there was a siren. Ilan's parents also caused us some problems, since his father wasn't willing to go downstairs to the shelter. So Ilan's mother decided to move into an internal room. We told her that next to the bedroom there is a shower stall where there is a closet and then a niche. There's a little bit of space between the closet and the niche. So she went to stand there. Then she called for Noa to come and stand there with her. So every time afterwards when there was a siren she went to stand there. Once when we were home, there were sirens and Katyushas falling. So we called Noa to come to the mamad. And what did she do? She stood next to a closet in the mamad. She called me to come stand next to her just like she stood with Ilan's mother that time we were at their house!

Kathy

I didn't have work during this time, but actually I had a lot of projects to do during the days. Besides getting Noam ready for the army, I had to get some photographs of the family ready and send them to my family in the States for a family gathering. So I was going through all these boxes of old photographs. It was really a great opportunity to do it, since I had nothing else to do. So I just sat there with all these boxes of old photographs going through them. My family was very happy about how fast I got onto the project and got it done.

Judy

That Sunday, even though Naphtali had been sick and was in Netanya with his family, he got a call from work and was told he was needed for the evening shift. He made arrangements to come North, but by then there was very little transportation to Nahariya. So I said okay I'd meet him at Lev Hamifratz in Haifa (where there is a bus terminal). At the end of the workday, Mayzie and I tried to find the right timing so none of us would have to wait around because that would be scary – never knowing when a siren would sound. Just as I got to the terminal, I called Naphtali to see where he was. He had just arrived at the Hof Hacarmel terminal (south of Haifa).

I told him to wait there and I would come and get him, even though that meant driving through Haifa. There was a two-day "cease-fire" after the Kfar Kana tragedy, so I felt less uncomfortable about driving through Haifa. Otherwise I was really scared. (In a normal time, the only consideration about driving through Haifa would be traffic or traffic jams!)

We drove north and luckily all was quiet. At the Acco intersection I saw a soldier with a large backpack waiting for a lift. So I pulled over quickly – luckily there wasn't much traffic on the road – to pick him up. I didn't want to leave a soldier with a big bag on the road. He had to get to Nahariya. So he piled into the back seat and off we went. He was thrilled to have a ride. I dropped him off at Faisel's market where he said he could walk home. I felt good that I was able to help someone out.

I usually eat a heavy meal for lunch at work while Leah and Naphtali usually eat a heavier evening meal before he goes to work the evening or night shift. With Naphtali home and working evenings I felt it would be nice if we could eat together. So I started cooking to have a full meal available at dinner. We didn't always end up eating together, but there was freshly cooked food every day. Naftali had supper at my house before he went off to work. He slept during the day in his security room between sirens and Katyushas.

Ishai

It happened once when I was driving to Shlomit, that a Katyusha fell very, very close to me – a few meters from the car – and for a few weeks I almost couldn't hear anything. My hearing still isn't 100% now a few months later.

The day after the Katyusha landed a few meters from me, I tried to convince Evelyn not to drive with me when I went to pick up the care worker in Shlomit. She didn't know about the Katyusha that fell next to me the day before. She insisted on coming and there were also some rockets that landed in the area this time as well. So I said: "Now I can tell you. Yesterday a Katyusha fell a few meters from me – like from here to that fence in the field. There was a very loud explosion and air shock waves, but no shrapnel."

Evelyn

About seventeen to eighteen seniors stayed most of the time; the rest came and went. They all knew that it was important to contact me or leave me a message when people came or left. There was also a list like that being kept for everyone in the Situation Room. I had a daily connection with them, sometimes twice a day, especially when there were a lot of Katyushas falling that specific day. That was part of my routine – to call everyone at least once a day to make certain they were okay.

We were still having our daily meeting of the Emergency Committee. But now, when the Hizbullah started to shoot between 17:00 and 19:00, it was really unpleasant to have to walk around outside. It's a very weird feeling – you don't know if a rocket's going to fall or not when you're outside. But I would go every day anyway.

We were outside and on the roads a lot – and it was better for me that way than to be sitting at home. It was unpleasant driving on the roads, but we did it. There were a few times when we had just driven to Shlomit when rockets fell. We saw the mushroom clouds very close to us – very unpleasant! But we did it. I wasn't afraid when we were out driving on the roads; it was more of an unpleasant feeling. Whatever will happen, will happen and that's it. We're doing things and that's it. I didn't think: "Okay a Katyusha might hit me!" I never thought about it. Usually when I drive with someone in the car I constantly say, "Don't drive fast," but now I said: "Drive faster, drive faster!" It really was like that.

Our children called us crazy and stupid during the war because Ishai and I went out and did so many things. We continued with our lives regardless of the rockets being fired at us. They would say: "You don't love us, you want to leave us."

Ronny

Sometime in the middle I decided that I wanted to help more. I realized that this conflict wasn't ending so quickly. So if the war has already become our routine, I thought that I should do something more effective and helpful. I thought about helping to distribute food to the shelters in Nahariya. I had to make a number of phone calls in order to find the person in charge. He didn't want my help – they didn't want women for that kind of job; then he said he had enough volunteers. He took my phone number anyway and said he'd call if he needed me. So I did what I could on the kibbutz to help the communal effort. I would have done more if I had been able to get in touch with the right people, or people who knew how to use my talents.

Lyn

A couple of times in that three-hour period in the morning, between 9:00 and 12:00, when the kids were at their activities, I asked if any volunteer work was needed around the place and I went to clean shelters and got different things done.

We usually talk about things together as a family. If we did go out on walks they knew the situation, so that if something did happen they knew how to get down and what to look for and how to try to be as safe as they possibly could. But we did try to go for walks when it was deemed safe. I mean, can you imagine not going out of your house for weeks on end?

Benny

There were places organized for people who wanted to leave Gesher Haziv during the weekends. I spoke with Bethe, when she was doing a shift in the Situation Room, about going to Kibbutz Sdot Yam. That was before Eilat. Then there was a rocket that fell very close to Sdot Yam itself, near the power station. And I said: "I'm not going to Sdot Yam because of the power station!" A prime objective would be to hit a power station.

Helen

We still had a lot of delegations coming to Nahariya Hospital. I routinely welcomed them but fine, what do you do with them? Now I showed them the fourth floor where the Hizbullah rocket hit the Ophthalmology Department and all the damage that was done. It wasn't difficult for them to imagine what the scene would have been like if the patients hadn't all been evacuated to the basement shelter. The main thing to show them was how the hospital actually functions underground.

Asher

One day I realized that there was a safer place to be than the designated area or my office. There is an internal room without windows directly across from my office. I started going in there when the alarms sounded. Other people from the immediate area of my office started using this small room as well. So that's what I did when the sirens sounded – stop work and go across the hall to this inner room and wait for the all clear.

At Tadiad, we weren't really working "as usual." There were too many interruptions throughout the day to really get deeply into a problem that needed solving. Most days there were three or four or more sirens. While my colleagues and I always chatted, now people exchanged stories where a rocket had fallen or who they knew who had been injured or caught in a predicament because of the war. There was a definite decrease in output. It was difficult to concentrate. I found myself (and so were others) checking the news sites on the Internet more than usual to see what was happening. We listened to the news more on the radio.

At some point the managers of the Miluot conglomerate began to worry about having too many people together in one place. So they decided to close the Dining Room. Now, food was brought to Tadiad (and the other factories on the site) already prepared in Styrofoam containers. While this solved our problem of having lunch to eat, there was not always enough.

Meshi

During the 48-hour cease-fire towards the end of the war, the Regional Council took us to the Mei'madion Water Park in Tel Aviv. The entire way there I was nauseous, but my friend Noa was so brave, she sat next to me the whole time. We stopped at Sdot Yam to pick up the older teenagers, including my sister.

The Mei'madion was okay. I had been there already, so it wasn't so exciting. But there was a "ride" that looked like you used a skateboard that had a smooth surface. I saw it and at first said: "Oh my, I'm not going on there!" But I wanted to go even though it looked really scary. The thing is you went up – you could do it with another person or alone – I did it with Noa. It turned out to be so much fun! It felt great to be out and to be able to run around for a change.

Shanie

To break the routine of everyday life (where we did relatively nothing) on the kibbutz, a seminar was organized by our youth movement counselors Rachel and Roi for the youth of the kibbutz (ages fifteen to eighteen). The seminar was held at Kibbutz Sdot Yam near Caesaria. The first day we had an activity about what had happened in the war so far and the mistakes that we felt had been made. We had a chance to finally go to the beach since Sdot Yam is right by the sea. (Our kibbutz is also right by the sea, but because of the war we were not allowed to go!) We were there for three days and then we returned north to the real routine, our routine of war.

Sometimes in the evenings, when there weren't any rockets being launched I went out to meet my friends, the few who stayed. Sometimes we met in one of the shelters and other times in the Ekonomia. We just hung out – talking, watching TV and eating whatever noshes were available.

Carolyn

I worked five shifts a week which is what I normally work. We didn't have to work extra. There weren't that many patients, especially initially, because there weren't that many wounded; there were more wounded at the end.

On the other hand the birthing rooms at Nahariya Hospital had less work. They usually have sixty births a day. They moved into the surgery – the whole ward – they had like about five births a day because nobody was here. Everybody, I guess, was giving birth in Tel Aviv.

And you had your regular staff – there was no problem with staffing. There really wasn't. The staff didn't really move that much between departments. Another member of Gesher Haziv, Rhona Tobin, works as a nurse's aide and stayed during the war, worked the whole time in Day Care, taking care of the children of staff. That usually has anywhere from thirty-five to sixty kids; now there were ten kids. We had a whole lot less business.

On my way to and from work at the hospital I always use the shortcut through Ragum. During this period I continued to drive that way, but I was definitely more frightened. They got hit a lot. Not too long ago someone was killed in that area when he was standing outside of a shelter!

Zvi

More than once I was on the street in Nahariya "working," when there was a Katyusha attack. Everyone learned that if you hear the siren, you take cover. By then they had the arrangement of the shahar adom– it senses the shooting of a Katyusha in Lebanon and automatically sounds the siren so that you know you have a few seconds to get to a safe place. This is exactly what they did in Nahariya at that time. At the beginning they didn't have that and a lot of people were hurt and there was a lot of damage. Into the third week of the war, they had this arrangement and people were much more relaxed as a result of it because when they heard the sirens, they immediately ran to places that they knew were safe; safe was even being in between two walls. Being next to a building was even safer than being out in the open street or, better, in a shelter. And that's what we did.

Tuesday, August 1; Wednesday, August 2; & Thursday, August 3

Numerous Katyusha hits on Gesher Haziv, Nahariya, and in the Western Galilee; fires in many areas and casualties. Katyusha hits in Acco, Safed, Ma'alot, Tiberias, Rosh Pina, Carmiel, Migdal Ha'emek, Afula, Shlomi, Metula, north Golan Heights; dozens fall in Kiryat Shmona. By 19:39 on Wednesday, 210 rockets are shot into Israel, with at least sixty casualties. By 18:40 on Thursday, 160 rockets have been launched into Israel with at least twenty-seven casualties.

Evelyn

One day, when Iris was giving an exercise class for the seniors in the central shelter, there were so many Katyushas being shot at us, and for so long, that we couldn't leave the shelter until close to 14:00. It was an unbelievable intensity.

Then Noa calls us from the Situation Room where she was volunteering as usual. She said that her mobile phone wasn't working. So I called the company and they said that the only place open where you could get it fixed now was in Acco, and that between the hours of 12:00 and 15:00 there would be a technician there. Noa was working an afternoon-evening shift in the Hamal and she couldn't leave, but then again she needed her mobile phone.

So Ishai and I went to take care of it. We quickly drove to Acco. There were just a few people in the office – two technicians, a security guard, and a few customers, but they wanted to shut the office. Two Katyushas fell in Acco then – one killed a father and his daughter on the road and another person as well. We saw how nervous the technicians were; they just wanted to finish up their work and leave. And they still had a few more people waiting for service. So they did everything fast.

I said to Ishai: "We're flying home." I think we went from Acco to Gesher Haziv in ten minutes (it usually takes close to twenty). Maybe we passed one other person on the road then. You're really playing with your life – roulette.

There were some seniors like Menucha who almost didn't leave her security room the entire time of the war. And to sit alone all day every day, day after day is awful; someone needed to speak with her a bit. So I would make certain that I went to visit her as often as I could, just so she could have a little human company.

Bethe

At this point, our lives were on hold. We were functioning as well as "living" or "existing," but that's about all. We were in this surreal space. For all the years that I have lived here, and all the times when I have "dealt with" being bombarded from Lebanon, the period of time was never so long.

When we were in the States all my family and friends said, "Stay" and I knew I had numerous places of refuge. But my life and family were here. I had two children here in Israel. How could I stay there? But it never occurred to me that this period of conflict would continue for so long! Then I thought the Middle was the End. Only after beginning to write this narrative do I realize how naïve I was.

We had a nice surprise on Wednesday morning. Lavie called at 6:00; he had "returned" to Israel after fighting in Lebanon for three days in order to begin the *Course Makim* (Squad Commander Course). The rest of his unit stayed in position on foreign soil. Lavie told me that he would be heading south to the base where the course is held and didn't know when he'd be home. Since I was already up, I went into my morning routine: drink cold coffee, read the newspaper, empty the dishwasher, walk the dog, tidy the house, and sweep the floor. I then turned on the computer to check my e-mails and sites.

This morning was just like any ordinary morning – birds were singing, the sun was blaring (it's always hot in Israel in July and August), and the Mediterranean Sea glistened invitingly. But we were at war and nothing was "normal."

The Hizbullah would normally fire a lot of Katyusha rockets between 11:00 and 13:00 for a couple of days running. Of course, there was always a variation on the theme with them moving the firing times from 9:00 to 11:00 or 14:00 to 16:00. Oh, they definitely kept us on our toes. The routine was the same – stay inside and close to "safety," when you hear the *whoosh* of the rocket coming towards you, take cover. The louder the whistle of the rocket, the closer it will fall.

The phone rang mid-morning, and it was Lavie again. He said he was coming home for a few hours and that he was taking a bus out of Kiryat Shmona. He wanted me to pick him up in Acco. I told him no problem. Then I called Asher at Tadiad to let him know that Lavie was coming home for a few hours.

The rockets were falling all morning and many fell in our area. I was sitting in front of the computer in the study (a room facing east in our house) preparing work. Suddenly I would hear the sound of rockets. I'd get up to go to the security room. Meshi was sleeping and my entering her room didn't disturb her. Skippy came right with me and settled himself down on the floor as usual. I'd wait a few minutes and then go back to work.

There were so many rockets fired that morning that there was no way I was going to take a chance on the roads. I thought I wouldn't be able to get out of the kibbutz safely. So I called Asher and asked him to pick Lavie up in Acco. They arrived home safely and we had a family reunion for a few hours.

I was out one evening alone feeding the cats around the kibbutz. Suddenly there was a siren signaling that I needed to get to a safe place. Well, I was in an area without a shelter and no place to take cover. However, there was one of the concrete constructions for the infrastructure nearby. So I ran there and crouched down. I waited a few minutes, didn't hear anything fall, and then went back to what I was doing.

Asher

Later that afternoon, I volunteered to take Lavie and Nimrod, a friend from another garin who was also beginning the Squad Commander Course, to the bus/train station in the south of Haifa – Hof Hacarmel. They needed to get a bus or train to go south to the new military base. There was no public transportation in the North during this period, so we picked Nimrod up at his sister's apartment in Acco and then drove south. This evening it was quiet and no rockets were being launched. This was good, because some of the long-range rockets hit neighborhoods in Haifa that I needed to drive through in both directions.

Hannah

Once, at lunchtime, it was very tense outside so I didn't go to Chava's to eat and my granddaughter, Sharon, brought me food.

Gilad

I brought a lot of movies from my house up to the Ekonomia to be shown for whoever wanted to come. It became a place where there was a meeting of people together, simply.

Meshi

I went to the Ekonomia a few times when they had movies playing. I went to see *Superman Comes Back*, but I didn't stay until the end because it was pretty boring. I also went to the comedy show one Friday night.

There was the Miri Maseeka performance that I went to. I didn't really like it because it was kind of commercial. The way she was acting was dollish, like something was holding her strings; it wasn't very real. I knew the music; it was all known music because she's a known singer. It was entertaining, but I didn't really like it. It was a nice change from the routine and I saw a few people there, but none of my classmates. After the Miri Maseeka show, there was another person's show. He was trying to get us all up and moving with different kinds of activities, but it didn't really work, it was pretty boring. Then I walked home alone, Shanie wasn't with me. I wasn't bothered by walking home alone in the middle of the day during a war, I didn't want to, but then again I don't like walking home from school every day.

Shai

I didn't go to see the movies that were shown at the Ekonomia. But once there was an event when someone came from outside, a stand-up comedian, and I went to that. It was also something spontaneous, the whole thing of the Ekonomia, it was really nice – it was very personal and good – it answered a need.

At the beginning of this crisis a lot of people left Gesher Haziv. After that there was a stage when people started to return because they couldn't be away anymore. Then we had some really difficult days here, so there was another round of people fleeing. It was like an accordion – leaving, returning, leaving, returning. There was a group of people who decided to stay at the beginning, but after a while decided that they couldn't handle it anymore and fled.

Danit

In the middle of the war an activity was held in the late afternoon for children in the Ekonomia when the movie *Narnia* was shown. Just when the battle scene between good and bad was raging on the screen, there was a siren and booming outside. A real battle raged outside. Some kids got up to get a hug from mom and then returned to the movie. It was a very interesting scene – in essence a bit of a bubble within a bubble. Reality within reality met and the two realities intermingled.

I think that one of the things that people needed and helped people cope was a connection between all the people who chose to stay. The Ekonomia answered that need. In professional literature the difference between trauma and non-trauma is the ability to refresh yourself (to get some space to breathe), the ability to converse. The connection people developed at the Ekonomia, I believe really helped people cope. The practice of coming together to see a movie or have a cup of coffee was a return to a better period or the creation of a new, positive period. It was an act of coming together, an act of assembly.

My parents live in Haifa and I was more in contact with them during the war than usual. Sometimes we spoke a few times a day. Every time a rocket fell there we spoke to make certain that everything was all right with them, even though they don't live near the areas where rockets did land. Haifa was perceived as a place where it was impossible to know what would happen during the war. We called also to make sure that they went down to the shelter during the bombardment and things like that.

At the beginning of the fourth week of the war something unpleasant stung Stav. I suddenly discovered that there were no pharmacies open in our area! And I had a feeling of helplessness – there weren't any doctors available in the area either. I managed to get in touch with a doctor via the telephone and he told me what to do. Then by mistake I gave Stav an overdose of the antihistamine medication and I got really tense.

One day I went to Lyn's house because she is a nurse, to get some cream for Stav. And speaking again of J.K. Rowlings, Stav imitated Harry's aunt who swelled up. Really! But instead of floating above Gesher Haziv she lay in bed and didn't feel well. When I returned home Stav was really tense because there was an electrical blackout. That was the time when Dave from Sa'ar was killed. I went to Lyn's at that exact time. When I was out looking for the medication she needed the Katyushas were flying and I deliberated whether to continue walking or not; but since it was much more imperative to get Stav what she needed I continued to Lyn's house. I didn't really think about what could have happened if that Katyusha fell near me and hurt me. Only later, after Stav received what she needed and she went to sleep and everything was all right, did I suddenly realize what could have happened. And then we heard that Dave had been killed. That didn't make us feel good at all since we knew Dave and liked him a lot. When we lived at Sa'ar we also got to know his children.

Stav

My knee swelled up from the bite, the exact knee where I now have a wound. And my fingers swelled up so I couldn't bend them.

Tammy

At some point, at the beginning of August, our son, Barak, finished his year of community service for the Noa"l – which of course he only finished at the very last moment. Then he came home, except he kept traveling back to Kfar Saba to do things. Originally he thought he'd have a week's vacation – but that didn't happen. And then he would get stuck along the way, he couldn't get back because of the Katyushas, so I had to drive to bring him home from somewhere – once in Acco and once in the main bus station in Lev Hamifratz in Haifa. The whole situation was really weird. Another time I had to drive to Nahariya to get him. There were two sirens along the way when I had to stop the car. Once I stopped opposite Alonit because there was a siren. I stood next to the bus top which was useless because it wasn't protected or anything. The siren ended so I got in the car and drove to Nahariya. Just as I got there another siren went off. So I got out of the car again and stood next to the *trampiada* (where people wait for rides) – again for nothing. The whole situation was quite frightening. I didn't lie down or crouch down, but I did get out of my car.

Barak felt that he still needed to do things in Kfar Saba.

When he was here on Gesher Haziv, Barak went with me to the performance that Miri Maseeka gave. She is a well-known singer in Israel and she came, along with other performers, to entertain citizens who didn't flee from the rockets, but chose to stay at home, like us. I didn't go to any of the other performances that came to the kibbutz. I didn't feel like it. I was tired in the evenings and didn't want to go out, even to the Ekonomia.

M

More of my fun as a fire-fighter: One day there was a fire caused by a Katyusha near the fields of Kibbutz Eilon that a few of us helped to put out. Eilon's fields are not far from Gesher Haziv's bananas and avocado groves. The plane put out most of it, so just a few of us got out there to put it out. We were missing beer when we went to fight the fires; that would have made the work better.

A day or two later I decided to go surfing in Hadera, in the middle of the week. Strangely enough, I ended up in the hospital because the surfboard hit my foot and I needed stitches. I got to Hadera because friends of mine from the kibbutz were staying in Kibbutz Sdot Yam.

Usually, what was good about the war was that there were no waves during the week, but there were waves in Tel Aviv during the weekend. This once, in the middle of the week the waves were big.

But I didn't want to take my chances there in Tel Aviv, so I got a ride north with my board and ended up with stitches in my foot. It was surreal.

Miri

Once during this period Noa got sick. I took to her a doctor who was on-call and who came to the kibbutz and he told me that she needed to take antibiotics for a week. And I said to him: "Where am I going to find a pharmacy now where I can buy the prescription?" So I said to myself: "Okay. I'll take Noa and drive to my father's in the Krayot and go to the Kiryon Mall." Ilan was worried that while I was driving a Katyusha would fall on the car and kill us. Anything's possible. We saw on the news where a person who was driving was killed because a Katyusha fell on his car.

I insisted on continuing as if this was nothing unusual. I put Noa in the car and we drove to my father's. Just as we arrived there was a siren for the Krayot area. So I said to my father: "Let's go to the Kiryon. I won't tell Ilan." I thought about Noa – how long can you keep a child in a house? She needed some type of fresh scenery and stimulation. So I bought her sandals and we had a fun time in the mall. Then we returned to the kibbutz.

A few days later we drove to stay with Ilan's aunt who lives in Ramat Gan. That was when a Katyusha landed in Acco and three people were killed. I said that I was going to take Noa to get ice cream on the main road. We got to an ice cream store and the man had a TV on. I asked him nicely for a scoop of ice cream in a cup. And he says to me: "Don't you know there's a war on and people are getting killed? How can you eat ice cream now?" I said to him: "Listen to me carefully, mister. I just came from Acco and I've just experienced rockets and now give me ice cream! All week we haven't had ice cream, so please give me ice cream now." So he said: "Really? You just came from the North?"

Benny

The first week in August we'd had enough and decided that we needed a breather. So since the baby was two and a half weeks old I said to Orit, we should go – it wasn't a trip we had planned beforehand. We made the decision from one minute to the next. I said, we have to leave here – for the children – even though they showed no signs of distress, if this was going to continue for a lot longer, we needed to give them something rewarding. They were missing out on summer activities like going to the pool and a vacation – and we needed to give them something else. So I went onto the Internet and found a deal at the Princess Hotel in Eilat for a few days. That same night, at 4 in the morning, after I had previously loaded all our things into the car, we "flew" on the road – we were the only ones on the road, by the way. We had to drive down (it's a seven-hour drive minimum from the northwest corner of Israel to the southeast corner) because there were no flights out of Haifa airport. The trip to Eilat – to leave the house – was an unpleasant feeling, although within two and half hours we were already in Beersheba where we made the first stop and fed the baby. Again, we were the only ones on the road, but until we passed Haifa we didn't feel safe. It was a tense drive. But I pushed hard on the accelerator.

We really enjoyed ourselves in Eilat. We didn't feel tense and we didn't have time to watch television, although every once in a while we received reports from my mother who chose to stay here on the kibbutz. The situation worsened while we were gone. But there we were with the children in the pools and it was really great. And that was it. The vacation ended. And it cost us a lot of money. It wasn't a situation where we had been invited for free, so we were headed for home.

While we were on our way home Thursday, my mother called and said that we really didn't have any reason to return to the kibbutz. She said: "Just get a hotel room. I'll pay for the hotel, get a room somewhere, like Netanya." Orit wanted to return home. I turned on the news and I heard about deaths that had occurred in Acco and deaths in other places in the North and I said to Orit: "Come on, we won't return, we'll find another place to stay for a few days, at least to spend the weekend in a hotel."

So we called some friends of ours, the Goldensteins who live in the third stage of the new neighborhood; they said that they have already been staying in Kibbutz Gan Shmuel for a week. They said that they would speak with their hosts there and see if they could arrange a room for us. We made a lot of phone calls, back and forth; in the end they said that they've organized something for us. I said: "Okay, why not, Kibbutz Gan Shmuel is on the way home anyway. We'll stop and see what available." So we stopped and they welcomed us very nicely. At 22:00 they managed to organize a room for us with beds and a kitchenette and a refrigerator full of food. They really went all out for us. We slept the night there.

Micha

Sometimes at work at Bermad there were days when there was a siren and we'd go into the security room for two or three minutes, wait, go back to work, sit for five minutes, then another siren. It was not easy. Out of an eight to nine-hour workday you'd get four or five hours, during which you could actually work.

I remember once I left Bermad I used to look up in the sky towards the North more than I looked at the road, to be ready to jump out of the car if necessary or drive faster. You never knew what was the best thing to do. I was never caught by a siren or Katyusha while driving.

One afternoon, when I was home early, I was walking to the offices when I heard the whistle go by, and I think that was the whistle of the Katyusha that killed Dave in Sa'ar. Because you hear the whistle and you hear the strength of the bang and you could work out that it hit Sa'ar. That was something I became quite good at, learning how far away the Katyusha fell from. I remember in earlier years, every time a Katyusha fell we had to know exactly where it hit. Now you stopped thinking about whether it was Rosh Haniqra or Betzet; there were just so many of them that you couldn't keep track of where every one fell.

We went to the Ekonomia when it was open, a few times, when there were shows there. Whenever Adar Sharif was on the kibbutz, it was open. The kids went there to see a few movies. We as a family saw a show or two.

Lyn

For the first few weeks of the war we didn't have sirens. But when the sirens started we were fairly strict about going into the security room. Only on one or two occasions was there a siren during the evening meal when we actually got up and went into the security room for our fifteen minutes and came back out and finished our meal.

When you have kids at home somebody has to be at home with them. Micha had the option of going back to work. He had that flexibility because I could be at home with the kids since the whole school system was shut down. But because I work for the Ministry of Health, if there had been something with biological or chemical weapons then I automatically get a Tzav 8 and I disappear from the scene and am sent wherever is needed. So then Micha would have to be home with the children. So this is something we are both aware of. This time it was him at work, maybe next time it will be me! Let's hope not!

I found that the first week in August (after that initial three-week expectation) was when it started to get hard for us. I think we were mentally prepared for three weeks and then the three-week mark came and went and that's when it started to get us down.

It was also difficult with Oren being away. He would call us up and beg us to bring him home. We didn't really want to do that because Oren is very active and being cooped up in the house all day would be difficult – we just saw him the first few days of the war, but then he was climbing the walls. He's used to swimming 4-5 km a day. All of a sudden doing nothing physical, he was just jumping out of his skin. We didn't want to bring him home.

One of the things that really angered me was the fact that the Hizbullah were dictating to me how I was going to live my life. And I started to feel a lot of anger – that this is my life and I should be able to choose the way I want to live. I shouldn't have to be dictated to by some people who are fanatical and who live across the border and who feel that they have the right to dictate to me how I am going to live my life!

Eugene

During previous wars with Katyushas, I would sit outside and do whatever I wanted to. And at the point, when I heard them getting closer, then I would walk into the house. But now they have missiles that were going to Haifa, which of course were no danger to us. But Shlomi got bombed, the Bedouin village got bombed and they're north of us. This time I was more careful. When I thought it was necessary, I would get up and go into the security room.

Carolyn and I didn't do much during this period. We watched the news and stayed in the house. Carolyn went to the Ekonomia a few times, though. We borrowed some CDs of movies that we watched at the time, but very few. That was our big social activity.

A lot of people called and wrote e-mails. We talked to relatives. One cousin in the States tried to raise some money – that was really sweet. And I felt very good about that. But that's enough "*shalom aleynu ve'al kol Yisrael*" (Peace be with us and all of Israel), that's enough! And the kids – please don't come home when there's a war.

Helen

I remember Wednesday, when one of the people I took around the hospital was the head of the Los Angeles Federation – literally while Katyushas were falling around us. And then he wanted to go out to Kiryat Shmona. His driver was looking at me and silently asking me to try to help him convince this guy to change his plans, which I managed to do. So I took him to visit David Coren (Asher's father), for instance. David might have been a little difficult to understand, but he is head and shoulders above a lot of people. And this man was greatly impressed by David.

Noa

Volunteering in the Situation Room on a regular basis gave me a lot of inner strength. I don't think I would be able to sit at home and do nothing and feel that I didn't give anything of myself to the community. I'm unable to sit at home and do nothing anyway. Afterwards things got organized and began to flow. I felt comfortable and good – it gave me the feeling that I was doing something useful and not just sitting around doing nothing. And I was definitely not sitting around complaining, "Oy! Look how bad we have it!"

Aliza

There's a war going on in the North and people in other areas of the country were going out to eat and going to the movies and everything. It was too incongruous to think that in our house this was happening, and here others are living the life of Riley, because our children are so scared for us. I understand their feelings.

That's another thing – we had more contact with family abroad during this period than I think I've had in the past ten years or so. Phone calls and e-mails and writing letters were also part of a way for us to stay in contact. It was nice when people responded to our letters with, "Thank you, thank you, thank you," even from guys whom I haven't heard from in a few years, and telephone calls.

Judy

On those days when I was home alone, sometimes I would get together with friends who live close by on the kibbutz, maybe eat a meal together or have some coffee or just sit and chat. But through a lot of it I was just home in the evenings alone. I kept in touch with the family by phone. I decided I was not taking Mayzie out for walks, though; I let her out. And anytime there was anything more – we had sirens by then – or anything happening, she was glued to me. She came into the security room with me as well. I didn't have to worry.

Sharon & Ronny

Once we went into Nahariya to go to the bank (the banks were all open), and since we were there we decided that we wanted a cup of coffee, so we went to the Penguin, which was the only place open throughout the entire war. All I wanted was a cup of coffee – cafe au lait – to feel that I was still alive. There weren't a lot of people there, a few reserve soldiers, a few foreign journalists, and some old people talking, surrounded by newspapers. Not so very usual for a coffee place in Nahariya.

CHAPTER THREE
The End

Friday, August 4 & Saturday, August 5

Numerous Katyusha hits on Gesher Haziv and in the Western Galilee. Katyusha hits on Acco, Safed, Ma'alot, Kiryat Shmona, Nahariya, Shlomi, Mr'ar Village, Carmiel, Hadera, Migdal Ha'emek, Tiberias, the Krayot, Haifa, with casualties and fires. By 17:05 on Friday, 140 rockets are launched at Israel. By 18:29 on Saturday, 194 rockets are launched into Israel, with at least twenty-six casualties.

Bethe

Teresa told me that she heard that the Uri Buri Restaurant in Acco was open for business despite the war. Uri Buri's is a first-class seafood restaurant now located on the water in the Old City of Acco. I called the restaurant just to make certain that what Teresa had heard was true. The person I spoke with told me they were open every day from 12:00 to 17:00, because those were the hours the official permit allowed. I wanted to go on Tuesday and have Asher meet me from Tadiad, but he had just eaten.

So we decided to go for lunch on Friday. The date was August 4th and it was our anniversary. I guess it was better that we went on Friday instead of mid-week since it was a special occasion. We were the only customers in the restaurant. But it didn't matter. The food was superb and the service fantastic.

A lot of people went away for the weekend and there weren't enough volunteers to staff the Situation Room with two people for all shifts, especially in the middle of the night. I volunteered to work the graveyard shift on Saturday morning, from 2:00 to 6:00 with a resident of the settlement named Baruch. I didn't know him, but I figured this would be a perfect opportunity to get to know someone new. I had a book with me to read, we had a TV with a wide variety of cable stations, but more importantly we had each other to speak to. Very quickly we found a number of topics to discuss and passed the time mostly in conversation. Our luck was that it was quiet on our shift and we didn't have anything to do. The four-hour shift was over before we knew it.

I went home at 6:00. My family was sleeping. I had told Asher that I would go to the hospital and be with David for breakfast. So I got into my morning routine. I emptied the dishwasher, swept the floor, and changed the kitchen towel. Then I sat down for a glass or two of cold coffee, took the dog out for a walk; afterwards driving to the hospital. Again the roads were empty. I went the usual way through the Ragum neighborhood and again I parked on the street outside of the hospital parking lot. I made my way into the hospital basement where all the patients were. I got organized with David so that he was comfortable. We spoke about what had happened since we had spoken or met. It's important for him to be up-to-date with everything outside of the hospital and his condition. I helped him eat breakfast and clean up afterwards. Then I organized his table so he could easily turn on the CD/tape/radio and listen to whatever he wanted.

I left the hospital and walked to my car. The roads were fairly deserted, as usual, even more so since it was relatively early on a Saturday morning. Just as I reached my car I heard noises that sounded like rocket blasts. I looked around for some safe place to hide; there was none, just a grove of avocado trees. I quickly walked in between the rows and crouched down. I knew I should lie flat on the ground, but I was wearing white pants, and I just couldn't. After a few minutes of staying in that position, but not hearing any shells fall I got into my car and drove home – safely, I might add, although I did feel ridiculous.

The Israeli army had stationed a few artillery posts in our area. They fired periodically into Lebanon from their position near us. It got to the point that we couldn't tell the difference between a Hizbullah rocket coming towards us, or one of our own rockets being fired.

Now I had the whole day ahead of me. But I couldn't go outside and work in the garden. I couldn't go for a long walk in the fields. I couldn't go to the beach. I was a prisoner in my home. I was "free" to go where I wanted, but I had to be certain that I was near a shelter if I needed it quickly. So I got into my daily routine – organizing, cleaning, reading, watching TV, writing e-mails and watching the news stations. So one of the things I did that afternoon was to send a long e-mail to family and friends. Here's a bit of what I wrote:

The Hizballah don't let up. They send rockets at us throughout the day in sporadic barrages. We have an alarm system that indicates when a "shooting" has been spotted in Lebanon, which gives us 1 minute or so to take cover.

Our troops are working slowly to clear Hizballah-held areas and uncover caches of weapons. We're working slowly for 2 reasons: to minimize civilian casualties (we could just bomb the villages from the air flattening what intelligence has designated as Hizballah strongholds) and to reduce negative public against us.

As usual Israel is in a lose-lose situation. For every Israeli civilian Hizballah kills it's a victory for them. For every Lebanese civilian Israel kills it's a victory for Hizballah.

The Lebanese government had 6 years to dismantle the Hizballah, it didn't. Instead they got stronger militarily and politically. They now hold seats in the Lebanese government. Hizballah wants UNIFIL forces to continue - they're ineffective and have been since 1979 when first mandated in Lebanon. They turn a blind eye. A multi-national fighting force is what is needed to keep the Hizballah from strengthening militarily again, when we pull out. Israel has no interest in occupying Lebanese soil.

Lavie is "out" of Lebanon and has begun his non-com course. Unfortunately they have been moved to the Golan Heights to do their training because Syria has been amassing forces on the border. We spoke with him last night and all is well. He managed to come home for a few hours on his way to the new base. It was good to see him - even for a short time.

Asher has been working. Not everyone comes to work, because the missiles and rockets can reach the area where he works these days. The summer semester at the university didn't open. I have work to do at home - an article to finish to publication, re-editing a textbook, and the completion of another article I started in May. Unfortunately with all the interruptions of sirens throughout the day, I don't get as much done as I would like.

The girls are fine. Shanie is a real "hero" - she volunteers to work hours in the "war room" of the kibbutz where all information is gathered and then spread to the public: when to enter shelters, when to leave, when certain services are open, when a performance from outside will occur, etc. She has also volunteered to go to the hospital to help out with her grandfather quite frequently. Meshi spends most of the days with me in the house: reading, doing Sudoku puzzles and other puzzles, and of course watching TV.

Meshi helps me every evening feeding the abandoned cats and dogs around the kibbutz and making certain that water is available to them. We found another abandoned dog with Nahariya tags; poor thing was hungry and scared. We passed him over to the proper group that is taking care of animals like these.

So that's the news from the front. Stay in touch - and remember - the media is only portraying one side of the conflict.

Then later that day Shanie wanted to visit her Grandfather David in the hospital around 16:00, so I agreed to drive her. The roads were fairly deserted, typical during this period. We drove through the Ragum neighborhood and saw people sitting outside the local shelter taking a breath of fresh air. I dropped her off at the hospital on the road near the entrance and drove home.

I was on the Nahariya-Rosh Haniqra Road going north. I had just passed Masaryk Street when I suddenly heard an extremely loud noise, which sounded like a loud *crack*. I pulled the car off the road immediately, turned off the engine, and got out. I didn't even lock it and left my bag on the seat. I ran around the car to the passenger side and crouched down in a ditch by the side of the road. A minute or two passed and I saw that there was a passage under the road for water drainage. I thought that would be even safer, so I went under there. I waited for another few minutes to see if any more shells fell. When the quiet continued I got back into the car and shakily drove myself home to the kibbutz. Just as I was about to pull out onto the road a police car passed me and turned onto a dirt road that leads into the fields to my right. I thought that was weird, but considering my state of mind at that time, didn't really wonder too long about it.

As I got closer to Gesher Haziv I saw smoke in the distance. At first I thought a rocket had fallen in our fields. Then I realized it was further north, probably in Moshav Liman. Then when I turned onto the street in the kibbutz that leads to my house and which goes south, I saw that there was another plume of smoke in the direction of the hospital.

I ran into the house and told Asher and Meshi what had just happened. I also called the Situation Room to let them know where I saw smoke so they could find out what had been hit. There was no way I was going back on the road at five to pick Shanie up. Asher went. When they returned he told me that the reason I heard such a loud noise was that a Katyusha had fallen about 50 meters or less from where my car was. He knew because he saw the smoke from the fire that it had caused. No wonder I was so shaken up! And that also explained why the police car I had seen earlier had turned onto that dirt road.

What an eventful Saturday!

Micha

During the first weekend in August, we went down south again. As we were driving through Nahariya – Lyn was driving – and I remember we were just about to stop for a traffic light at the main traffic lights in Nahariya because it was flashing green, when a siren started and I said: "Lyn, hit the gas, go!" and I think we actually went through a red light. There was hardly any traffic in those days and the roads were empty.

On another note – when I was walking around the kibbutz, I didn't think of the shelters, but every time I was walking I kept looking where there might be a place to hide if I suddenly needed to; where there was a place to crouch down or drop down or something.

Lyn

We all drove down to Wingate on Friday, August 4th to pick up Oren and bring him home for the weekend. But before heading north we took Alon and Ela, along with Oren, out to ten-pin bowling just so they would have a treat. We went to one of the malls there. And that was a real surreal experience coming from the security room to a mall where the people are going about their everyday lives. They're not in a state of war, they're just living their everyday lives. It was very strange.

The kids were sort of like: "Why aren't they worried here?" and I tried to explain to them that it was like a coping mechanism – it affects them, they watch the news, they are aware of what is happening in the North, but this is their way of coping – living their lives as normal. If something starts to happen here then they get stressed about it – like when the buses were being blown up in Tel Aviv – people were more stressed about getting on buses and things like that, because that was what was happening to them and that was their reality. Our reality is we're sitting in a security room and they don't have the concept of that. Just like when we were at home when the buses were being blown up – we were aware of it, we knew it was happening, but it wasn't our reality. I think they understood this. But it was still strange for them. To go from seeing almost nobody in the kibbutz – which was like a ghost town – and walking into a mall which is shoulder to shoulder with people shopping and chatting and laughing and sitting in restaurants and drinking coffee and everything and it was like "*Wow!*" That should contrast their perspective.

On that day up at Gesher Haziv, families started to come back because they were tired of being with other people, tired of not being in their homes, just the whole thing.

Since Oren was home this weekend, he could actually see what it was like sitting in the security room most of the day. He enjoyed being on his computer or whatever, and he enjoyed being with the family, but he realized that it is actually quite boring to do that. And we had so many Katyushas that weekend; he really got a show!

We had Kabbalat Shabbat with *Saba* and *Safta*. We really tried to keep the things that we could. We really tried to do a Kabbalat Shabbat every Friday, more often than not with Chaya and Zvi; we had them come over. Normalcy in an abnormal situation.

Paul

Today is Saturday, and as usual I drove out to the banana and avocado groves for a spin to check out the situation. I heard that there were things happening in the Ekonomia, but we decided not to go.

I was a little bit more concerned driving on the roads than usual. I had this feeling of vulnerability being in the car, I guess. But I'd be driving out in the fields all the time and it didn't bother me. Now, for some reason, driving between here and Nahariya was scarier. I don't know why, it's not logical. Maybe because we were driving faster and then if something hits you, you might lose control, I don't know. It's not like I was sitting in the shelter all day and then rushing into Nahariya to buy things and rushing back. I was outside all the time anyway. There's no real logic to my being more scared.

Kathy

I usually work in the garden when I can. I have a lot of herbs and things growing. Although I'm not afraid of the Katyushas, I didn't go outside to work in my garden during this time as I usually do. Now my garden is a total shambles.

I was watching a lot more TV than usual. I became a news addict, but then again I always am. But this was way more than usual. We had FOX news on the satellite channels we were able to get during the war, so I watched that a lot. Thank God they took it off; I need blinders to watch that station.

I'm not scared of Katyushas, so I wasn't scared being in the car and driving. I'm much more scared of traffic accidents. I wasn't scared on the roads. We didn't have any incidences of rockets falling close to us when we were driving, although I know people who did.

What was strange is that I didn't really go into Nahariya during the war at all. In fact I never even went to see where the Katyushas fell in Nahariya. We went straight to the Krayot when we needed to do major shopping. Paul used to go to Sabri or Dekel sometimes to get a few things. He went wherever it was open. He always does the shopping anyway, so that wasn't unusual for us.

Carolyn

I found the war depressing more than scary. And it overwhelmed me. It took a long time to get over this depressing feeling. We were inside. We didn't go anywhere. We didn't spend any money. And we watched the TV. We had no social events. A friend came over once and we ended up being in the security room. We went to friends another time and we were in their security room. We didn't have dinners together with friends. I even went to Bethe's once and we ended up in her security room because a siren went off!

Most of the time we reacted and went into the security room when we heard bombs falling, or the sirens. We spent a lot of time in the bedroom, which is our security room, much more than normal.

Terry & Teresa

We went to Migdal Ha'emek to visit Gabi again. This had become our Saturday routine. Just like last week, as we were driving through Kfar Yasif there were rockets landing in the Nahariya area. We must have reached the hospital a few minutes after the attack. We saw smoke from the fires caused by the Katyushas landing in the fields in a couple of spots on our way to the kibbutz. Later Bethe told us that she had been on the road on her way back from dropping Shanie off at the hospital, when the attack happened.

Judy

At the end of the fourth week, Leah decided she wanted to come back. Since so few of my co-workers were planning on going into work that day, the office didn't open. Again, I drove down to Netanya to be with the family. Again, I saw the same traffic patterns of traffic going north on Saturday night.

Aliza

One Friday night there was a Kabbalat Shabbat in a shelter and that was very nice. There were around thirty people there. An SMS message announced the event. We just sat around and sang songs. It was very simple and very nice. This put a bit of normalcy into our bizarre situation.

After the first few times a Katyusha falls you sort of become – you don't become immune to the noise, but you live with it. You just come to a point where it's not a question of whether you are terrified – you are scared, but at the same time that's life, that's it, this is the situation. You know what I mean: "Dear God don't let it fall on me! Let's go ahead and do what we have to do."

We spent one Saturday morning in the Situation Room; they were short on people, and we were down there. It was towards the end, so it was very quiet. Not exciting, just the fact that you can do it or that you are wanted.

Tammy

We had gone away sometimes on the weekends – that was also something we deliberated about, to go or not to go. Gesher Haziv is our home and we didn't want to leave. Our daughter Karen's boyfriend's family has a hotel in Bat Yam (near Tel Aviv) – and all the time she kept saying, "Come." "Come." "Come." And we kept saying, "No." "No." No." Until we finally broke down and called Karen and said, "We're coming."

On the fifth of August we all (my entire family – Yehuda, myself, Manor, who came up from the South where he is working at Kibbutz Be'eri, our daughters Ayala and Karen, and Barak) met in the Center and had lunch together in honor of Barak's military draft. That was nice.

M

One thing you could tell was that weekends were getting very, very crowded in Tel Aviv. A lot of people from the North were going to Tel Aviv then. It was basically blooming. Some of my friends in Tel Aviv tried to convince me to stay there, but I didn't want to stay in Tel Aviv. It was comfortable staying here on the kibbutz. I had more of a routine here than in Tel Aviv and it was kind of amazing because in Tel Aviv nothing changed.

Eugene

Towards the end I had just had enough, especially when I was eating a meal. I said: "I'm going to finish this meal – I don't care." At that point it didn't matter how intense the shelling was!

The bottom line for me was that being in the house with Carolyn was not difficult. And thank God we don't have any small children.

When I wasn't glued to the TV watching news, I passed the time reading. I read fiction as usual. There was no change in my choice of reading material during this time, however tense it got.

Since we were doing all of our food shopping at the Alonit, I didn't have a lot of occasions to drive on the roads during the war. But again use common sense on the roads – if the road sign says 60 and there's no one ahead of you, then go 80.

Benny

The first two days after our return from Eilat were difficult for me. I was tenser than the others, even though I didn't show it externally, I think. There were sirens now and more Katyushas falling than at the beginning. We maintained our routine in the house, though, and the children were fine.

Many times we would be notified that there was a "window of opportunity," but within ten minutes or so there would be a Katyusha barrage. So it was really impossible to know when it was safe to do anything outside.

When we went outside in the evenings, it was really very pleasant. The air outside was refreshing – both early in the mornings and in the evenings – to go outside and breathe in the fresh air was wonderful. And I said: "We have our newborn daughter and we can't stroll around with her in the carriage." Also, there was total quiet around us.

We had our routine during this time, but our lives were so totally different from normal. You have to understand that everything is connected to chance. One of my neighbors is a police officer. Every once in a while he would arrive, usually at night, and report to us where the Katyushas fell in this area. We spoke about what had happened in Acco, how he knew the people who were killed. He was sent to all the places where Katyushas fell in this area. And we're standing there, in the middle of the road, totally unprotected. My wife thinks I was stressed. If I was really stressed I would have isolated myself inside a room and not gone out.

Orit

Our children usually like to play together if they're not with their friends. They did puzzles, played board games, and watched TV. We heard the usual complaints from the children – like he's bothering me - but we'd rather have that type of behavior than if the child was scared or introverted. So being in the mamad many hours during the war wasn't so unusual for them, and didn't cause any major problems.

Helen

A senior kibbutz member named Menucha routinely volunteers in the Gesher Haziv Library, which she has been doing for many years now. I also volunteer there. I thought it was a great victory when I said to Menucha: "You've got to start coming to the Library!" in order to get her out of her house a bit and see other people. She came a couple of times and it was a big event. I worried about people like her because she doesn't really have a lot of contact with others on a daily basis. But there is a limit – if someone says I don't need help, I go away. But I stuck with it with Menucha to make sure she was okay and taken care of.

I was getting sadder and sadder as the war dragged on.

Sharon

One afternoon Ronny and I drove to visit friends in Shlomit. Coming back we decided to take the coastal road (from Rosh Haniqra to Achziv) instead of the main road. We found some soldiers there on the side of the road with their commander, you know, right before they were moving into Lebanon – boys who are eighteen and nineteen and they're in a fighting unit. They were sitting there drinking some vodka and they asked us for a few cigarettes, so we gave them some. Then another car drove by and stopped. Two people got out and opened the trunk, which was full of food. How those people knew where to find the soldiers, I'll never know! They were soldiers who had been at Gesher Haziv; they said that they were sleeping at the Sulam Tsor High School and were from a Golani unit. I always imagined Golani soldiers to be bruisers, but these were regular Israeli soldiers. It made the whole war return to reality; these men were someone's sons.

Towards the end of the war I started calling the border "the volcano" (*har ga'ash*) not because it was burning (as it had been at the beginning from all the fires started by rockets exploding on our side of the border), but because of what was happening on the other side. Now it's impossible to rely on the border as being secure any longer. We'd been in this surreal situation for weeks now. On the one hand, it didn't look like there was any end in sight. On the other hand, Ronny, the politician kept saying that there's no way that this war won't end before the beginning of the school year. As if we had some kind of deadline. This was a long period. I'd had enough.

Ronny and I had a lot of fun together during the war despite the fear and aggression against us. We calm each other down – I'm much more hysterical than she is, but I also helped Ronny not to become hysterical. We could tell each other what to do and what not to do – don't walk around during those hours, for example. We have been close friends for many years now. When Ronny first came to the kibbutz she lived with me for about two months. She didn't find a place so quickly – so we knew how to manage with each other at such close quarters. Before that, however, when I originally decided to leave the Center, I lived with Ronny for a month before I decided to come north to Gesher Haziv. So we've done this before. We also have different personalities, which helps us get along. Except, that this time it was much more intensive.

Shai

When I'm not traveling somewhere, I usually make certain that I have time to eat lunch between meetings around 13:00 to 16:00 depending on my schedule. I make certain that I have at least thirty minutes when I go home to eat. During the war I did manage to eat, but not within the same framework. If there was a Katyusha strike or there was some other event that prevented me from getting home, then I didn't get home when I wanted to, but later, but I did try to get home to eat. Part of this time I was alone, because my family wasn't on the kibbutz, so sometimes I would go and eat at my parents' house (they also live on the kibbutz). My parents stayed at the beginning, but after the Katyusha fell not so far from their house they left for two weeks, but then returned again.

Since I've lived under Katyusha strikes all my life, I didn't feel any less safe on the roads than I did in the kibbutz. I had one incident in the latter part of the war, when I drove through the Krayot on an internal, secondary road, and there was a siren. And I saw all the cars stop immediately and the people get out of the cars and go into the buildings, so I found myself doing the same. If I had been alone on the road, with no other cars around, I think I would have just continued driving. But I did what everyone was doing.

I didn't drive that much during this period, so I really wasn't in a position to get caught by sirens while driving. I drove to a few meetings or to briefings at the Regional Council, and a few times to the kibbutzim where residents from Gesher Haziv were staying in order to see that everything was all right. Also every once in a while I'd drive to take my children from one place to another, but not a great number of trips on the road.

Ilan

There was a Saturday when we decided to cook outside. I said: "No one will see us." There were no neighbors around us. So we got organized and ate like proper people for a change, the way we wanted to.

Miri

Towards the end I even infected Ilan a little with my need to do things. I just can't stay in a confined area for long. We barbecued outside and planted plants in the garden. I was standing outside with Noa in my arms and things are happening all around us. We saw helicopters in the air shooting. You see them shooting! A police car passed us by and we saw them staring at us. They couldn't believe that we were outside in this mess! And we were just standing there outside, watching the show. Katyushas were falling here and they were falling there and the helicopters are in the sky. I was just waiting for someone to come and take us away to the crazy farm.

Sometimes I had strange thoughts when I was in the house. I like to lie on the large sofa in the living room and right behind it we have a big window that faces north. Sometimes I thought to myself how easily a Katyusha could come flying from the Lebanese border directly into our living room. I had thoughts like that one because there were stories like that that did occur. Once there was a family in the Krayot who went to sleep in their mamad and a rocket hit their house – nothing happened to them because they were in the mamad, but their house was destroyed. Maybe I'm not normal.

Hannah

What was different about being in the shelter is that I don't usually watch television in the mornings. I work a little bit in the Accounting Department and then I have things to do around the house. I don't have time to watch television. So after my afternoon nap I watch TV. In the shelter, the television was without the cable connection. Later YES was hooked up in the Situation Room, but we didn't have it on the TV in our room in the shelter. We also couldn't sit in the Situation Room because they were busy and they watched the shows that they wanted to watch. So we only had the regular channels, not what I usually watch at home. Okay. So what we watched the most was the news. I don't think that any one of us asked for YES to be hooked up on our side, at least I didn't ask.

I don't usually read books. I read the newspaper on Fridays. It takes me a while to go through all the sections. In the afternoons I usually watch television – I really like nature shows, and of course the news. So now I was watching television all the time.

Sunday, August 6; Monday, August 7; & Tuesday, August 8

Numerous Katyusha hits in the Western Galilee; fires, casualties and injuries. Katyusha hits in Acco, the Krayot, Safed, Carmiel, Ma'alot, Nahariya, Metula, Kiryat Shmona, Rosh Pina, Upper Galilee, Tiberias, and the Golan Heights, with some casualties. Haifa receives a direct missile hit causing at least 200 casualties and fires. By 19:31 on Sunday, 160 rockets have been launched into Israel, at least forty in the area of Kiryat Shmona alone; numerous casualties, including the Kfar Giladi tragedy. By 18:57 on Monday, 160 rockets launched against Israel. At 9:17 on Tuesday, it is reported that since the beginning of the war the Hizbullah have launched 3,050 rockets and missiles into Israel, 750 of them in residential areas were there have been forty-nine civilian deaths so far. By 15:50 on Tuesday, ninety rockets have been fired at Israel.

Danit

In the fourth week of the war, we went to Tel Aviv for an outing. There was a great feeling of fear among some people we spoke to there that rockets would begin to fall in Tel Aviv as well; people spoke about rockets and missiles landing in Tel Aviv. We were less terrified than people in Tel Aviv because we were more trained in dealing with rockets falling near us, I guess. We had an advantage over the people who live in Haifa or in the Krayot or in Safed. We've been living with the fear of Katyushas for years and we know how to cope with them better.

When we were home filling up the many hours we had every day proved to be relatively easy. Sometimes Stav had friends come to our house to visit and play. Other times she went to the activities organized in the shelter every once in a while because she was kind of too old for the activities there. She helped me distribute the mail, which was very good and important. Stav drew and painted a lot during the war. In the Alonit, I found canvas panels for acrylic drawing that she used. She wants to be a fashion designer. So she used the time during the war to create a very impressive portfolio because she had a lot of free time.

Otherwise, my husband Shlomi continued to drive to work every day. He went to his base as usual on the other side of Haifa Bay. However, now the base was being heavily targeted by the Hizbullah. As souvenirs he would bring us some of the little balls that the rockets were filled with, since they were different rockets than the Katyushas that fell here.

Stav

My experience in Tel Aviv during the war showed me that there were people who got stressed from the war and then there were others who were totally disconnected from the war – they had no idea what was going on.

I didn't just draw during the war I also created. The war was the fun part of my summer vacation from school. I hadn't signed up for any of the summer camp programs. Two of my best friends from the community decided to leave with their families – they flew abroad. They hadn't planned the trip though.

Gilad

There were a lot of Katyushas fired at my father's base. And none of them hit. A few fell on the beach or the shore close by, though.

So what I did throughout the war, more or less, was to be in the Situation Room during the days and do what was needed there. I spent a lot of time on the computer during the war.

Ilan

The last week or so, we were kind of emptied out in the way of food products and other household items. So I think it was Saturday, we drove to Faisel's market to get what we could and what we needed. And there were incessant sirens going off and I don't remember hearing any rockets hitting, but the sirens were non-stop. And the bottom line is that Faisel's is really only a large shed. You might be between the shelves and feel safe and protected, but in reality you're not. So we continued to buy what we needed and then drove home trying to maintain some kind of normalcy.

Zvi

We didn't let the continuation of the war become a factor in our daily lives – like giving in to depression. As long as you're busy, as long as you have something creative to do, whatever that is or how insignificant it may be, as long as you have your routine and you're busy.

Sometimes to get food I went to the supermarket in Nahariya, the Hypernetto it was once called, since it was open. Once I was in the supermarket the siren went off. The staff was well trained already. They gathered all the people in the store and took up their positions; very good. And all the customers went to a place that was a shelter;

about fifty or sixty people were crowded into this shelter. And then we sat there for about five minutes, then everybody went out and on their way.

And less than five minutes later the sirens went off again. Everybody went back in, but this time someone on the staff started opening bottles and serving drinks to everybody, which was very nice. The atmosphere was very nice, people taking care of each other; you're not just a customer, but something more.

Hannah

People asked me if I wanted to go anywhere, and I didn't. First of all I felt safe in the shelter; if it is true or not, I don't know, but I felt safe. I also felt that I didn't have the desire to be out. I knew I wouldn't enjoy myself. There are a number of people who went and had a good time. I would have found myself some place to sit and I wouldn't do anything else and I wouldn't have a good time and I didn't want to use the possibilities that arose. I know that Evelyn and Ishai went away for a week after the war ended and really enjoyed themselves. But they were a couple. I'm alone. Normally, if there is an organized trip then I do go and participate, even if I am the only one going from the kibbutz, because we walk and it's organized. I don't need to look for entertainment then.

Benny

After the weekend ended and the next week began, we attempted to resume our normal lives, especially taking the children to the activities from 9:00 to 12:00 every day. It was important that they were able to get out of the mamad in the house. They didn't show any signs of distress at all throughout the entire war. No panic, nothing. After Eilat we allowed them to go outside in the yard once or twice when there was a "window," to play. But besides that they were in the house, in the mamad, most of the time.

When I was driving on the roads I would drive very fast, first of all because I had the opportunity – the road was empty and open. Even inside the kibbutz I would drive fast, as if driving faster would get to me a safe destination faster. But it's impossible to know – even if you drive fast a Katyusha can hit you – perhaps if you had driven slower you would have been saved.

Towards the end of the war, I called the Human Resources Department of the Electric Company again and I explained the situation here one more time. I said: "Someone who lives in Haifa, even with all the rockets that fell there, doesn't understand what situation we're living in here. Don't expect me to come in to work."

And the truth is I acted according to the decisions of the Civil Authority (*Pikud Ha'oref*). I wasn't willing to chance driving the long distance into Haifa on the roads and I also couldn't leave my family. I felt that I needed to be here. How could I leave four children, one being a newborn, with my parents and wife? So from that standpoint it turned out well for me – there were some people who were forced to return to work or had their permanent status at work threatened with being fired.

We kept hearing from some who had fled that they were in this park or in that mall and how great it was – and here we were in the kibbutz under bombardment. But I had this feeling that I was guarding the outpost, especially the new neighborhood because there were almost no residents here. I felt like a patriot who was guarding the place. Other people who left called relating to us their difficulties, especially with their children who were totally confused by the situation – they weren't at home, but they also weren't on vacation. They weren't sleeping in their own beds. They were wandering from one mall to another in order to keep busy, totally going crazy. I considered those people who fled from their homes as the miserable and unfortunate ones – to be forced out of your home for a month. And my children, who were at home, were fine and managed with the entire situation. And that made me happy, really. Our children's behavior also helped us endure the war.

Once I went to Nahariya to buy things and afterwards I said that I wasn't going to do that again. I went to Dekel after a Katyusha fell on a parked car outside the market. I asked them if they had a shelter. One of the workers in the fruit and vegetable section said they had a shelter in the basement. Just as we finished this conversation, there was a really heavy barrage on Nahariya. I found out later that one of the Katyushas fell into the sea. It sounded as if it had hit an apartment building. An unbelievable explosion! So I ran to the shelter – it's some type of warehouse – and I was certain that when I left the building I'd find my car full of holes from the shrapnel, it was that close! I said to myself: "That's the last time I do something that ridiculous like going to Nahariya for supplies." Orit had told me not to go to Nahariya, go to the Alonit instead.

Noa

When I'm in a car and there have already been rockets that have fallen – I won't stop the car and lie on the ground, because you don't know where the next Katyusha will fall – on this side of the car or on the other. So I believe that you just need to continue driving, fast, in order to get to where you need to go. I had this really surrealistic feeling because the roads were almost empty.

It was unpleasant on the roads. We know the Hizbullah are there and that at any second they can shoot a rocket at you and you don't know where it's going to land. It's a more intense feeling than if you're at home or in your kibbutz. So if you happen to be outside when a rocket falls then you crouch down, but when you're on the road it's different.

I didn't eat much during this period. My parents got me some of the things I needed when they went out shopping for the senior citizens. I didn't cook much either during this time, but I normally don't do a lot of cooking since I don't like to cook. On the really long shifts, which often occurred on Fridays, I asked my mother to bring us something hot to eat so that we could feel that it was a special day. And there was always food to nosh on in the Situation Room and beverages to drink.

Once or twice I went on an organized trip south to the Center with the whole community. This specific time we had gone to Kibbutz Ga'ash. What was memorable was that during our return journey we had a funny experience on the bus. When we got to the area of Haifa there was a report on the radio that there was a siren in the Krayot, which was in the direction we were headed. So we circumvented the Krayot as much as possible. When we got to the Krayot, the reports of sirens were then for Acco. We got to Acco and everything's quiet. Then they announce that there were sirens in Nahariya. We get to Nahariya and we say (and got):"Quiet." We just wanted to get home to Gesher Haziv. It was really funny.

Lyn

On that Sunday, we had lots of rockets – 170 rockets. That was the day that the twelve soldiers were killed at Kfar Giladi.

I will say that come the last week of the war I had some thoughts about leaving because we were starting to go stir crazy around here. I am an outdoor person, so the idea of having to be confined inside pretty much twenty-four hours a day was very difficult for me. That was probably the most difficult aspect of the war for me. The house sort of tended to become a jail towards the end. I just want to go outside. I just want to go outside.

The activities for the children continued throughout the war every day from 9:00 to 12:00. It was only in the last few days that they had soldiers come in to do activities with the kids. That was a nice change. The kids couldn't concentrate enough to do things like homework and projects and things like this that they were assigned to do over the summer. We tried to do just little bits. They would concentrate for half an hour on their homework and that was enough. They really couldn't concentrate more than that.

The diary I kept was a day-by-day thing. I normally keep a work diary basically; it's mainly in Hebrew when it deals with work and when it's more family things I write in English. I started to use the diary as a journal during the war. I guess that was my way of sort of dealing with it – we sort of survived another day, write it down. I don't have rocket counts for every day, it was just the days that there was extremely heavy fire – fifty, sixty, seventy rockets a day became a normality! It was when it started to get over the 120-plus, 160, 170 – things like that.

A more normal entry reads: "August 7th. The kids went to activities from 9:00 to 12:00. I washed their school bags out and changed the sheets and put the laundry away. The kids did some of their homework that they were supposed to do over the summer."

The kids used the computer a lot and they got really into doing handicrafts. At the time this new plastalina book came out – how to make models with this material and all that sort of thing. So I managed to get them the book and they spent hours making models and painting, lots of board games. Alon and Ela learned how to play sheshbesh – backgammon – and games like that. And I was playing with them. We had a lot of time together.

Miri

The last week of the war, or so, I started to feel very uncomfortable not being at work in the bank, because other people were coming in to work. They were coming from the Krayot and from Carmiel and they were being bombarded just as much as I was. I said to Ilan: "Everyone's going into work, and I'm the only one who isn't!" I work at the branch in Kiryat Haim. So I said: "When Ilan isn't working, then I'll go in to work at my branch."

So I drove to the Krayot one day to work. Except that when I got there I wasn't really working, because during the last days of the war there were really heavy barrages in the Krayot. So every minute there were sirens and I had to leave my desk and go to the designated safe area. And we weren't sure what was happening. Are we going to open the main doors so that customers can come in or not? So I said, I'll go home. Then Ilan called me and said, "Don't come home." And I thought to myself "So what am I going to do?" The days I went to work Ilan stayed home with Noa.

When I drove to work it was really weird. The roads were empty. And there I was standing at an empty intersection. I think it was Sunday. I hear a siren, but I didn't really hear it because the air conditioner was going and so was the radio, and I think I really didn't want to hear it. And Ilan calls me on my cell phone and says: "Miri, I debated whether or not to call you and tell you that there was a siren. What was better – to have you under stress?" It's a red light and I wasn't certain what I was supposed to do. So I waited, after all it was a red light. And I thought that when it turns green I'll continue on my way. Afterwards, Ilan thought that I should have pulled over to the side of the road. I said: "Really. You want me to stop the car and lie down on the ground according to the instructions?" At the time it just didn't seem appropriate.

In my branch of the bank they organized mobile units and bank tellers drove in them and went to all kinds of out-of-the-way places. The people who worked in these mobile units were volunteers, and I have to give them credit, but it was crazy. The van they were in wasn't protected or anything. It was just like a taxi.

One man who works with me, he's an older man, was told that he needed to volunteer to work in one of these mobile units. During one of the days when I went in to work he sat next to me and asked me what I thought. I told him: "Are you in your right mind? Who told you that you have to go?" And he replied that he was told by our superiors. I replied: "Then if whoever told you that you have to volunteer goes with you in the mobile unit and sits beside you; maybe that makes sense." That was really something! On the one hand you want there to be bank services available because people need money, on the other hand you need to do things that make sense.

And it became a really crazy routine where I drove to work and Ilan stayed with Noa. One day Ilan said to me: "Miri, do you get it? We're driving to work in the Krayot under barrages of rockets or in possible target range." But we went. I don't know how to explain it.

During the last week of the war, there were times when Katyushas were falling nearby all the time. We were in the mamad with Noa, but I just couldn't handle being in that room anymore. I said: "I don't care any more. I'm going to sit at the dining room table and eat dinner like a civilized person and then I'm going to sit in my living room and watch TV!"

I think people's responses are extremely individual. Ilan was a little more cautious and thoughtful than I was. In the end I think we sort of balanced each other out. I became a little more cautious and he became a little less serious. But the war didn't end and it didn't end.

Sharon

The routine was to be at my parents' house and hang around. Every once in a while I needed a break, so I'd go away for the day, usually somewhere in the Center. When I was on my way back in the car, close to Acco, a siren sounded. And that was weird because everyone was looking at everyone else to see what the others did. There were about six cars in the area. I started to slow down. In the end everyone stopped and then we remembered the tragedy that occurred at Kfar Giladi so we all started to distance ourselves from the car. But then the sirens stopped.

Everyone looked at each other kind of embarrassed. So we all got back in our cars and drove off. I was driving north, so I decided to drive relatively slowly thinking that if something was coming at us I'd see it and be able to stop in time. There's really no place to hide. I was very afraid to drive, or to be more exact, to be on the road, and so I only went out when I really had to. And to tell you the truth the calm mood on Gesher Haziv suited me.

My routine changed some during the last week of the war. I didn't work any shifts in the Hamal at all. To get to the Situation Room you have go down some stairs, and then down another flight, and down once more. And after a while it became difficult for me to go down there. So I stopped volunteering. But, the last week of the war I found this little female kitten and adopted her. Her name is Guri.

This last week was very difficult for me. Without paying attention I found that Ronny and I were awake at the same time only about four hours a day. She went to her own house more. But anyone who's gone through something like this war with another person is bound to come out with a strengthened relationship. I saw her in situations that I'd never seen her in before. But the six weeks of the war were definitely enough.

I stayed awake later at night, so that I could sleep later in the mornings because the mornings disturbed me the most. My son lives in Moshav Liman and during this time he delivered one of the daily newspapers early in the morning on his motorcycle. So, every morning in my almost unconscious state, around 6:00, I'd hear him drive down the street on his paper route. It was so quiet that I'd hear him at the beginning of the street. Then I'd know he was safe and fall into a deep sleep.

Judy

That Sunday I went to work as usual. I decided to take Mayzie with me, even though Leah was home. I figured it would be better off for Mayzie to continue her regimen of going up to work with me, especially since people at work didn't seem to mind having her around.

A lot of mornings I'd drive up to work saying to myself: "Why do you want to be brave, why are you doing this?" Right. And I'd answer myself "I don't know, but I feel that I can do more at work anyway." I had a secure feeling at work, a more secure feeling than being at home. I also enjoyed being with other adults instead of being bundled up at home alone. I didn't want to be with kids. And even adults who didn't have little kids weren't around; they had gone away. So this way I at least had other adult company and could get some work done. I still wasn't always sure why I wanted to be brave. On the other hand,

I wasn't comfortable with the option of not going to work in the office and staying at home to work on-line. I also didn't want to go south or anything like that. As for convenience, I saw that the supermarket in Me'eillia was open. So if I needed something I could stop there on my way home.

Shanie

One evening my father and I went to visit my grandfather in the hospital. We were still in the basement shelter, but on our way out, we saw a person running at full speed straight at us. So we asked him if there was a siren, but he said no. So we went out of the hospital building. And as we did we heard rockets landing. It sounded like they landed close by. The next thing we knew a police officer was yelling at us to come into the auxiliary building where he was. He acted as if we had broken the law since we hadn't reacted to the siren, which we hadn't heard. We waited for about ten minutes and then drove the short distance home.

Shai

My office is not secure at all; it's on the second floor of a building. Fear is a relative emotion and it's difficult for me to think back to those days and time. But I think that the part of me that was fulfilling a job was stronger than the personal side of feeling fear. I remember going to the location of a hit and Katyushas passing by fairly closely and them hitting, and I remember crouching down and waiting for them to pass and then continued walking. There wasn't that feeling of having to seek cover or go into a security room or anything like that, because the need to do my job was stronger than my need for personal safety, if you want to call it that. I don't remember any feeling of fear, no personal fear.

Orit

For our children, summer camp was to go to the activities in the shelter. They went in the mornings for three hours, and sometimes they even stayed after for a bit. In the afternoons we would make a play date with other parents and children to meet in the shelter, even though there was nothing organized then. So they were in the shelter playing for a few hours in the mornings and a few hours in the afternoons, and then go to sleep later in the evenings. So it wasn't so awful for them as it seems. When you're on the outside, in my opinion, it appears a lot worse. During the few outings we went on it did appear much worse than when we were here.

Tammy

Barak was drafted on August 7th. He managed to get what he needed here and there, in Kfar Saba, for example, because nothing was open up here. Yehuda took him to the Hof Hacarmel station in the south of Haifa the morning of the draft. He wasn't on his way to work; he went there especially with Barak.

At work during the days throughout this entire time I was in my office as usual, which is on the second floor and totally unprotected. I had a constant internal debate: "Go downstairs or stay upstairs? Move my things downstairs or not?" I wanted to work in my office where I feel comfortable. But every time there was a siren I had to go downstairs. So I was constantly going up and down the stairs. It was a catastrophe. I finally had enough running downstairs for safety every time there was a siren or barrage of Katyusha rockets. So when the war was almost over, in the last few days, I finally did move my things downstairs and work there. Towards the end I also told Effie that I just couldn't do the Duty Roster for the Situation Room anymore. Then he organized Noa and Niria to do it; to run after people all the time for work during the day and shifts at night – who was here and who wasn't and who returned, etc. It just wasn't pleasant to have to keep asking people to do the difficult shifts at night or during Fridays and Saturdays.

When I was at home and there were Katyushas falling or a siren, I went into the security room, but I walked there, I didn't run. I stayed for a few minutes and then went back to where I was – usually in the living room area. Yehuda and I always said that above us there is another floor, so we're not all that unprotected. But when there were Katyushas that fell close, I dropped onto the floor. Yehuda felt that he didn't need to hurry into the security room when there were Katyusha barrages. And I told him: "Listen, we have four children and for them we need to safeguard ourselves." Our children were really worried about us. They kept saying, "Come." "Come." "Come." "Come." They really didn't like the fact that we chose to stay here.

Carolyn

Towards the end you were already more uncomfortable. It was a long war for us and it was very noisy and a lot of bombs, more than the usual. I barely watered my garden and I always water my garden, but I wasn't comfortable. We're here and we'll just put up with the Katyushas. I don't think that makes us big heroes.

We didn't have anything to do, like when the kids are coming home and you have to go shopping, or begin cooking or whatever.

Our lives just went into a different dimension. We were home. And I really think I was lucky that I went to work, because it broke the monotony of my daily routine. We went to Alonit quite a few times and that became a way of breaking the monotony as well. I definitely drove faster than normal, I wasn't crazy, but you were allowed through red lights – that was kind of fun.

The war really depressed me. And the longer it continued the worse I felt.

Teresa

One day Bethe called and suggested we go food shopping in Yarka (a Druze village in the Western Galilee). We took Bethe's youngest daughter, Meshi with us. It felt great to be out of the kibbutz for a change. It was a lovely clear day, but rather hot, since it was Israel in the summer. The supermarket wasn't very crowded, and since we'd never been shopping there before, it took us a while to find our way around. But we weren't in any hurry or anything.

On the way home we decided to eat at a humous restaurant in Kfar Yasif that Bethe knew of. There were other people in the restaurant, both Arabs and Jews, and the food was great.

The supermarket in Yarka didn't sell fruit and vegetables, for some odd reason, and we both still needed to buy some. We didn't see good quality goods at either the vegetable store near the supermarket or in Kfar Yasif, so we decided to go to Faisel's market a bit south of Nahariya. On the way to Faisel's there was a siren. Bethe decided to stop the car. We all got out and looked for a place to crouch down. Bethe led us behind a low stone wall. Meshi said that we needed to lie down, but I didn't want to since there was horse manure all over the area. I said to her: "Go on then, you go first;" the three of us just crouched.

Bethe

The Hof Hadekel food store, where I usually go shopping, was really getting low on supplies. The last time I was there the shelves were even emptier than before and the produce looked ever worse. The optimistic side of me says: "At least you have food to eat – it might be frozen products or a limited selection, but at least we have food."

However, I felt that I needed a break in routine so I called Teresa to see if she wanted a break as well. I thought about going to the Druze village, Yarka, where there is a big supermarket. Shanie was off at another seminar, so Meshi was our only child at home. She wanted to come as well, which was great since there was no way that

I was going to leave her home alone (she stays alone quite often during normal times, and has no problems being in the house for a few hours by herself) with Katyushas and sirens all the time.

The supermarket had everything we wanted and more, but they didn't sell fruit and vegetables (which I thought was strange). We had to go to another little store a few meters away that was a greengrocer. Even there I couldn't find fruit and vegetables that were fresh, so I didn't buy what I needed! Then on the way home we decided to stop for lunch at a humous restaurant. I looked for a grocery store and there once again the produce wasn't worth buying. We ended up going to Faisel's. The selection was varied there and I finally purchased what I needed that was also of a decent quality.

While driving from the village to Faisel's we got caught by a siren. We were just south of the main street in Nahariya, which had been heavily bombarded since the beginning of the war. To stop the car or not – that was my dilemma. On the one hand I had Teresa and Meshi with me and had to show responsibility. On the other hand, I wasn't certain that I wanted to be out in the open in that specific area in case a Katyusha did land close. Crouching behind a stone wall didn't really give us a lot of protection. But we went through the motions anyway. Luckily nothing fell anywhere near us, so we got back in the car and went on our way as if nothing out of the ordinary had happened.

The Sulam Tsor Regional Junior and Senior High School is located on Gesher Haziv. And since the war was on and still going strong I guess the army got permission to use the facilities for soldiers. So we started to see a lot of military trucks pull up and unload both equipment and soldiers. When Asher and I would walk Skippy at night we'd pass by the soldiers. We always say hello to people we pass, so we spoke to them as well. They were with the Golani unit and had been in some of the heaviest fighting in Lebanon. Now they were taking a break.

Since I would drive around the kibbutz and feed the cats every evening, I realized I was getting low on food, so I called Yulia, who was handling the distribution of food donations for animals. A colleague of hers said that I could come to Nes Amim to get some. I don't know why, but maybe because he was there at the storeroom and it was difficult to catch them, I decided to drive there then. It was around 12 o'clock. My daughters were sleeping. I left the house and drove. I had a very weird feeling on the road. As usual during this time the road was empty – it felt as if I were the only person around. But there was also this abstract feeling of threat since the Hizbullah could launch a Katyusha at any time. I drove very fast, got the cat food, and drove home very fast.

Yehudit and I were still working from our respective homes using Skype. We were managing to get a good number of articles covered, revising and creating new questions for them. We worked for an hour or two, sometimes more, each day. However, our concentration was often broken by having to stop for imminent Katyusha attacks or sirens. We'd have to stop what we were doing immediately and take cover. I went into the security room. Yehudit, who didn't have a security room stood next to an inner wall as far away from a window as possible. Sometimes there would be a siren near my house and I'd leave for a few minutes. Other times there would be a siren near her house and she'd leave for a few minutes. And other times we'd hear the sirens at the same time.

Every day I checked the news sites and some of the foreign newspaper sites. I guess this was part of how I attempted to deal with the tension. I also wrote tons of letters to news stations protesting the one-sided coverage of the war. I went "ballistic" about the coverage of the Kfar Kana tragedy. It was a tragedy that civilians lost their lives, but how can only Israel be blamed? Not only did we announce a warning (get that – we announced to the villagers that they should leave because something might happen – and I never *once* had the Hizbullah announce to me that they were about to shoot rockets so I could take cover); but these people had allowed the Hizbullah to use them as human shields. Anyway, I was reading a lot of reports about media manipulation with pictures and facts. And I realized that although many people did die, their bodies were being used as propaganda. How awful! What about sanctity of the dead?

Meshi

When we were driving on the roads I felt like: "Let's just get there already." I didn't really want to get on the side of the road and duck, it happened when we went with Teresa to the market. I wasn't scared, I was excited! My father did that a lot – get in the ditch and stuff – I didn't do that except for that one time. You have to have a little experience of everything. If you are in a war at least do it properly!

M

Even after some of my friends got drafted into the reserves, it didn't change my routine. I still got together with Avner and Eran from the village and I'd go swimming at the village in the small pool. My regimen didn't really change much because I was up during the nights in the Situation Room and during the day catching up on sleep a bit. I'm beyond doing reserve duty so this is what I could do. Basically I passed the time by having friends come and have coffee in my apartment, or I would go to them. And whoever was here functioned. It's probably easier when you're with other people.

I actually saw my neighbors more during this time than ever before and I got to know them better. They were here quite a lot and they have three kids.

I went to the Alonit for food shopping. During the day anyway I basically drink coffee and that I brought from Tel Aviv. And evenings I went to my parents – nothing really changed; this is my usual custom, except that I didn't work in my normal job. Once I wanted to go down to the Alonit to buy some food. I had just started my scooter and the siren started, then I heard a loud *whoosh.* I turned around and went back home. Basically I was playing a game – stepping in, stepping out.

Being out was not as scary as sitting inside and not knowing where the Katyusha barrage was coming from. And at some point you didn't know if it was ours, or theirs. This whole situation became surreal because we didn't know when the war was going to end. And at some point I started worrying about my paycheck.

Asher

My routine continued week after week – I'd get up, drive to the hospital to take care of my father, go to work, drive home, walk the dog, watch the news on TV in the evenings. In reality, this was almost exactly my routine in June before we went abroad and before the war. The only difference now was that we were at war. I never thought we'd still be bombarded after so many days. This situation had never occurred for so long in the past, even in all the times we'd been attacked by terrorists in Lebanon (first the PLO and now the Hizbullah). And I never believed that it would go on for so long!

One of my clients is a large factory that I have been writing software for, for over ten years. The factory is now located near Carmiel. And while the factory made a decision to continue working throughout this conflict, Carmiel was hit on numerous occasions by Hizbullah rockets. As usual I had many conversations on the phone with my contacts there. But, it happened that on a number of occasions, I called the computer office about work and no one answered. So I called my contact on his cell phone. He said that he couldn't talk because he was in a shelter due to a rocket attack or a siren sounding.

One evening I had an eventful drive home from work. When I was close to Nahariya the sirens sounded three different times. Each time I heard the alarm I went into Katyusha routine mode – stopped my car, got out quickly and lay down in a ditch by the side of the road. I'd wait a few minutes and then continue on my way. The first time I thought, "Okay, no problem." The second time I had only driven a few kilometers north when the sirens wailed again. Once more I went into Katyusha routine mode. The third time I'd had enough and didn't know whether to laugh or shout, although I stopped the car once more and lay down in the ditch. By the time I got home my clothes were full of burrs from lying in the undergrowth by the side of the road.

I went into Katyusha routine mode not from fear, but to minimize risk. You never know where the rocket will fall. There were a few other cars on the road at the same time. They didn't stop, but passed me at great speed. It was if they knew where the rocket would fall and by accelerating could thus get out of the area as quickly as possible.

I took Skippy for a walk almost every night. In normal times Bethe and I walk him along the security road, which surrounds our community. It's approximately a 4-km walk. Since the war, Bethe walks the dog in the morning and I walk him in the evening. I sit in an office all day in front of a computer screen, so I want to walk in the evening; Skippy needed a walk and I wanted the exercise. The Hizbullah had been into a routine of sending rockets at us between 17:00 and 18:00. I usually didn't go out before then. Once or twice it happened that there was a siren during the walk. I found a hole nearby, off the road, and lay down there. Skippy was on top of me and dripped saliva onto me. Yuch! Then after a few minutes wait Skippy and I continued.

Aliza

I wrote a few e-mails to family and friends during this period, to let them know we were okay. Towards the end of the war my cousin used some of this material in the letters I wrote and he made a big speech at a fund-raising affair in Scranton, Pennsylvania, where he lives. They gathered something close to $180,000 – anyway a large amount of money. Then he writes me: "What do I do with the money?" So, at that time there wasn't anything immediately needed by the kibbutz. I have a copy of his speech – it was really a riot! So he made a contribution to the hospital in Nahariya. His rallying speech contained what we had written about concerning what was going on here in the North during the war. That was good.

Paul

I went shopping at the Hof Hadekel this afternoon for some food and things. It was the usual wartime afternoon with rockets bombarding us late in the morning. Later I heard that a Katyusha had landed right outside the entrance.

The fact that Katyushas were falling when I was out working in the fields didn't bother me. It only bothered me because I knew that

that was the end of the workday because the workers would leave. My philosophy is that sitting in my living room or standing out in the bananas is more or less the same level of danger, so I might as well be out there. So I continued my routine – day in and day out – of going to work in the fields.

I think during the war I was out there (in the fields) until 14:00 or 15:00 in the afternoon until Kathy would call me – especially when there had been a lot of Katyushas – and nag me to come home already. So, I'd come home and rest for an hour or two and then return to see where they'd fallen. Something like that was my usual practice during the war. I'd work until 13:00 or 14:00 in the afternoon and then go back again at 16:00 or 17:00 for an hour or so and do a "*sivuv*" (spin around the fields) more or less.

Kathy

I didn't have any work and I went to the security room every time there was a siren. And then if it sounded close I'd call Paul on the phone and ask, "Are you still alive?"

Terry

I remember one day, sometime in the middle of all this, I was down in the fields with Paul late one morning after the contractor and the workers had left. We were tying banana bunches onto the open "train" carts near the shaded loading area (the "*shachha*") between the bananas and avocados. And then there was a barrage of Katyushas. Of course, there was no place for us to get shelter out there in the open. There'd be explosions going off all over the place and we'd just carry on.

Teresa & Terry

One day mid-week, sometime late in the afternoon we decided to go food shopping. We needed some food in the house, but the outing was more as a break from our daily routine than really needing food. We decided to go to the Hof Hadekel market this time – again as a break from our regular habit of going to Sabri. There had been Katyusha rockets falling late this afternoon. So we waited a bit after the barrage before we set out. The Hof Hadekel market is located in the northern area of Nahariya right on the sea. That street had already received a number of hits so far. As we turned onto the road where the market is located we saw a hole in the road where another rocket had probably fallen. Then as we drove on towards the south, we saw a lot of commotion. It appears that a Katyusha had made a direct hit on a car parked directly outside of the market. There were police and fire trucks and lots of commotion. We realized we would never be able to shop there that day, so we continued south to our usual market, Sabri's, instead.

And then one night we wanted to break our routine a bit, so Teresa and I dropped by to visit with Bethe and Asher. We stayed for a bit and then left. Suddenly I felt hungry. We didn't feel like going home, so we decided to find someplace to eat. The first place we stopped at wasn't open. We ended up driving to Acco where we found a Middle-Eastern folk restaurant near the main bus station open. It was an Arab restaurant – there were all Arabs in it; besides us there were no Jewish Israelis there. They had the TV on to the Arab stations, speaking Arabic. There we were, in the middle of the war, in an Arab restaurant. It felt a little bit strange since everyone was speaking Arabic, but they didn't treat us any differently or hostilely. At some point a soldier came in and we felt better. It felt like we were in the enemy zone, you know.

Helen

I was driving on the roads relatively a lot – going back and forth from Nahariya or to the hospital or to the Alonit. I was puzzled by the instruction that was put out if you hear a siren get out of your car. And I thought, "Why should I get out of my car? I'm in the middle of nowhere. What am I going to do?" So a friend told me that the rationale was that if the Katyusha hits the gas tank of the car then you're dead because you're in the car. But these instructions, it seems, were aimed at people who live among buildings and then you try to get behind a safety wall or something. I wasn't near any buildings. I was going from here to Nahariya and back. I really was lucky and I was on the road reasonably a lot.

On the other hand, we knew what the Hizbullah routine was – more or less – so you tried to do your errands either early in the morning or evening, or later at night to avoid the late morning or 16:00-19:00 slot of rocket attacks.

Each day was different for me. It depended on the shift in the Situation Room or what my previous commitments were. I wasn't sitting at home, whether sitting in the mamad or not, and watching television, which drove me crazy all together. I read a lot of mysteries, I've got to admit, rather than serious literature. I was really not concentrating on Dostoyevsky or anything like that. What I needed was something totally mindless. I can't even tell you what I read because it went in one ear and out the other, or in one eye and out the other.

Wednesday, August 9; Thursday, August 10; & Friday, August 11

Numerous Katyusha hits on Gesher Haziv and in the Western Galilee. Rocket hits in Nahariya, Acco, Ma'alot, Carmiel, Misgav, the Krayot, Kiryat Shmona, Safed, Beit She'an, and the Golan Heights, with some casualties and numerous fires in various areas from Katyusha hits. By 15:50 on Wednesday, 130 rockets have been launched into Israel. By 18:37 on Thursday, 155 rockets have been fired at Israel with seventy-six casualties; at 17:40 it is reported that 750,000 trees have been destroyed, with the cost of afforestation approximated at NIS 60 million. By 17:30 on Friday, there are forty-five Israeli civilian casualties and by 20:10, approximately 120 rockets have been launched at Israel by the Hizbullah.

Asher

Lavie called and said that he would be home for the weekend. The problem was that public transportation was sporadic at best because of the war. He would have to take a bus from the Golan Heights, where he was stationed, to Tiberias to Haifa to Nahariya. It was easier and quicker just to drive to Tiberias to pick him up since it only takes about an hour each way. Shanie decided to go with me for company.

We met him and Nimrod near the community of Migdal, north of Tiberias, and drove to Carmiel where Nimrod lives. He took his things and said farewell. Just then there was a siren. Nimrod hadn't had time to move from the car across the street so he stayed with us. The four of us lay down in the ditch by the side of the road. It was made out of cement so it was relatively clean. We waited for a few minutes and since nothing had fallen we separated from Nimrod and went on our way home.

Shanie

I was pretty excited when the attack at Carmiel occurred because I was finally able to react when a Katyusha attack was imminent. Lavie warned me that the ditch was probably disgusting because tons of people use it as a lavatory. But I lay down anyway and it didn't smell like urine. I guess my brother was just trying to unnerve me.

Helen

It was interesting how the cats took their cue from me. They knew it was calm here. The gray one did her usual rounds at night.

They weren't happy when I wasn't at home, which was a lot. They were very happy when I came home. Usually the reaction would have been: "Oh good, you're home, where's the food." Now it was: "Oh you're here, we need to be petted." And for the both of them to react that way was a lot since they don't usually talk to each other and when they do its adversarial.

Ronny

I was scared driving on the roads. Once when I was near Acco there was a siren – I had to make a decision, go forward, stay here, or go back. If I went forward it was going to be "*duch*" (straight ahead *fast*) – for life or for death – and that's what I decided to do. I lowered my head when I got to the area of Nahariya because that was a dangerous area and pushed straight ahead to the kibbutz. I prayed a lot and anything else that might help as well.

It doesn't matter how brave I think I am or that this situation is one that I can definitely handle – or whatever – it's frightening, there's no doubt. It's a feeling of hopelessness. You've got no idea where that rocket is going to fall – in front of you, behind you, next to you – until it falls you just don't know. But I believe in statistics and the statistics are still with me, so that's a bit calming. And I continued to drive when I needed to.

Evelyn

There were a few times when we were on the road and a Katyusha fell close to the car. You're on the road and you can't do anything. We didn't stop the car, we continued to drive. We had a mission to do and we did it. When we went south in the direction of Acco we knew that the care worker was waiting for us – that was what we had to do, to pick her up or take her home – so we didn't think about anything else. Ishai could definitely have driven alone, but I often went with him because I didn't want him to be alone. God forbid if something should happen.

I felt that the fact that I was doing something during the days – distributing papers, driving to get the caregivers for the old age home, being in touch with the seniors and visiting them, etc. – not that I'm important – but it gave me a lot of energy. I barely slept.

We don't have a security room that we can sleep in – it was torture to be in that room since it doesn't have an air conditioner. I had constant arguments with my husband who refused to go into that room – I said that he wants to leave us as a widow and orphans. Even if I said they're falling close by, let's go into the security room – he refused. He preferred to stand on the front porch and see what's going on around us – he felt responsible to report where the rockets were falling. So I said if he's outside, then I'm going outside as well. If you die, then I go as well. This argument went on all the time. But this is an old argument between us.

I have to say that we were greatly surprised by the intensity of the shelling this time. We're "accustomed" to being shot at by Katyushas from Lebanon. If twelve Katyushas were shot in the past, we said "Wow, what a quantity!" This time, I was astounded by the numbers of Katyushas that were shot at us, especially toward the end.

I honestly believe that there is something that protects the radius of Gesher Haziv because the rockets don't fall inside the community often, but mostly in the fields around the periphery of the kibbutz. This also happened to us during the 1982 war – Katyushas fell around us and not inside the residential areas. Something up there is protecting us and it should stay that way. And when you consider just how many rockets were shot at us during this war, it's remarkable!

Ishai

Sometimes I drove alone during my daily trips to pick up workers. Once, just as I got to the city, there was a siren. I had one caregiver who I had to drop off in Acco and immediately go fetch another caregiver for a shift in the old age home. The minute the siren went off, the people who were on the road stopped their cars and crouched down by the side of the car. I couldn't help myself, so I stopped my car as well. I went over to one of the drivers and I just had to ask him: "How you know that the Katyusha is going to fall on this side of the car and not the other?" Then I got back into my car and continued.

Lyn

On August 11th, we were going to visit Oren at Wingate and stay for the weekend. It was Ela, Alon, and me in the car. But just as I got to the intersection at Nahariya a siren started. The light was turning orange. And I said, "I'm sorry, I am just not stopping at a red light in Nahariya with the siren going." So I just continued through. And I said, "If they send me a ticket for this, I am going to have them check on their computer that there was a siren going at this point." And I was not stopping. I made sure that it was clear, but I am pretty sure that it was quite red when I was entering the intersection, but I was not stopping. I feel a moving object is harder to hit and if you're hit in a moving car then your number is pretty much up. I knew that there had already been two Katyushas fall near that intersection – so I was not stopping.

On a daily basis, I found myself going to sleep later than normal because I wasn't doing the physical activity that I normally do. So physically I wasn't tired. There was this sort of mental feeling which was tiring.

Well, I thought, I have all this time at home and there are lots of projects that I can do, like this album that I am now doing for Oren's bar mitzvah, for example, but the thing was that I found that I couldn't concentrate. I'm certain it was due to stress or whatever, but I just could not concentrate on these projects. I read a lot of good books during this time. I read things that were mostly easy to read and interesting. I used the Library quite extensively– more than usual. Also the kids – they used the Library quite a bit.

Micha

Even at work we weren't always able to keep things as normal as possible. There was a day or two when people were sent away from Bermad when there were high alerts, when they thought there would be more bombarding and Katyushas than usual. Or they cancelled the night shift. On some days when there were lots of sirens, there were a couple of times when they didn't provide lunch.

We tried to stay as calm as possible and live as normally as possible, not to show the children how stressed we were.

Judy

The last week we actually worked in the office in Tefen on Thursday. I had what to do and I wasn't running off to go anywhere. It was very strange to finally work on a Thursday. That probably sounds weird since a "normal" workweek would include Thursday, but what we've been going through wasn't "normal," it was surreal.

That Friday, the 11th, I had to get my car inspected, which is something every car owner must do once a year. I decided I was going to Yarka, I like going to the inspection station in Yarka anyway. I set out in the morning and hoped for the best. I got there fairly early and took care of what was needed to make the car pass the test. Since my car is fairly old it always needs some "tweaking." I also went shopping at the supermarket there. I drove home and had lunch with Leah and family. They went to their place to rest. I finished cleaning up just as I always do. We must have had a siren at that point because I went into the security room. I lay down on the bed there because I suddenly felt exhausted. I just wasn't feeling right. I woke up later and I called Leah and told them not to come over for dinner because I just wasn't feeling well. I just drank a lot of liquids and didn't eat. That was the beginning of the infection in my leg.

Danit

Once, when I was on my way to work helping distribute the mail in the Main Office Building, a rocket flew overhead. I looked up and said to myself: "Who has authorized someone to fly a model airplane in the sky?" Afterwards I got to the Mail Room and I said to myself: "Wow, it didn't have wings at all!"

On the one hand everything existed, on the other hand, we needed to protect ourselves. Except for the cracks here and there, the war wasn't really concrete. What happened – in therapeutic terms there's a "thing" called disassociation, which is a mechanism that protects people – I had never encountered it myself until this war. There were times when we felt that this was happening to other people, not really us. Or that it was happening in a movie, as if we were in a movie, all the Katyushas. I never internalized what was happening.

Towards the end of the war, on Thursday I think before the cease-fire, I drove to Alonit and I saw an ambulance leave the area of Polyziv because a Katyusha had fallen there and two people were injured. The ambulance was just passing, so I stopped my car and waited until it passed and the road was clear.

I looked at the mountain opposite (Sulam Tsor) and I saw the remains of fires like bald spots or wounds on the mountain. And I thought to myself: "What for?" In other words, it might sound like diluted philosophy, but that was what was in my head at the time. I think that was the first time that I stopped for a moment to ask, to think about what was going on around me. Before that, I tried not to think too much, not to see too much, not to hear too much, and not even to get into those questions that make you feel bad. I think it is a type of survival mechanism, not to go too deeply into what is going on; let it pass, and hope that it passes next to you or opposite you and not affect you, and continue on. And try to have as much fun as possible. And I think that's what we did the entire war. We tried to pass through this entire war with a smile on our faces. It's true that we put our heads in the sand a bit, but at least our mood stayed positive.

Paul

I went to the supermarket Hof Hadekel today to do some shopping. I'd been there the same day that the Katyusha fell right next to there the last time, but about an hour or two before. But when I went back there afterwards and there was a siren I'd say to myself, "Shit, this is one of the Hizbullah targets," but it didn't really move me that much. I continued going there when I needed to.

As the weeks went by I had the feeling of "enough is enough," basically. This situation just sort of wears you down after a while. I'd been used to it from the past – a week or a few days or something like that – it's almost fun when it's a week or so, but when it drags on like this it becomes very nerve-wracking. Also at work the fact was that everything was falling behind, I was just losing control. I still haven't regained control months later.

Aliza

Zvi and I decided not to go on the outings from the kibbutz. At the end they offered us something in Jerusalem, but it was at a place where we couldn't park our car, and there weren't any organized trips or anything, and we would have used those few days just to visit with people. I didn't want to go out, but I was glad that they managed to get other people out. The people who did go really enjoyed themselves; they got that relief they needed. After we came back the second time from Tel Aviv we didn't move until it was all over, we didn't go away on the weekends. So by the end we were here for close to three weeks.

Tammy

My daughters didn't come up here to visit during the war as they usually do. Ayala said at some point that she wanted to come and we persuaded her not to. Karen didn't want to come at all, and that was fine. So we met them in the center of the country.

Helen

I worked a lot of shifts in the Situation Room throughout the weeks. What was for me the most rewarding part of working in the Hamal was the opportunity to meet people who I would never have otherwise met. And since we were doing shifts with two people, sometimes overlapping with three, I worked with many different people including people of different generations, including youngsters I had never exchanged two words with before this. I discovered that they were amazing young people who really took on leadership in every sense of the word. Maybe some of the kids are kind of spacey in other things, but for the work they had to do in the Situation Room, they were terrific. Reliable. It was just wonderful. I met people from the two communities when we were matched to work. Physically I live in the new neighborhood, but I really belong to the kibbutz. But meeting people from the neighborhood on that basis was also a positive experience.

Sharon

This is my home and you want things here that are yours, even if it's only the garden. My routine was the garden. If I didn't have the garden I wouldn't have held together. I was afraid when I was working outside, but I still went out to work there, because I was also afraid inside. So what's the difference? When I sat inside and watched TV I realized how much glass there was around me. If I went into the security room there wasn't glass, but the feeling was not one that I wanted to deal with for long.

Bethe

One day (who remembers when), Yehudit and I had to stop working every five minutes or so because of so many sirens going off. After thirty minutes or so of "this" we just quit working for that day, it was too frustrating. Trying to think rationally and clearly about texts and questions is difficult during a regular day, but during a war it was close to impossible. However, actually getting into this regimen of working almost every day, even if it was for only an hour or two, helped keep us focused on something other than the surreal situation we were in.

I woke up one morning to the sound of Katyusha rockets landing in the vicinity. I didn't get up and run into one of the security rooms in the house. In fact, I continued to lie in bed and went back to sleep. I couldn't be bothered to move. I felt that if a Katyusha was going to violate the sanctity of my home – then welcome. I was tired of the constant concern that this war was forcing into my consciousness.

Later that day I went to the Hof Hadekel store to buy provisions. There again I saw the results of this lengthy conflict. Many of the shelves were empty, the fruits and vegetables were in pretty bad shape, and the store was almost empty of customers. The cashier told me that they couldn't get their usual suppliers to deliver anything so that they were running through whatever stock they had in their warehouse. On the one hand I can't say that I didn't have food, but on the other hand I didn't have the selection that I normally have.

Hannah

Towards the end, fewer people came and went through the eastern door in the shelter, the one closest to the new neighborhood, so the disturbance was less. For the most part we got along. We all knew what the situation was – it wasn't my house and not the usual group of people who I am with. Not too bad.

Miri

One evening I had just cut up salad and we were about to eat dinner when the rockets started falling. Ilan said to me: "Come, we'll go to the mamad." And I said: "No, enough. I'm going to eat my dinner here."

Our friends who live off the kibbutz were in contact with us all the time. They invited us to their houses and were really worried. They always asked if we were all right. We really didn't meet much with friends who live here during this time. We saw Leah once or twice; she came to our house once also, mostly so that the children could play. Maia was alone and so was Noa. Not that many of my friends stayed here, so I didn't really have anyone to visit with.

Kathy

This war is really dragging on and I've had enough. For me it hasn't been traumatic or anything – I wasn't scared and I wasn't uptight. I didn't have many responsibilities. But this is not my "normal" life and I've had enough. The house was a mess; I didn't feel like cleaning it.

Teresa

Whenever I needed to go food shopping – which seemed like every day – I'd go in the mornings. The roads around Nahariya were virtually empty. I was able to drive as fast as I wanted to. The police weren't giving out tickets, since they were busy with other things. I drove fast out of sheer pleasure and the ability to do so, finally. I wasn't scared when I was out, though.

Carolyn

You would think that if I'm a nurse at a hospital near the front I would get to take care of a whole lot of soldiers at Nahariya Hospital. Unfortunately, most of the soldiers went straight to Rambam in Haifa. So we took care of a lot of wounded civilians. But since I work regularly in a trauma unit, I got to be in the Emergency Room a few times; that's when I got my picture in *Time Magazine*. It's really nice taking care of soldiers by the way, that's what I remember from Shlom Hagalil, that it's much nicer treating twenty-year-old kids because they do so much better than the usual hospital patient. If you've got to be nursing in a war you'd feel better if you get to treat wounded soldiers. Of course, I was lucky to be in the Emergency Room when they brought in a lot of wounded people if that was my shift. I remember saying to my head nurse that we're all going to get really fat – I was eating all the time. It's very easy to sit and eat. Eugene doesn't nosh, but I do.

Saturday, August 12 & Sunday, August 13

Numerous hits on Gesher Haziv and in the Western Galilee. Rocket hits in Nahariya, Shlomi, Ma'alot, Acco, the Krayot, Haifa, Kiryat Shmona, Safed, Shlomi, Emek Yizrael, Upper Galilee area, and Carmiel. By 15:18, the police reported that since the beginning of the war 3,650 rockets have been launched at Israel by the Hizbullah; 835 were planned to land in residential areas; there were 1,874 civilian casualties; Kiryat Shmona suffered 930 hits, 730 in Nahariya, 584 in Ma'alot, 448 in the area of Safed, and 181 in the area of Tiberias. By 19:18 on Saturday, sixty-five rockets have been launched at Israel since the morning hours. By 18:15 on Sunday, 230 rockets have been shot at Israel on that day (a record number) and over 3,800 rockets and missiles since the war began.

Lyn

On Saturday we were still in Tel Aviv. I asked the kids if they wanted to stay another few days. They were talking about the cease-fire and that it would probably be on the 14th. And I asked them: "Do you guys want to stay here until it finishes?" And they said "*No! No! We have our things to do on the kibbutz!*" They had their own routine and that was their way of dealing with it. The thought that they would miss their activities on Sunday – they couldn't deal with that! They were going to their Sunday morning activities from 9:00 to 12:00, have me pick them up and bring them home and have lunch together and then do something together in the afternoon. Have the evening meal.

I was surprised. We tried to make it fun when we went somewhere. We would go bowling or go see a movie like a holiday – away from the situation – so I was surprised that they didn't want to stay longer. They really didn't. They had their routine and I really think that was their way of coping.

There was only one day when Bermad sent the employees home after they started back to work, and that was on August 13th. That was the day when we had something like 250 Katyushas strike. I also counted twenty-six sirens that day. They just couldn't deal with it in Bermad. People were going in and out of the security room with every siren. It just got to the point that they weren't getting any work done, so they just said, "Look, just go home." So Micha came home.

I don't know what the last weekend was like because we went to Tel Aviv, but we came back that Saturday night for the grand finale! I was not traveling during the daylight hours at all. And we woke up to the incredible number of rockets being fired at us! I would go into the security room when there was a siren or I might already be in there playing a game with the children. But it was just non-stop that day. I counted that day because it was really starting to get on my nerves that the sirens were just going off like that. It was right before the end and it was really bad.

That last night we slept in the security room with our children, but we banished Ela's hamsters to Alon's room! Apart from that we had been sleeping in our bed and the kids had been sleeping in the security room. And it was probably the most sensible thing to do.

There had been Katyushas coming over all that morning as well as really heavy artillery from our side. The echoing of it here was something else. So I didn't have a lot of faith that the cease-fire was actually going to go into effect.

Then everything fell silent. And it was actually quite eerie. After weeks of this constant background boom, boom, boom – the silence. You could say that the silence was deafening. It was quite strange. It was quite a surreal experience really. All of a sudden it's quiet. We were still on alert, which was that we were supposed to stay in our security rooms at this point basically because I don't think anybody was really sure what was going to happen. We weren't going to release people. Micha went to work of course, as usual.

Judy

That Saturday my leg started hurting me. I took Acamol and just felt awful. On Sunday, I finally took my temperature and saw it was very high. I called work and told them I wouldn't be in that day, not because of the war, but because of the temperature. I rarely get sick, so this was definitely abnormal. I decided that I was going into town to see the doctor. I was feeling bad enough that I was willing to have Leah drive me into Nahariya. But that was the day when they were firing a lot. Any time we made an attempt to get into the car with the kids there were more Katyushas, more warnings and more rockets falling. I finally told her to keep the kids at home – don't risk it.

I started driving into Nahariya alone. There was a Katyusha siren just as I got to the gate of the community. I stopped the car, but I didn't quite get out. I put the car near the guard booth hoping that if anything did fall close by the booth would protect me. I waited until I heard all the boomings finish and kept driving into town. I really wanted to see the doctor, I felt that bad. Waiting to see a doctor was a terrible experience. There were sirens all the time I was at the HMO Kupat Holim Clalit. With every siren that sounded I had to debate with myself whether to go to the shelter in the building or not. The walk down to the shelter was difficult for me then – back and forth and in and out for a while. I finally got to see a doctor and he said, "Well, it's a little infection, it's nothing." He gave me antibiotics and told me to go home. Later that afternoon another one of my daughters, Lior, came from Jerusalem, and helped take care of me. (Note – it was only after the war ended that I was able to see my family doctor and really get the infection taken care of!)

Asher

One evening I was out on my regular evening walk with Skippy. We left the house shortly after an attack. The rockets sounded as if they had landed close by. But since we hadn't received an SMS message from the Situation Room, I figured that even if it had landed in Gesher Haziv, it was probably in the fields or in an open area. I was walking along the security road on the east side of the kibbutz (close to the new neighborhood), when I saw smoke about 100 meters from the security fence in the field. Then I looked west, in the direction of the houses, and saw Ronny and Sharon sitting on the porch of their house. I asked them if the smoke had been caused by a Katyusha rocket. They said yes. They had watched it as it fell so close by.

Helen

One afternoon I was working on the computer and my calico cat reacted; obviously she heard the whiz of the Katyusha before it landed, again close by. She had been sitting between me and the keyboard, which is her favorite place, although it does make it very difficult for me to write that way. In those few seconds or whatever it was, her body language changed immediately as if she was saying: "Well, something's happening," because it was a different noise than she had registered before. Then we heard the whoop, which was a big whoop, but she'd already jumped before that. In other words it was that thin sound, which I'm sure animals are much more sensitive to than people. Anyway it was interesting.

Ronny

Sometime towards the end – there was already a lot of talk about a cease-fire – everything we heard in the media was connected to a cease-fire. That was the operative word. We're sitting on the porch, as usual, and suddenly Adar Sharif came for a visit. He'd been in Tel Aviv for a while and had come back. So he sat down with us and asked: "So *nu*, how is it in your daily routine? Is there anything fun to do? Is there any adrenaline or excitement around here?" That must have been the "discussion" in Tel Aviv as to why people chose to stay in the North.

So we said that there is definitely some amount of excitement to be had at the front and to be in the middle of it. And I started to tell him that a few days before I was sitting in that exact place on the porch when a Katyusha fell about 200 meters to the east of us behind the row of cypress trees past the fields. I saw the smoke and the small mushroom cloud from the explosion. The noise really causes you to have the shivers. And just as I was telling him about the noise – that's what we heard. Was that a rocket just being fired? Sharon said no, that's a whiz (meaning it was already in flight and close to us). And then there was the explosion. Another Katyusha must have fallen to the north of us at almost the same time. But this one fell 50 meters from us in the field. That was extremely loud and intense. After the initial shock of the explosion the next thought in my head was, "Where's the camera?"

Sharon

We dropped to the ground and got under the table. I think we felt the shock wave as well. My entire body was shaking. I heard the whiz before the Katyusha landed and I knew it was very, very close. I ran into the security room and we didn't get any pictures. Then one of the neighbors came out of his house and drove through the fields around the road to get to the site. He brought a shard of the rocket to us as a souvenir.

Benny

One day a Katyusha fell close by. I went outside and saw where it had fallen because there was still smoke emanating from the hole.

I told Orit that if it continues like this we'd need to find another place to be. I started to look on the Internet for kibbutzim that were hosting refugees from the North, in places located further south than Tel Aviv. In the end we got to Kibbutz Revadim. But they wanted full payment for the rooms – this was close to the end of the war. We went there Sunday, August 13th and returned on Tuesday after the cease-fire began. But once again I didn't feel comfortable that I was leaving so close to the cease-fire. I said to myself: "Why are we leaving the house now? Now of all times?"

We arrived there. We didn't have such a good time because the place is not as good as Eilat. It was difficult to get accustomed to the atmosphere, although we went to "Little Israel" and met people from the kibbutz who had come on a bus. That was great for the kids to meet some of their friends again whom they hadn't seen in over a month.

M

Towards the end of the war I had this feeling that it was going to end really soon. But relatively there were more sirens then and close hits – it was very noisy here the last two days, but I think I probably went to the security room less. I got used to it.

Every time you go out of the kibbutz you can just feel how apprehensive you are – if there is a window shaking a little bit, you feel like it's another Katyusha hitting. But basically, if you hear it hitting, you're okay.

Danit

In the last two days of the war we were staying at a friend's house in Beit Yehoshua (near Netanya in the center of the country). There was already discussion of a cease-fire, so we allowed ourselves to go away, along with our dog, which was also one of the reasons we decided to stay at home. The places where we could have been evacuated to didn't allow animals, and our dog is a part of our family.

Ilan

The last days of the war, the days before the cease-fire, were really difficult because a lot of rockets were launched and fell on us or in this area. We got out of our little bubble, and I just went outside, put on gloves, and planted some trees in our garden. I planted vegetables such as cherry tomatoes, or other tomatoes. And even with all the action going on around us I just got into planting our garden. I know it wasn't rational, but I had just had enough.

Micha

My boss, he was on reserve duty and he was in Lebanon some of the time. You think about the people who were in Lebanon as well. I was very sad in Evron the few days before the war ended when the helicopter was shot down. The pilot was from Evron; he was a *ben meshek* (a son of the kibbutz – born and raised there), so it was a time of sorrow and sadness. That's when it hit as well – I didn't know anyone else who had a close relative hurt in this war, other than this family from Evron. I work with his mother very closely in the offices.

Miri

There was some discussion of a cease-fire. Then one day we drove south to Dor Beach to meet friends. The entire morning it was quiet. We were in the water and on the beach and having a great time. Around three in the afternoon we drove home. And then the barrages started. We had already begun to think that we would have a quiet evening as well. Unfortunately, we would have to wait another day for the quiet.

Bethe

I took Skippy for a walk late this morning and I suddenly noticed how long the grass had grown in the public areas in the center of the community. He's gotten into the habit of flipping himself over and rubbing his back in the long grass. The gardening crew hasn't been at work for weeks now, and the long grass is just one of the signs of their absence. It's as if time has stopped on the one hand, but on the other hand the hours and the days are definitely passing by.

We finally decided to break our routine a bit and take advantage of the offers for residents of the North throughout the country. The Cameri Theater in Tel Aviv was offering a half-price discount on theater tickets to residents from the North. We managed to arrange a day and get tickets when all of us (Asher, me, Shanie, and Meshi) could go. It turned out that this day was the last one before the cease-fire between Hizbullah and Israel kicked in. There was heavy rocket fire throughout the morning and early afternoon, so that when there was a sudden cessation of fire, we decided to leave earlier than we had planned taking advantage of the situation and moving quickly.

The play was a comedy and quite delightful. We had decided beforehand to drive home that night (we often do that), however we expected a rough night between the two sides – last licks or who can do more damage in the shortest amount of time. We expected to be up and down all night running in and out of the security rooms. But no, we were able to sleep soundly.

I don't think we really believed that we had had a quiet night in the morning when we awoke. Asher did his "thing"; got up and went to work. I got up with him and did my "thing" around the house. Then everyone just kind of waited until 11:00 when the cease-fire was to become official. Nothing happened to change the sudden quiet. We kept waiting for the bombardment to start again. Just to make certain, no one was "dancing in the streets" or even walking around freely outside as we once did before this period in our lives.

Tammy

At the very end, the last week of the war, the Regional Council organized a trip to Jerusalem and so Yehuda and I decided to go. So during the last days of the war I wasn't here. I felt great being in Jerusalem and not being on Gesher Haziv. We heard that the last days were really difficult with major barrages of Katyushas and a lot of sirens. So it was great to leave for a bit. I can't remember when we left the kibbutz – whether it was Sunday or Monday – but we came back on Thursday because Barak was supposed to come home from the army for the weekend.

Monday, August 14

At 8:00 the cease-fire goes into effect according to U.N. Security Council Resolution 1701.

Shanie

The day the cease-fire was scheduled for I had a seminar organized by the Youth Movement in Rosh Ha'ayin (in the center of Israel). I wanted to return with my parents after the play the night before because I wanted to sleep at home. I wanted my own bed and surroundings. At the seminar the organizers made certain that we were kept informed of what was happening – that the cease-fire really happened and what was happening at the political level.

I was there for three and a half days, so I missed the final adjustment period on the kibbutz. When I came back everyone was happy and alive. There were cars and people. The *Oref* (the Home Front or Civil Defense), our gathering place on the kibbutz, was suddenly full of people.

Judy

The day of the cease-fire I felt relieved that I didn't have to be brave anymore. I felt a little bit, and sometimes a lot, disappointed – if that's the way to describe it – we started this whole thing because we were going to free the two soldiers and we didn't do that. We lost a lot of lives, people I knew or friends of people I know.

Micha

I think we, Lyn and I, only slept in the security room the last night. We were debating yes or no, just before the cease-fire, because we knew that both sides would try to shoot at each other as much as possible. At about 4:00 or 5:00 o'clock in the morning there was a lot of activity and shelling. The cease-fire was supposed to start at 8:00. That day at Bermad we didn't start work before 10:00 or 11:00, just to make sure, because they were also expecting heavy bombardment in the last hours. So we started late that day.

Shai

"M" sat in the Situation Room Sunday night. Monday we had it working on minimal staff for just one more extra day, a spare day. We knew ahead of time that the cease-fire was beginning Monday morning. We deliberated whether to have the Hamal continue working that Sunday night or not, but we did.

We informed people that we were going to close down the Situation Room at 10:00 in the morning. And an hour or two before that, two or three people and families arrived one after the other, from the new neighborhood. They came to the Situation Room and told the people who were working there at the time: "We didn't have the opportunity before to say thank you. You made the entire war so tolerable for us, since we knew that we had people who were thinking about us. And you deserve a thank you." They didn't tell me; I think Helen and Niria were the ones working during that last shift – they were there. I looked into Niria and Helen's eyes and saw just how much it meant to them to receive that thanks. They received an answer for all they did during the war. And I think that until that exact moment they hadn't really understood what the other side felt about having that Situation Room behind them.

This last week, the Regional Council organized a few days in a hotel with a limited number of places available. So we decided to give the option to those people who were busy during the war – to those formal and informal jobholders who did a lot. So there were ten couples that went to Jerusalem. And it was very good and important to give those people a good feeling about their work. After that there was a gathering at the beach that the Regional Council organized to go over the crisis and how it was handled.

The direct translation for Hamal is War Room, but it wasn't a War Room, it was a Community Room. It didn't function as a place that made military decisions. It worked as a back up, as a response for personal and community needs. I think that the real story of the war was the Hamal – the people who volunteered and worked there – they listened and gave answers. From my perspective that is the story of this war on Gesher Haziv.

Throughout most of Monday we had one person working in the Situation Room most of the time. Then around noon or early afternoon we decided to keep the Situation Room open until 22:00 that night. We informed everyone by SMS and then at 22:00 we closed it. During the last hour or so we were engaged in dismantling everything – moving the refrigerator and all the other equipment. That's it, we closed it.

The whole thing ended in one second and the energies dissipated – that's how it goes with these kinds of things.

Bethe

Monday, August 14, 2006 was the day that the cease-fire took effect. I keep waiting for the rockets to start falling again. The noise and the fear and the surreal situation has been going on for so long that it's hard to believe that it's really over. People still aren't acting "normal" – but then again what is normal now? Our routine has been dictated by the Hizbullah and their rockets for over five weeks and that surreal reality has become what we know and expect – in essence, reality.

I went outside to work in the garden that first afternoon of the cease-fire. It was eerily quiet outside – no artillery, no people walking about or sounds of life. I knew that it was "okay" to be outside – the threat of a Katyusha rocket catching me suddenly unaware and unprepared was minimal, but I couldn't totally relax. I still didn't feel safe.

CHAPTER FOUR
After The Cease-Fire

Helen

We at Gesher Haziv were lucky, so it is easy to see this as a positive experience socially, even as we deeply regret the tragic situations that occurred to others. A lot of tragic stories happened to people we know well or peripherally. Considering that 4,000 Katyushas were fired at us in Israel, and the damage that could have been caused, as a country we were lucky. I was bleeding for those people in Beirut and throughout Lebanon – I'm not saying that it could have been done differently. Not only wasn't I rejoicing, but I was very unhappy. But thank God I'm not the prime minister or the defense minister and I don't have to make decisions, just take care of my own little corner. It was all very surrealistic. I don't think it will ever end. I don't see any constellation in the foreseeable future of it getting any better – the Sunni/Shi'ite civil war will have tentacles that will get longer and longer. We are the only unifying factor. We're small potatoes, but the fact that we might just get roasted to hell is part of the ironic situation we're in. In my opinion, the cease-fire should have been three days earlier. The cease-fire – in the short term I believed it would work, but I don't believe it will in the long term.

Lyn

I was quite apprehensive about this cease-fire. I didn't have a great deal of trust that the Katyushas were going to stop, when they said that at 8:00 o'clock the cease-fire was going to go into effect, particularly since we had such heavy shelling that morning as well.

There had been Katyushas falling that night as well, the night before the cease-fire, which was probably the first time that we had Katyushas coming over during the night.

After the war, when the kids returned to school, the teachers did a lot of activities with the kids about the war and stress and everything. I actually got a phone call from Ela's teacher saying: "Ela drew this picture today that we're a little bit concerned about." She drew a picture of the security room – a square box – with her in it crying. And I asked her why was she crying in the picture? And she said because the Katyusha fell on the school and it frightened her.

So we had a chat about the Katyusha falling on the school and I explained to her that yes, it was frightening, and yes, she's right it was a shock to us when it happened because we weren't prepared – it was the Big Bang – that was the start of the war really for us – the Katyusha falling on the school. And I asked her was she frightened being here. She said she was frightened with all the bombs. So I said okay, fine. I asked her: "Are you frightened now?" and she said: "No."

So I said to her: "If it starts again do you want to stay at home or do you want us to try and go somewhere else?" And she thought about it – she didn't give me an immediate answer – and she said that she thinks that if it happens again she would want to stay here again. Because she feels safe in the house, so she actually feels safe with what we did.

I tried to put it into some sort of context for her and I said to her: "More people have been killed on the roads in Israel than in all of the wars," or something like that. "You're not frightened about traveling in a car are you?" And she said: "No." So I said: "Look, it's true that a Katyusha could have landed on the house" – it's a possibility. She knew that one landed just behind us and we had damage and they were here when that happened. So she knew. And I said you can't let it rule your life. You have to live. Everything you do is a risk – crossing the road is a risk, driving to Nahariya is a risk, eating fish is a risk if you get a bone in your throat or whatever. With everything you do you take some sort of risk; there is a consequence to every action. You can't let it stop you living.

And that was part of the reason that we stayed, because we chose to live here. We discussed it long and hard before we left Australia, when we made the decision to come to Israel – a permanent decision – because we knew that once we came here the children would have the language here, this would be their culture, their friends would be here, the education, everything. And it is very difficult to pull a child out of that, and try to give them a separate culture. So we knew that when we came here it was as permanent as permanent can be.

This is part of living here. We knew that Katyushas fell on Gesher Haziv; we knew that we're 4 km from the border.

It's not a surprise to us, but we did try to minimize the risks for our family as well. It's not as if we went for drives along the border or anything like that. We really tried to be sensible in a non-normal situation – what can I tell you – minimize the risks. But at the same time I did mow the lawn and do things like that because I guess it was my defiance. This is my life, this is my home, and I am going to mow my lawn and I am going to pull the weeds out of my garden. I felt that was my way of defying what was trying to be imposed upon me.

When it is looked at in the final analysis it was a very boring experience. It is very difficult to explain that to somebody like my mother who lives on the other side of the world and was getting CNN reports and the BBC and the SBC, and everything else – she was being bombarded by all this information. She's been here, she knows the names of places, she knows Nahariya and how close Nahariya is and when they're talking about the bombs falling and when it hit Nahariya Hospital and the rest of it; she is very well aware of how close these places are. It is very difficult to explain to somebody when you're sitting at home in your security room that it is actually quite boring. It is stressful, yes, but when all is said and done it was really very boring. I would really rather have been at the beach swimming or something else – but not sitting here missing my nice Israeli summer.

That is probably my kids' biggest complaint now – that they didn't have summer holidays! Sorry guys, I was very happy to see the school year roll around!

I really feel that it took a couple of weeks after the war for us to get back to normal – to feel normal again – it wasn't an immediate thing, it was progressive, one foot in front of the other before we really got back into our normal routines and started feeling comfortable doing our normal stuff. The kids – I found it very strange – when they could go out of the house, they had got themselves into such a routine of being in the house – it was like, "Go outside already guys! Take the ball outside and kick it around a bit or something." It was almost as if I forced them out of the house at the beginning.

It probably took two weeks for us to really get back to feeling comfortable. And even now I have this feeling that it's not finished – that there is unfinished business here somehow. It's not something I'm happy about that I have this feeling, but there is something in the air that it's not finished. Hopefully it won't go back to an armed conflict again. But I just don't know, I just don't know. Already Nasrallah is telling us, "Until Israel leaves all Lebanese soil it's not finished!" So I don't know. We'll see what happens.

Shanie

What I can tell you that really bothered me was the indifference of the world towards us (the Israelis). Over thirty days we were sitting in shelters, seriously – over thirty days – or in rooms or our houses or in our kibbutz, feeling trapped in our own country, our own environment and I think that is what really broke me personally. That's what made me feel bad about the whole war – that, in addition to so many soldiers dying. We needed to defend ourselves, but there were too many things that I don't think we handled correctly. We still haven't gotten our kidnapped soldiers back (at the date of this writing), the Ministry of Education didn't do anything to help all the pupils in the North with their matriculation exams, and the government didn't take care of the citizens in the North who were under attack for so long.

Judy

I think that the first few days after the cease-fire I was wondering if something would happen. But the truth of the matter is that at that point I was sick and with the infection in my leg I was fairly miserable. At the same time I also developed an abscess and I was in total misery. My own personal health was occupying my mind far more than what was happening outside. I just wasn't worrying if the cease-fire would hold.

I figured it would hold as long as we kept our side of it. But we didn't achieve the initial goal that we went in for. I don't think it was so bad that we cleared out a lot of the stuff they had aimed at us. They obviously had a lot. They say they've re-armed already. I think all these years we've been in a constant cease-fire we haven't been at peace.

Sharon

At this time my parents were supposed to return from abroad. Throughout most of the war Ronny and I stayed in their house, and we had a great time there. We were two people in this nice, big house. But what would we do with more people around, especially if all of us had to be in the security room. In addition, we'd been here for more than three weeks already and I started to think, "Maybe my luck's running out." But there was no need to worry. The cease-fire began, they returned from abroad and we each returned to our own apartments. Anti-climax. It ended.

This was a trial by fire, literally for us. Maybe because we're people from the city and bit more closed than the kibbutzniks; it's not easy to come from the city into a community like this one. But this war really helped us to connect into the community, to connect with other people. You learn that you can rely on that person afterwards. All of a sudden the community seems smaller and more intimate. There are some really nice people here. The community was relaxed, considering the tensions.

There were a lot of positive experiences in the very large negative situation; at least something very positive came out of the bad. I feel much more connected to this place now. Look – we really didn't do anything. Here we were working in our garden and then bang! It's not like living in the city and not knowing what's going on.

Ronny

The cease-fire was a real anti-climax for me. You get up in the morning and it's announced that there's a cease-fire. The following day the return to normalcy was almost 100%. And I was left with this feeling that suddenly I was left hanging up in the air. Also, I really didn't have a daily routine to return to because just before the war the work I was doing ended. And throughout the war there was nowhere for me even to begin looking for something new. I was already unemployed and then this further forced unemployment for another five weeks really left me with a feeling of helplessness. And no one can guarantee that this period of unemployment won't influence my chances of future employment in some way.

A return to routine here in the North is difficult anyway because employment opportunities are minimal to begin with and now it's even harder. I had a feeling, and I thought, that maybe now after the "situation" of the war there would be financial investment in this area and more resources, so that employment and development opportunities would arise. It doesn't appear to me that it's happened yet. It doesn't seem that the government or businesses are looking for new projects because there's suddenly money available – there is no money.

Awful as it might sound, and scary as it was, the war was fun. It was a really wonderful opportunity for us since we're new to the community.

Kathy

It was weird when the war ended and we could finally go upstairs and use the whole house again. And it was a mess. All the suitcases from the trip were still out. Right before we left for the States, Noam had just come home from his year of community service. He just dumped all his stuff and then we left. So I had plenty to do.

I've been living on Gesher Haziv permanently since 1973 when we officially came to Israel on aliya just before the Yom Kippur War.

We had been here a year before then in 1972, and there were no clues of tension or hostilities, so the Yom Kippur War was just out of the blue. We were twenty then and already married. It doesn't make sense, but I always managed to be surprised whenever there's another escalation or war. I think there'll be peace and then they do it again!

Ishai

This war had attributes that were different from any other war we've had in the past. It was definitely different because this time it was more the civilians who fought and not the soldiers on both sides of the border for the most part. It was the civilians who suffered. Who knows what will be in the next war.

We had a meeting of the senior kibbutz members after the war. All of those who left had their own stories. And all of those who stayed had different stories. The feeling among some of the seniors who left was one of guilt – as if they are guilty of something – they exaggerated in their stories in all kinds of details in an effort to equalize their stories with the ones who stayed. At least that was my impression.

Evelyn

Those seniors who stayed were really "10." Shortly after the war, there was a research study done via the Matte Asher Regional Council by social workers. It found that many of the seniors felt better (health wise) after the war than they felt before the war. I thought this was very interesting research.

After the war I felt the need to convene all the senior members of the kibbutz. I felt it was important for them to meet together and tell their individual stories and experiences, a type of closure. We hadn't seen each other for close to six weeks. I tried to explain to those who left during the war and after, that anyone who didn't have a position to fulfill or something to do for the community, there was no reason for them to stay. The fewer seniors who stayed, the less pressure there was on those who had to help them out. But this war left us strengthened – the people who lived and worked here and were active here during the war – they were really "10." It gave us a lot.

At the very end of the war, the week that the cease-fire began, we received a week of a vacation in Jerusalem as a donation from the Regional Council. It was only after we arrived in Jerusalem that I realized how tired I was. It was as if someone had taken a pin and pricked me – suddenly all the air flowed out for a few hours. After all the tension during the war, I finally felt it leave me. It was a great vacation. And then when we returned a few days later, it was as if nothing had happened, really as if nothing had happened.

Eugene

After the cease-fire I went outside and did things, but I didn't feel it was over, not at all. I'm not even sure now. In terms of the reaction to the cease-fire and the threat of 10,000 more Katyushas, I definitely don't feel as if it's over.

I was sad, not depressed during this war. This feeling is fading less quickly than in previous wars, except for the Yom Kippur War when five kids from the kibbutz were killed. This war is not quite over because the threat is still there – that's where it is – in the back of your mind.

During this time I watched a lot of television news, not shows, to get information – a lot more than normal. I was glued to what was happening. I was switching around not focusing on one station. I watched it all. Getting information from the news was my best source. But I didn't believe what I saw because I was hearing stories already from Shelley's boyfriend, Navo, about the lack of food and him being in this house in Lebanon and doing nothing. And things that came out with the cease-fire and the so-called end of this war were as he described.

Once I might have reacted to my grown-up children's demands for certain things by saying *no*. Now, I think – have a good time – not because I think the world is going to end tomorrow, but because, number one, they all deserve it, especially all the soldiers, and secondly because I honestly believe they should have a good time and enjoy life; a limited good time.

Carolyn

I remember going into a Super-Pharm store a few days after the war was over, for nothing special, and the lady said: "Do you want to buy this?" and I said "Oh, okay!" And then she said "Do you want to buy this?" and I said "Oh sure." And I realized, this is fun, I hadn't bought anything in more than a month! And I spent like 300 shekels. It was just fun because I hadn't done it in a long time.

After the cease-fire I went to the beach, the afternoon of the same day, but the beach was closed, which was upsetting, so I went next door. It's nice and then you're not sure. I still think the whole thing was very depressing. It took a long time to get over it. I think it would have been better if we were better organized. Over time the depression dissipated. This war was terrible actually. It was much more personal. I saw the entire northern border up in smoke day after day; it was horrible. I found that most upsetting. I am taking a drawing class and I painted two pictures to show how I felt. And in Hanita, a friend of mine could hear the Hizbullah talking on their walkie-talkies. Really!

In the past my kids had a few Katyusha experiences, but nothing traumatic. But this was traumatic for them. Shelley's boyfriend was in Lebanon; all their peer group was in Lebanon, they knew people in the army and people getting killed. It makes you appreciate your children more and the soldiers very much. And I was very glad that it wasn't any worse. I think they were lucky that there hasn't been a war here for six years, because our children grew up with Katyushas. I remember one of my kids saying to me a year or two ago: "Mommy, I never thought a Katyusha was a bad thing." But yes, someone is trying to hurt us. You know how many Katyushas we had when our children were growing up. My kids spent three weeks under the kitchen table in Invei Za'am – they thought it was a gas – a doll's house.

Noa

The cease-fire was on a Monday and the following day I was supposed to go back to work. I called my boss and told him that I was taking a few days off to get my life together for myself. My son, Kfir, was supposed to return from his stay in the center of the country with my sister and I wanted to be at home. The following Sunday I returned to work and the other worker in the office and I exchanged experiences and stories from the war. He had stayed in Nahariya during the war, so he had stories to tell.

The day after the cease-fire it was if nothing had happened – that everything returned to normal. After the war I gave myself the right to sleep and not to think, or to sit outside and talk on the phone, which I really hadn't been able to do throughout the war; the right to quiet and the right to enjoy the quiet.

The experience was a very positive one that attributed to my development as a person. I was able to meet people I had never met before and get to know them. I always believe that every experience in life can be positive – you just need to look at the positive side – to find the inner strength that we all have which might be buried beneath the fears and all the attempts to cope. My son wasn't here for a month and I missed him. In addition, I had to learn how to deal with my parents' (Evelyn and Ishai) tendency to move around outside during the periods that were critical and not quite safe, which isn't so calming at all. I had to find the inner strength. But with all the pain and suffering that occurred during this time, I was fairly positive about what I was able to get from all of it. To take it to the place where development occurs – I saw it as extremely positive.

Another aspect is that the war broke the normal routine I was in. It demanded that I use certain traits or parts of me that I don't use in my day-to-day life. I had to learn how to deal with being alone in the neighborhood because all of my neighbors had left or the ones who were here were closed off in their homes and I didn't see them or have contact with them as usual. There was a lot of soul-searching that only enriched me.

M

I went back to work for Kupat Holim probably within a week or a week and a half because business started picking up slowly. This was because of the type of clients I work for through them – we had to wait for the clients to start scrambling back. I think people were a little bit out of money. But basically I went back to work pretty quickly. Two days after the cease-fire people started calling me for private treatments.

The big uncertainty was that because I didn't work, what kind of monies would I get back? In the end, it turned out that I actually got reimbursed. My compensation was good, so for me this was a period of time when I didn't work but I still got paid.

The one thing I actually felt was that now there were too many people here on the kibbutz. I actually liked the quiet and the fact that there weren't too many people around here during the period of the war. I was glad to get back to swimming in the ocean.

Immediately after the cease-fire nobody really knew what was going on and what to do, so I think I did one more night in the Situation Room. I was ready to do another night and then basically they stopped everything because it was decided that there was no need. Should we sit there or shouldn't we sit there? I had already had enough of the Hamal, though.

Relative to anybody else my life is pretty flexible. So I didn't really experience any problems returning to normalcy, it didn't make a real difference. The only real difference was maybe that it was easier to get to Tel Aviv – at the time I was going to Tel Aviv at the weekends – so finally there were trains so I didn't have to look for rides. I can't remember when the trains came back to full function, but that really made a difference, now that they were reaching Nahariya.

The days after – for about two weeks you are still jumpy – every time a window shook you were kind of feeling a little bit…, your nerves were a little bit on edge. It took a while before you realized that things were quiet. You'd see a difference between people who were here for the whole time and those who weren't. In Tel Aviv you'd hear something and I found that I was a little more jumpy than other people. Finally, I got used to not having to be on alert for sirens or explosions.

Now, when I look at things from the perspective of time, life is kind of back to normal in Israel. Israeli mentality can be a little bit of backstabbing or in your face. We were hoping that the war would change things somewhat, but it doesn't look as if it has. We're still aware of corruption that happens at all levels and it seems as if people are hopeless since no one is doing anything about it, and the people who should be punished are being promoted. So that's back to normal. The thing is that it's a kind of realization that heads should have rolled and they didn't roll, and it's back to the Israeli mentality of the people who shout the most get the most. I'm lucky that this time I got basically compensated for my work time that was lost, but I really think there is basic stuff that should change – the banks and politics – the people who have the least are paying the most and the people who have the most are getting more or they're basically not affected.

I hope the cease-fire will hold, but it probably won't unless things change drastically – both here and there – the whole world is a mess. Basically, you can't live your life in fear. So you live your life as if there's not going to be another war, and yet be prepared that there is going to be another war. I think that in the next war we're going to be less threatened – I think that Tel Aviv is going to have problems. I made a conscious decision to stay, but also part of the conscious decision was comfort. And it's not that it wasn't a hard decision to make because I don't have children and I think that made a big difference, I think, I can only guess. People who I know that I grew up with here, who have children have much more responsibility. So on that optimistic note I'll end.

Danit

I didn't find it easy after the cease-fire. I had difficulty making the transition, because I suddenly returned to work and I went back immediately to help people who had been "damaged" by the war. Bam! And I went back to work! From the standpoint of resources, there was a lot of money suddenly available and I had to write a lot of project proposals for funding right away. I suddenly fell into a double workload.

And together with that, I had to make certain somehow that my children returned all right to their routine. I felt as if I was running after my tail. Also, there were still loud noises in our area, so we checked out what the boomings were so Stav would be more relaxed – they were both the loading machine that weighed the trucks and the explosions of the many Hizbullah bunkers on the other side of the border being destroyed.

I had a lot of things happening all at once. It was to re-live what we had just passed through and to enter into what I needed to do with all the energy possible. I think that was the difficult part, emotionally less, but according to my daily schedule, it was much more. It was to connect two completely different realities together. And that connection was not easy at all!

I also found that the way that the war ended was difficult for me. This war happened. And I think the citizens gave the government a very wide mandate. But in the end, the war ended one step backwards from where it began. The war supposedly began in order to give the civilian population of the northern border security, and that security hasn't been re-established. Another goal was to release the kidnapped soldiers, and we still don't have any information about their fate.

Also, frustration and disappointment has developed because when you believe that you go through certain things for a good cause, it's a whole lot easier to suffer through the immediate situation. But when you discover in retrospect that the objectives weren't achieved or that the objectives weren't for the cause you believed in, then the feeling of frustration develops. And this is the frustration that I experienced. Then the frustration turns into something non-operable. I didn't manage to achieve the professional goals set after the war or projects that I designed because of something outside of me that didn't get results. And at some point I started to feel angry.

I think that what happened here is that a lot of people were killed on both sides, regardless of whether we won or lost. This is the third of Stav's possible endings to a war – that even if we win or lose, a lot of our people will be killed and on the other side as well. It matters that people were injured in this war. Fortunately we didn't feel this intensively here on Gesher Haziv.

But the war wasn't all negative. There were certain things that we were able to do during the war that we might not have done otherwise. There are always those projects that you push off to another time when there will be more time – well this was the time when there was time! So from this perspective I was quite apprehensive about how we were going to return to normalcy.

Reality was a bit like being in a Luna Park – reality didn't really get to us all the way to the end with all the various meanings that we attach to it – there were just a few times when reality did invade our lives though.

I think that the return to normal life was more difficult for Gilad, because from the first day of the war he was in the Situation Room whenever they needed help. He also went to check shelters, then he went to bring a saw in order to cut off the branches that had grown over the entrance to a few shelters; he also brought mattresses to the shelters. He helped computerize the Hamal and helped type in all the information for the SMS program. Then he started doing shifts in the Situation Room. Sometimes he did two shifts in a row, and the adrenaline was flowing! I worried a bit because he's still a boy, he's not quite sixteen yet, and to return from this place to being a youth still going to school and normal activities is really difficult. It's like going back a few years in time. He said it was difficult for him, even though we didn't see the difficulty on the surface. It looked as if he slipped back easily into his former role, although he was quite sorry to, I must say.

After the war we went away for a few days to refresh ourselves.

Today, when I look at the war in retrospect, I understand so many nationalities and ethnic groups that did all kinds of things and then asked: "Where was everybody?" Today I am capable of understanding them – the same people, the same ethnic groups – they just survived. They must have endeavored to create within the few meters that they had around them that were safe, some type of island of sanity. Even if they were isolated for a time, that island of sanity kept them going. You understand what I mean, don't you? Today I can't judge others the way I once did – not in Kosovo or in other places.

The community and the way our community deals with this kind of situation gave strength and support. We are also a community that doesn't easily give in to panic. We know how to control ourselves. I know about friends and people from outside who went through situations of evacuation and even those who stayed who suffered from a lot of stress. They spoke together and fed off the fears of one another. In Gesher Haziv people smiled and spoke with others. There was a lot of positive interaction, even though we were in a state of war. That isn't to say that people weren't tense, they were, I saw them, especially those who had a Katyusha hit close by. There was that feeling that Death came to visit – he didn't do anything, but he was here. And they didn't smile during those moments; but they did again later.

There were difficult situations throughout this period, and each one of us had his own individual moments of crisis as well as those moments within the community. But we also know how to "catch" one another when needed. We also knew how not to let the reality of the war to permeate or seep down into our everyday lives. An example of this was Evelyn and Ishai when they returned from Nahariya with all the packages from the shopping trip. They were smiling. The entire atmosphere was one where there was no demoralization; in contrast it was one where people were managing.

Another advantage was that there was a wonderful quiet in the community during the war, like a sympathetic Yom Kippur. It was nice outside, most of the time.

Tammy

I'm optimistic and I thought that the cease-fire would hold. I wanted to believe that it would hold – and it has until now.

It was good that I had the break in Jerusalem. On that Sunday I went back to work – but it wasn't as if I flipped a switch and everything was back to normal. There were still a lot of "leftovers" from the war that didn't start again right away. For example, all the work on the infrastructure in the kibbutz had been stopped during the war and it took the contractors close to a month to get back to work. Things were slow in returning to normal – almost a drop at a time. At the beginning I didn't have a schedule that was really tight – like always. But it was all right. I was working more hours during the war that I usually do, so I was happy that it finally ended.

Throughout this period, I got to know some people who I never had contact with before such as Sharon and Ronny, Baruch – who got involved – and that was very nice. There were a few people from the new neighborhood as well, but not many. Danit and Moshe Bartal have always been active and they did a lot during this period as well.

Benny

When we returned from Kibbutz Revadim, Gesher Haziv was still relatively empty. Only a third of the residents had returned yet. Slowly, slowly we'd see cars arrive packed with suitcases and unload. It was really quiet. The quiet of no sirens and no Katyushas was a nice feeling, maybe even a little bit strange.

I didn't have any problems when I finally did return to work after the war. The Electric Company is very organized and works according to the rules and regulations.

The Monday after the cease-fire, at 10:00 o'clock at night, my department manager called, because he knew that I was scheduled to be at a demonstration on that Thursday, so he wanted to know when I was coming back to work. I told him that I'd get organized and Wednesday I'd be back at work.

I am a person who likes to take chances and I believe that someone is protecting us from above. I don't go to the synagogue, but that's what I believe.

I have to say that the internal organization of the community was great – the Situation Room and the SMS messages, especially – and deserves to be applauded. It went very smoothly. It was wonderful. When I began to get the SMS messages I was really surprised. I hadn't expected it. All the messages and reports – such as: "In another 15 minutes enter the shelters" – they were excellent. And the messages really helped, because it was another source of information. You felt that you're not alone. Besides Orit's parents who live next door, we were alone here on our street in the neighborhood.

Orit

I definitely didn't have it bad here during the war. It sounds weird to say that, but I didn't have a hard time of it. I did have difficulty with the fact that the war dragged on for so long.

I know that other people I work with had a much more difficult time. They were forced to continue working. In the middle of the war, the workday was lengthened to 13:30. Towards the end, in the last two weeks or so, there were employees whose entire families were in the South, like in Ashdod, and they would come to work by train and return that way.

Benny was more uptight than I was and my mother-in-law was even more stressed than Benny. His personality is one where he can't sit still for long. So this period in the summer was difficult for him in some ways, but easier in others, since he was home with us for over a month and could spend time with the family, especially our newborn.

There also weren't any traumas afterwards with our children. We were at the pool after the war and there was a boom from something, I guess it was the Navy, and the children were totally relaxed because they know that if they hear a siren then they need to go into a security room and since there wasn't any siren, then there was no reason to get tense. My son even said that he thought it was shooting from the Navy ship – he made that connection.

However, even after the war ended, I felt some kind of fear when I was on the road, at least at the beginning.

Hannah

I was forced to leave the shelter – they really expelled us! We were told that there was a cease-fire. It was probably late in the afternoon when we were told to leave. We were even willing to stay one more night because it was so sudden – from all the noise and mess of the war to suddenly go home seemed... So we were willing to stay the night to see if it really was correct that there was a cease-fire. Lilach, Noga, and I were the ones in the shelter at the end. Giora's things were in the shelter, and he had a bed, even though he wasn't there very often. But we were told: "No, you can leave; even the Situation Room is being closed down." I don't know how long the Hamal was still working – that evening or that night. So I went home.

I usually don't sleep in my security room and that first night home I slept in my bed. I felt fine. But the change was too sudden for me. Either they're correct that there's a cease-fire or not, but I wasn't about to stay in the shelter alone in the dark. Everyone else had gone. I went home and went to sleep and when I woke up in the morning, everything was back to normal. There wasn't anything drastic that happened during those first days after the cease-fire that I can remember. But the suddenness of the move from the shelter caused me some problems.

Aliza

We were lucky – both of us got jobs that kept us going until the end of the war. There is no doubt in my mind that if we hadn't had those jobs that we could keep ourselves really busy, I don't know how long we would have lasted either. But the fact that we had what to do and we saw people and met people and we were in contact with people made a difference.

What we have today – there is still something left over. The way things were going at the end I believed that it would work out, not that it wouldn't work out.

But there was another problem when the stories started coming in at the end of the war, the stories of "*fashlot*" (mistakes), that was a blow! The army's mistakes, that was such a knock on the head that I remember being extremely upset by them, more so than the daily living under the Katyushas, because of the future. They started talking about the next war. And even today there are remains; we still haven't gotten out of this – the blaming and getting our act together again. We got through this thing, as absurd and insane as it was – we got through it fine. But we're left with a mess.

I don't accept some of the accusations that things weren't being handled here as they should have been. At the summation meeting, there was criticism: why didn't we at Gesher Haziv organize things for the children like other kibbutzim did. First off, other kibbutzim in the area don't have as many children as we have now – we have the children of both the kibbutz and the new neighborhood and it's a huge number. The other kibbutzim could take their forty or fifty children and make an arrangement with another kibbutz outside this area, and they went and stayed there. Here at Gesher Haziv we couldn't. But they did try to find places for people who really wanted to get out. And I was amazed at the way people like Tami and Micha and Rifi, and the girls who were taking care of the kids – they were just marvelous!

I found extreme reactions coming from myself and my children. In my down moments I found myself saying: "This isn't what I came to Israel for. I'm tired of living this life of war," and so forth. And then I have some of my children who think that there's no future for the country, but they're here. And some of my children who live abroad and look at us as if we're crazy continuing to live here. All kinds of such extreme reactions. These reactions were exacerbated and heightened.

Meshi

When they said that they wanted to delay the opening of school I was really against it, because we do have shelters at the school. We've always been under fire, so I do think going back to school as planned was necessary because we needed to socialize after more than a month in shelters or security rooms. So I really wanted to go to school, which is strange, if you ask me. At the end of every summer you kind of want to see your friends again even though you don't really want to go to school. But for me it was even more since this was a new school for me – I was beginning the seventh grade! And even though I've known Sulam Tsor all my life because my mother taught there and when her students had tests (matriculation exams) she would come home and take me to the Alonit and buy snacks and then we'd wait for the students to finish, I was excited. But this was going to be a new experience with new kids and new people and new teachers and stuff. I did want to go! In the end the school year did start on time. We started on September 3rd because the 1st was a Friday.

I think the cease-fire is only going to hold just for a while. In a few years I think this war is going to start again because just like the last time they collected weapons and in at least six years there will be another war. The Lebanese government won't stop the Hizbullah from collecting more weapons; they're doing nothing! The U.N. forces aren't doing anything either! They're just sitting and watching, but they're not doing anything, so what's the point? I mean they're just sitting there. It doesn't scare me thinking that there might be another war. I just don't want to be in the States when it starts.

Micha

I think I did believe that the cease-fire would work because we can say whatever we want to say about the Hizbullah, but Nasrallah was usually true to his word – when he said he'll do something, he would usually do it. It wasn't good things for Israel, but I did believe that the cease-fire would work, at least for a day or two. I wasn't sure it was going to last much longer, especially when it was just a cease-fire, and it wasn't that the Israelis were coming out of Lebanon since some Israeli soldiers stayed in Lebanon for a while. I thought there would be more shooting at soldiers in Lebanon. And I thought that the Israelis would have more casualties in that time until the last troops pulled out. Luckily, it didn't happen.

As far as it is now, I suppose we are as vulnerable as we ever were. We will never be secure as long as the Hizbullah are getting stronger as they are in Lebanon. I think we'll know when it will start again. The Hizbullah are getting more into politics and trying to get hold of the rest of Lebanon and not just south Lebanon. It's a bit of a worry. But we chose to come back here, and we know what's here and it's part of living in Israel and we're staying here.

My strongest memory from this war is the driving. All I really remember from this war is the driving back from work at 16:00, which was the heaviest time of Katyushas falling on almost empty roads, and looking up at the North. I think this is what I will remember from this war.

I think the older people who stayed here survived it and managed to live through the surreal life that we had here. Like I say, walking around showed me what it was like deserted – everything was deserted – only a few people were around. People are trying to estimate if ten percent of the people stayed here, or thirty percent or fifty percent. It was hard to tell which people did stay here, because it was really difficult to tell who was at home and who wasn't.

Shai

Getting back to normal was relatively quick. I think that within a few days, maybe a few hours or a day or two, we got back to our routine of quite a number of business meetings or committee meetings as if the war had never happened. I still have some questions about whether we as a community are more prepared today than we were in the past. I am strengthened by the fact that though we weren't ready during this conflict, when we needed to, we managed to deal with the situation. So if I have to choose between readiness and capability, I'd prefer capability. As long as we have the capability – and capability isn't one specific single individual, it's not built on one person, but on a lot of people and in the community and the "personality" of the community that is willing and knows how to take on responsibility. And I hope I'm not proved wrong in the next crisis, if one occurs, though I hope it won't.

I think this entire period of the war, this month, was extremely important, important not from the standpoint of it being "good," but important because even though it was an awful period from any perspective – of damage, of personal loss, and fear – it was an important period because from the distress we suffered there came support. I can identify the importance of this period in various circles.

It turns out that when there's a crisis people help out. There isn't a vacuum – people are willing to help, not just worry about their own family unit. There were a lot of people who helped – and it doesn't matter what they did – whether it was to sit in the Hamal or to help with the activities for the children or the Emergency Squad or the Fire Brigade or anything else. People really helped. Once we asked for volunteers to help clean shelters people volunteered. In an hour of need we must try to activate the community through volunteers – it isn't always easy, and there aren't always a lot, and it is also connected to the duration of the situation and the seriousness of the situation.

In the family circle, the war helped me a lot personally to strengthen. There was much more cooperation or partnership between myself and my family – when you're distressed or in crisis the partnership can get much stronger. The deliberations were much more difficult, the togetherness we had was much stronger – to decide what to do or what path of action to take. Our children had many fears – there were all kinds of things happening, but the family unit got stronger. Even though a lot of the time my children weren't physically present, it strengthened my family unit – everything got stronger and tighter. Feelings got stronger – the need to give love or to give a hug, for example. Support got stronger and from my personal circle it got much stronger during this period.

From the second circle, the circle of my formal responsibility as executive director of the kibbutz, a great deal of trust was created – everyone I worked with knew his or her territory and what he or she needed to do. It gave me a feeling that I had people I could work with and that I can handle crises like this in the future within the framework of the existing people in this community.

In the wider circle of the community, my feeling is that the community profited during this period because a large number of problems that we had as a community – the lines between the kibbutz and municipality and things like that were blurred because we dealt with events and problems equally together. The way we passed on messages, the way we got organized internally, the internal events that occurred, I think it strengthened everybody's feelings that we are one community with one structure that is equal for everyone.

The day after the cease-fire, I asked myself, will this whole thing "fly with the breeze," or will something of it remain within my three circles? And I think that something did remain from each of them – I can't say how much remained because that is a good question. But I think that in the lower circles, the family circle and the circle of functioning and responsibility, I think there is a feeling of strength. In the external circle, there are still some question marks.

Bethe

The day after the cease-fire went into effect I called Yehudit and we planned on meeting at the college to work on the textbook later that morning. I couldn't wait to get back to normalcy – even if I wasn't teaching. We have a computer and printer in the English Office at the Western Galilee College so that we could work together in the same room looking at the same screen instead of through Skype. We were there every day for the next week. Then the authorities at the college decided to open the Summer Semester English course – better late than never – so I volunteered to take a class. That was one more step for me to return to a normal routine.

However, every day I would read the Israeli papers and the articles I read would throw me back into that ambivalent state of absurdity. The Hizbullah and the Israelis were now involved in a verbal propaganda war – each side claiming to have "won" the war. There were too many deaths and too much destruction on both sides for either to claim victory, although we definitely came out stronger. The Hizbullah were posturing and making demands, even after they had agreed to the cease-fire and the Israelis were looking for scapegoats to blame for our own military mistakes and other problems that arose during the conflict.

I would drive into Nahariya to run errands and shop, as usual, but with each excursion I found more and more places that had been damaged by Katyusha rockets. Pocket holes – large and small – on the road showing where a rocket had landed and how the shrapnel had scattered; a stone wall that had crumbled from a hit. Then when I saw the upper floor porch of an apartment building that had been totally destroyed I felt really bad. That was someone's home and now it was unlivable. Had people been killed or hurt in that attack? I went to buy coffee beans from the store in the alley that I always go to only to discover that a Katyusha had fallen in the middle of the alley shattering all the glass windows of the stores and pocking the walls from the shrapnel. Later I discovered that Danny, the nice older man who worked in the coffee store had been critically hurt and had lost part of his leg from the hit. Even now, months later, I still find new places where rockets hit.

A few weeks later, Lavie came home from the army for a few days leave. It was his birthday (September 9th) and we asked him what he wanted for a present. He decided that he wanted a spa visit. He had never been to a spa before and some of his friends had recommended it. So I began calling around to the different spas in our area. One that is located in Nahariya was closed for repairs because it suffered a direct hit during the war. Another spa that I called was open, but working minimally. A third place I called was The Hacienda Spa. It is located in a hotel near Ma'alot and the hotel was currently closed because it suffered three hits during the war and all the windows had shattered. The clerk who I spoke with told me this up front, but since the spa was open and the price was good, I decided to reserve two places for Lavie the next day. After a lot of personal deliberation of who to take with him, Lavie chose his friend, Ziv, who was also home from the army. He told me later that evening that it was really weird driving up to the spa because as they pulled in to the Reception area they saw all the windows were empty and the place looked deserted.

Maybe writing this book is my way of coping with the war. I don't feel as if I was traumatized. It was just that my normal life became part of an absurd, surreal reality, and anyone who wasn't here can't even begin to imagine what we felt, how we acted, and how we lived through this period of time. The media definitely didn't portray our lives or our existence.

Will the cease-fire hold? I hope so. At least at the writing of this narrative it has. Is this the end to the conflict? Unfortunately, I think not. The Arab world won't give in so easily to accepting our small state, especially not a small Jewish state, in this region. The Palestinians are an example of that belief. They could have had a state of their own many times over (from 1947 to today) with a viable economy and society, but they refuse to accept any solution except their own, which is the total destruction of Israel. I hope the Lebanese citizens are able to strengthen their government so that they can live in peace, which will enable us to live in peace as well. There is enough war in our world; it's time to end it all.

About the Author

Bethe Schoenfeld was born in Yokohama, Japan, to American parents. Living in New York for a few years, she and her family moved to Baltimore, Maryland, where she spent most of her youth. After graduating from high school a year ahead of her class, she attended the University of Maryland where she received her B.A. in English. She then traveled around Europe, eventually going to Israel.

Working as a volunteer on Kibbutz Gesher Haziv, she met Asher Coren. Bethe decided this was the person she wanted to spend her life with and the life that she wanted to live. She subsequently immigrated to Israel. She worked on the kibbutz and studied English Literature at Haifa University where she received her M.A.

Bethe taught English at the Sulam Tsor Regional High School (located on Kibbutz Gesher Haziv) and lectured in the EFL Department of the Western Galilee Academic College. She received her Ph.D. from Anglia Polytechnic University in the UK. The dissertation is entitled *Dysfunctional Families in the Wessex Novels of Thomas Hardy* and was released in 2005 in a book of the same title by University Press of America.

Since then, Bethe has had two academic articles accepted for publication, has co-produced a series of computer software programs to teach English to early learners, and co-authored an EFL academic textbook for the advanced level of B.A. students.

The Routine of War is her first non-fiction narrative.